BOOKS BY BARRY TARSHIS

THE "AVERAGE AMERICAN" BOOK

WHAT IT COSTS

TENNIS AND THE MIND

THE STEADY GAME (WITH MANUEL ORANTES)

SIX WEEKS TO A BETTER LEVEL OF TENNIS
   (WITH DENNIS RALSTON)

TENNIS FOR THE BLOODY FUN OF IT

THE CREATIVE NEW YORKER

THE ASPHALT ATHLETE

JULIE HARRIS TALKS TO YOUNG ACTORS

The "Average American" Book

The "Average American" Book

BARRY TARSHIS

ATHENEUM/SMI NEW YORK **1979**

Library of Congress Cataloging in Publication Data

Tarshis, Barry.
    The "average American" book.

    Bibliography: p.
    Includes index.
    1. United States—Social conditions—1960–
2. National characteristics, American.   3. United
States—Population   4. Public opinion—United States.
I. Title.
HN65.T33   1979   309.1'73   79-50964
ISBN 0-689-11010-3

Published simultaneously in Canada by McClelland and Stewart Ltd.
Composition by American Book–Stratford Press, Saddle Brook, New Jersey
Printed and bound by R. R. Donnelley & Sons Company,
Crawfordsville, Indiana
Designed by Kathleen Carey
First Edition

PREFACE

Strictly speaking, the "average American" is a 29-year-old hermaphrodite (slightly more female than male) who stands about five feet four inches tall, weighs about 150 pounds, earns close to $17,000 a year, and eats a hamburger three times a week. He (she? or it?) is married (though not as likely to stay married as in the past), has 1.4 children and an IQ slightly over 100, and watches television about 2.5 hours a day, unless he happens to be a college graduate, in which case there may be only 1.2 children in the household, IQ is probably higher, and the television set is on for less time. Which is understandable, since a college graduate is more likely than a noncollege graduate to be reading, jogging, playing tennis, or attending an est seminar, anyway, unless, of course, he lives in the South, in which case he is more likely to spend one day a week in church than he would if he lived in the Northeast, where his chances of being mugged on his way home from church are higher than they would be if he lived in the Midwest. More or less.

All of which is another way of saying that there *is* no such thing as the "average American," and probably never was—not even when the country was populated solely by Native Americans. (Did the "average Apache" hold powwows as frequently as the "average Iroquois" or "average Sioux"? I doubt it.)

So, why a book entitled The "Average American" Book?

The answer, briefly, is that while there may be no such thing as the "average American," there are certainly living patterns, habits, attitudes, tastes, and, to a certain extent, traits that are shared by millions upon millions of men, women, and children who live in the United States. And what I have tried to do in this book is to offer an overall glimpse of these patterns, habits, attitudes, tastes, and traits through the medium of numbers— to present, in effect, a portrait in numbers of the American people as we approach the ninth decade of the twentieth century.

Virtually all the information that appears throughout is statistical, and each number, each ratio, and each percentage relates in one way or another to some aspect of American life.

With only a handful of exceptions, none of the data that appear in this book are original—that is, the data do not come out of surveys or studies I myself devised and carried out. Rather, they come from the organizations and the people who specialize in gathering this kind of information: the U.S. government, public-opinion-research firms, market-research departments of corporations, industrial associations, research groups in universities. Much of these data are in the public domain, having appeared in reports, magazines, books, and pamphlets; but this is the first time, to my knowledge, that (a) a mix of this kind of information has been put together in one volume, and (b) the data have been organized and presented as they are in this book.

Insofar as the data in the book reflect what my sources found in the way of results and numbers, the data are accurate, but their reliability and validity are something else again. It is not being unduly cynical or unreasonable to question whether the answers given by a national "sampling" of 1,500 (the typical number in a public-opinion sampling) can accurately reflect what is going on in the minds and lives of more than 220 million people. Yet, on this very premise is based a multimillion-dollar industry whose influence on political leaders and corporate heads continues to intensify each year. And with good reason. For the growth, prosperity, and influence now enjoyed by the opinion-research industry are probably the best endorsement of the reliability of its product—which is not to overstate the case. The general feeling throughout the opinion-research field is that with current knowledge and technology, a well-designed survey should, in theory, vary only four points in either direction from what the results would have been had the entire population been surveyed. And if the pollsters were not on, or close to, the money most of the time, nobody would pay them any mind.

Then, too, when a number of different opinion-research organizations do attempt to measure the same set of attitudes or patterns, the results tend to be similar, give or take a few percentage points. Indeed, it is one of the peculiarities of this industry that each of the organizations within it has a vested interest in the public credibility of its competitors. General Motors executives may respond with relish to the news that 50,000 or so Ford or American Motors cars have to be recalled for some factory defect, but there is no joy in the house of Gallup when a Louis Harris or Roper survey comes in ten points or so off the mark. As Alec Gallup of the Gallup Poll explains it: "If any of the major public opinion research companies loses credibility with the public, it hurts all of us."

But even granting the statistical reliability of sampling procedures, there are other, and more nettlesome, aspects to the business of gathering survey data. Take the manner in which questions are asked. Nobody knows better than a professional pollster how easy it is to manipulate responses simply by shifting words or adding a qualifier here or there. For example, if you were to ask a national sampling the question, Are you a prejudiced person? the picture you would derive about prejudice in the United States is much different from that picture you might derive were you to phrase the question, Would you say that certain racial and religious groups are born with traits that have a bearing on how they act and view the world?

Something else, too. Even if you put together a statistically reliable sampling and phrase your questions in a nonmanipulative way, there is no way of knowing for certain if the people who give you the answers are telling the truth. To illustrate: Official voting numbers matched against U.S. Bureau of Population estimates show that about 54 percent of Americans old enough to vote did so in the 1976 presidential election. Yet a survey taken among a national sampling of Americans in 1977 showed the proportion of Americans *saying* they voted, to be about 59 percent—a differential of about 11 million people.

Public-opinion professionals are hardly blind to these problems and are willing to grant what the *New York Times*/CBS News Poll chooses to call "a margin of additional error resulting from the various practical difficulties in taking any survey of public opinion." This is why the major opinion-research firms take pains to explain *how* they choose a particular sampling, *how* they obtain the results, and *how* they weigh the results. It is also why survey data based on a sampling of only 1,500 can carry more weight than a survey with a sampling of 20,000, if the data from the 1,500-person sampling were gathered on the basis of personal interviews and the data from the larger sampling came from mailed-in questionnaires.

Not that these observations about public-opinion surveys and statistical-gathering techniques are meant to undermine the information that appears in this book. I mention these things mainly to put the information into the proper perspective. *The "Average American" Book* is not a scientific work, and the information in it is subject to a variety of interpretations. I have tried to make the book both informative *and* entertaining, and except for some editorial liberties in the selection and presentation of data, I have tried to let the numbers speak for themselves.

And what, exactly, do the numbers say? Well, I venture a few personal observations in the Introduction, but for now it is enough to say that the picture of Americans that emerges from the information in The *"Average American" Book* is one that pretty much confirms what sociologists and psychologists have been saying about us for a long time: that is, the one thing most Americans have in common with one another is how much we differ from one another. "Americans feel on common ground without having to behave alike," Ted Morgan (formerly Sanche de Gramont) observes in *On Becoming American.* And paraphrasing Erik Erikson, he adds: "We are the sum of our disparities, and yet we are linked, we form a community."

To be sure, there is diversity to be found in most countries; but as Morgan reminds us, no nation in the world has as large a constituency of people who are comfortable enough and secure enough to devote a good-sized portion of their lives to individual needs and desires. There are more amateur photographers in the United States than there are Irishmen and Irishwomen in Ireland, and more Americans who bowl than there are Italians living in Italy. The number of Americans who scuba dive or climb mountains, though representing a minuscule proportion of the American population as a whole, is larger than the populations of nearly a dozen different countries in the world. And even though the United States could hardly be described as a fountainhead of intellectualism or culture, the amount of money Americans spend on books, lectures, and concerts each year is more than the gross national product of many countries.

So it is important to bear in mind as you read through the various sections of this book that even when we are talking about a very tiny proportion of Americans—less than one percent, say—we are still talking about two million people, nearly a third of the population of Switzerland. Like most Americans, I was always vaguely aware of the richness, the diversity, and the scope of this country, but it was not until I began assembling the information that appears in this book that I recognized how much about America I have always taken for granted, and never really knew.

As far as the actual putting together of this book is concerned, it was, by and large, an enjoyable and certainly enlightening experience, although I have never worked harder on any single project in my life. Assembling the data was in itself a mammoth chore, but more difficult was the task of organizing them and putting them together in a readable way.

Certainly, I could not have completed a book of this nature without the help and cooperation of a great many people, chief among them Ken Bowden, who came up with the original idea for this book and whose involvement (not to mention patience) throughout was of paramount importance in the completion of the project. I am grateful, too, to Ken's wife, Jean, who did work on the manuscript; to Arlene Restaino who was immeasurably helpful with the research and the bibliography; to Martha Durham, who also helped with the research; and to the dozens of people who helped me secure information that I could not get on my own, among them Richard Atkins, Richard Auletta, Richard Ballinger, Norman Karr, Robert Connors, Peter Craighead, Sheldon Fireman, Alice Fixx, Alec Gallup, Ira Garey, Bruce Gershfield, Charles Lehman, Clara McMichaels, John Murphy, Jane Rogers, and Earl Ubell.

Finally, I should offer a word of thanks to my wife, Karen, and to my two children, Lauren and Andrew, as well as to my close friends, all of whom served, not always willingly, as indispensable sounding boards as I became increasingly (and, I suspect, boringly) consumed with the material I was gathering.

April 1979   Barry Tarshis

CONTENTS

PART IV OUR GENERAL ATTITUDES

PART V OUR TASTES

PART IX OUR LEISURE PASTIMES

PART X HOW WE SPEND OUR MONEY

PART XI ON THE JOB

PART XII OUR PROBLEMS

PART XIII SOME AVERAGE AMERICAN TYPES

BIBLIOGRAPHY

The "Average American" Book

INTRODUCTION

•AMERICA SINCE THE 1950S: HOW MUCH HAVE WE CHANGED? You do not have to be a sociologist to recognize that life in the United States is a far cry today from what it was twenty years ago, when we were bidding goodbye to the 1950s. We no longer look the same, or dress the same. We eat differently, drink differently, listen to different kinds of music, laugh at different kinds of jokes, go to see different kinds of movies, play different games, and entertain ourselves in different ways. We think differently about a lot of things, too. Virginity in women is no longer the virtue it used to be, divorce no longer the disgrace, and marijuana smoking is no longer perceived as a symptom of moral decay. Our views on the role of women in society have changed. So, too, our views on race, communism, child rearing, and homosexuality, not to mention our attitudes on how much muscle the United States should throw around in dealing with the rest of the world, which are now notably less macho.

Whether the changes that have taken place in America over the past twenty years have improved or worsened the quality of life for the majority of people who live here is no simple question to answer. Superficially, it would appear that things are getting worse, that the country is on the skids, that the American dream is rapidly souring. Look at all the crime and violence. Look at the divorce rate, at the rising number of alcoholics, at the inflation rate, at the financial condition of some of our biggest cities, at the gas lines we had to sit through in the summer of 1979, at the lack of confidence that Americans now express in basic institutions.

It would be nice to report that the concerns most Americans now voice about the quality of life in the United States are *not* substantiated by the statistics relating to social and economic trends over the past twenty years. But the numbers, alas, only serve to underscore the dispiriting patterns. The number of violent crimes reported in the United States in 1978, for instance, was three times the number reported in 1960 (violent crimes are committed in the United States at a rate of about one every 31 seconds!). The divorce rate has more than doubled since 1965, with the latest figures suggesting that the average new marriage today has barely a fifty-fifty chance of surviving past the seventh year. The proportion of Americans committing suicide is higher than ever, too, and the number of alcoholics in the United States—about 10 million at last glance—now exceeds the combined populations of Denmark and Norway. Finally, the percentage of Americans who say they have confidence in the ability of our basic institutions to solve the problems that face us is today lower than it has ever been since public-opinion pollsters began questioning people on this issue.

That is the bad news. The not so bad news is that not *all* the numbers from the past two decades paint so bleak a picture. The average life expectancy in the United States, for instance, has risen from 69 years in 1969 to close to 73 years in 1978, with the life expectancy for women now close to 77 years. The infant mortality rate is almost half what it was in 1960, and the proportion of Americans living below the so-called poverty level is down from 22 percent in 1960 to 11.5 percent in 1977. More American young people than ever before are graduating from high school, and more than 40 percent of them are going on for higher education. And even with the onerous inflation rate of the past eight years, the amount of discretionary income available to the average American family was higher in the late 1970s than it has ever been in our history. If this was not so, we could not afford to spend nearly $200 billion on leisure and recreation.

So, it is not really surprising that in spite of all the problems we seem to be having, the most recent surveys show that a good 70 percent of the American population are highly satisfied (yes, *highly* satisfied) with their lives, and the percentage of Americans who say they are dissatisfied with the ways their lives are going, while substantial—about 10 percent—is not much higher today than it was in 1960.

But forgetting for the moment whether life is better or worse today than it was twenty years ago, the fact remains that the past two decades have hardly been lacking in eventfulness. Clearly, the 1960s were a more explosive decade than the 1970s, but it is tough to relegate to second billing a decade that witnessed, among other things, the end of a war, the downfall of a presidential administration, double-digit inflation, the first mass suicide in American history, rapprochement with China, a Middle East war, a Middle East peace treaty, and the country's first major nuclear-reactor accident.

Yet, it is not so much these specific events, historic though they are, that gave to the 1970s their distinguishing character.

Rather, it is a number of social trends—the women's movement, the sexual revolution, the rising divorce rate, the fitness and nutrition boom, the consciousness raising movement—all of which, viewed as a whole, suggest profound changes in the value structure that underlies what we normally think of as the American way of life. It will probably not be until 1981, at the earliest, before social scientists get around to making any scholarly comparisons between the 1960s and the 1970s, and probably a few years later before we can get a fix on the impact the social trends of the 1970s are going to have on the character of future American life. Then, too, it's still too early to gauge the long-term effects of the most recent chapter in the energy crisis. But a few preliminary observations, it seems to me, are not out of order at this relatively early stage.

First of all, it would be wrong to assume that Americans have completely discarded the values that have long been considered central to the American experience. Most Americans still value family as basic to personal happiness, still subscribe to the work ethic, still believe in transmitting to their children a sense of honesty and morality. What has changed, though, is that values that were not quite as important in the past have now become key priorities. There is a lot of disagreement among sociologists, psychologists, and public-opinion analysts about how we should interpret the prime social trends of the 1970s, but just about everybody agrees that the underlying trend in American life in the 1970s has been a turn *inward*—a growing preoccupation with self: health, money, happiness, self-fulfillment; and a corresponding drop in the concern once felt for so-called public issues: the environment, racial inequality, poverty, foreign policy.

Views differ on why this change has occurred. Some analysts see the inward drift as an inevitable pendulumlike reaction to the turbulence Americans experienced in the 1960s: Things were happening too fast and too soon in that decade, and so we have gone back to reconstruct some of the bridges we burned behind us. As Arthur Miller, study director of the Institute for Social Research at the University of Michigan, puts it: "People feel too much has been changing. There's a feeling that somehow everything has to be brought under control."

But let us not forget that this rising wave of self-involvement has been paralleled by (a) a precipitous drop in the degree of confidence in such basic institutions as government and education, and (*b*) an unprecedented rise in the degree of dissatisfaction with certain basic areas of our lives—jobs, communities, interpersonal relationships. The question, though, is whether this growing sense of disaffection and dissatisfaction is the reason for our preoccupation with self, or the result of it.

My own suspicion is that the disaffection and distrust of basic institutions that Americans are now experiencing cannot really be separated from the inward drift of priorities that has been gradually rising since the start of the 1970s. Given the succession of events that occurred in the United States between 1963 and 1973—the assassinations, the riots, the war in Vietnam, the Watergate scandal—it is hard to see how public confidence in our basic institutions could *not* decline, how people could *not* begin questioning old values, could *not* begin seeking new avenues for attaining peace of mind. On the other hand, the inevitable by-product of this inward drift is a concomitant retreat from the public part of one's life, and an increased sense of impatience with, and distrust of, any institution or situation that might serve to impede the inner journey. To put it another way, one of the most bothersome aspects of inflation—now the number-one concern of most Americans—is the mere fact that it *is* bothersome: It's in the road. It's cramping our style.

In any event, this inward drift is evident, to some degree at least, in virtually all the trends that have drawn attention throughout the decade. The running boom, the enormous popularity of books like *Your Erroneous Zones* and *Looking Out for Number One*, the fact that an organization known as est could become remarkably successful peddling psychic relief in much the same way that manufacturers of hemorrhoid products peddle temporary relief of pain and itching—none could have happened if the 1970s had been a time when Americans felt right about themselves and their country. It can be argued, too, that (*a*) the galloping divorce rate is less an indication that marriage itself is an outdated institution than it is a case of people simply wanting more from their marriages than they are getting; and (*b*) the sexual revolution, far from signaling an end to the Puritan ethic, is simply another variation of the self-betterment theme. Indeed, the most recent surveys suggest that for all the changes that have taken place in American sexual habits over the past fifteen years, the relative importance that Americans attach to sex has changed very little.

Exactly where this new drift in American life is taking us is not clear. Some observers, like the historian Christopher Lasch, are worried. In *The Culture of Narcissism* Lasch frets that the "survival mentality" of the 1970s bodes ill for the future of American society: By paying too much attention to ourselves and by becoming increasingly "ego-maniacal and experience devouring," we are exhibiting the symptoms of a "dying culture" whose chances for survival grow slimmer with each new narcissistic exercise.

But other analysts of American life see things differently. Sociologist Joseph Veroff of the Institute for Social Research, for instance, feels that by relying less on established social roles for behavioral models and more on a "very personal integration of experience," Americans have brought more stress upon themselves but have developed, in the process, "an enhanced self-confidence" that has made us better able to "cope with difficulties." Veroff supports this view with evidence from a study carried out in 1976: It was found that a much higher percentage of Americans reported feelings of anxiety and stress than did so in a similar study done in 1957; but the overall numbers of those relating a sense of individual well-being remained essentially the same. "People seem more anxious about a world they feel less in tune with," writes Veroff, "but more optimistic about handling distress, perhaps because of a more personal interpretation of their experience."

Having spent the better part of a year living with the numbers on which people like Christopher Lasch and Joseph Veroff have predicated their views, I should be in a good position to comment on whose reading is more accurate. But I shall make no such comments. There is no reason to disbelieve Veroff's assertion that the disaffection Americans are feeling with our social system has produced a self-orientation that has, in turn, resulted in a higher level of self-esteem. But even if this were true, it would not necessarily refute Lasch's argument that what makes us feel good about ourselves is not necessarily what is needed to keep our social system from self-destructing.

I wish I could say that the numbers that appear throughout the book give us clear answers. The fact is that they do not. They tell us where we have been and where we are. But they do not necessarily tell us where we are going. Or whether we'll have enough gas to get there.

April, 1979

I AMERICANS AT A GLANCE

HOW MANY, AND WHO, WE ARE

If everything goes according to U.S. Bureau of the Census estimates, the United States will show a 1980 population of about 222 million people, which makes us the fourth most populous nation in the world, behind China, India, and the Soviet Union.* This projection represents an increase of 41 million over the 1960 population but a rise of only 17 million from the 1970 numbers. So, while the size of the American population is growing, the rate of growth has dropped from 13 percent between 1960 and 1970 to 9 percent between 1970 and 1980. Here are some other numbers relating to the general makeup of the American population:

1. *Women*—about 51 percent.
2. *Whites*—87 percent.
3. *Blacks*—12 percent.
4. *Hispanics*—6 percent.
5. *Asians and Indians*—less than 1 percent.
6. *Five-year-olds and younger*—7 percent.
7. *Five- to 16-year-olds*—22 percent.
8. *Eighteen-year-olds and older*—70 percent.
9. *Thirty-five-year-olds and older*—44 percent.
10. *Sixty-five-year-olds and older*—31 percent.

Our marital status:

1. *Married men*—71 percent.
2. *Married women*—65 percent.
3. *Single men who have never been married*—21 percent.
4. *Single men between 25 and 29 who have never been married*—28 percent (up from 21 percent in 1960).
5. *Single women who have never been married*—15 percent.
6. *Single women between 25 and 29 who have never been married*—18 percent (up from 10.5 percent in 1960).
7. *Divorced men*—4.5 percent.

* The figures cited throughout this book are approximate, and in most cases percentages have been rounded off to the nearest fifth. Thus, a percentage that originally read 6.2 percent would appear as 6 percent, one that read 11.8 percent would appear as 12 percent, and so on. Also, unless otherwise indicated, the proportions listed are for American adults 18 years of age and older, which is approximately 155 million.

8. *Divorced women*—6.0 percent.
9. *Widowed men*—2.5 percent.
10. *Widowed women*—4.5 percent.

Trends? The ratio of males to females in the American population has stayed pretty much the same over the past ten years, but the proportion of blacks in the population has risen over the same time, from 11 percent to 12 percent. The population in the age-groups 25 to 34 and 65 and older is well up from the 1970 level, the former because of the "baby boom" in the late 1940s and early 1950s, and the latter because Americans, like nearly everybody, are living longer than ever before. Meanwhile, the number of divorced persons in the United States has nearly doubled since 1970. For every 1,000 Americans in an intact marriage in 1977, there were 84 divorced persons—a jump in the divorce ratio of 79 percent, compared to an increase of only 34 percent during the entire decade from 1960 to 1970. Women (101 per 1,000) had a higher divorce ratio than men (66 per 1,000), and Americans under 45 had higher ratios (91 per 1000) than Americans 45 years and older (76 per 1,000). The reasons: (1) women have a lower incidence of remarriage than men and tend to stay divorced longer before remarriage; (2) the bulk of the recent increase in divorce has been among younger couples.

• **N A T I V E S T O C K S .** Some 96 percent of American citizens were born in the United States, but 16 percent have—or had— at least one parent who was born somewhere else. From the 1970 Census, this look at the background of first and second generation Americans:

1. *Italy*—12.5 percent.
2. *Germany*—11 percent.
3. *Canada*—9 percent.
4. *England*—7.5 percent.
5. *Mexico*—7 percent.

As far as overall ethnic ancestry goes, specifics are tough to come up with given the ethnic mixtures that characterize most American family trees. But roughly speaking, about 80 percent have ancestral roots in Europe and about 28 percent have an ancestral link with Great Britain. Meanwhile, the fastest growing ethnic group in the United States are Spanish Americans, who, say some demographers, will overtake blacks as the nation's largest minority group by 1990.

• RELIGIOUS BACKGROUND. Two out of every five Americans with a formal church affiliation are Protestants, but Roman Catholics are the largest *single* religious group in the country (23 percent). Jews constitute just under 3 percent of the population. In terms of pure numbers, as of early 1979, the ten largest religious groups in the United States were:

1. *Roman Catholics*—49.3 million.
2. *Southern Baptists*—12.9 million.
3. *Methodists*—9.8 million.
4. *Jews*—6.1 million.
5. *National Baptists*—5.5 million.
6. *Lutherans*—2.9 million.
7. *Episcopalians*—2.8 million.
8. *Lutherans (Missouri Synod)*—2.7 million.
9. *Convention of American Baptists*—2.6 million.
10. *Presbyterians*—2.5 million.

• IN SCHOOL. The student population in the United States (kindergarten to college) has been averaging about 62 million a year for the past ten years, which means that just under three of every ten Americans go to school. The breakdown:

1. *Elementary-school students*—50 percent.
2. *High-school students*—33 percent.
3. *College students*—17 percent.

• INSTITUTIONALIZED. Approximately 1.6 million Americans are confined to a "long-term care" institution. The breakdown looks like this:

1. *Nursing-home residents*—63.0 percent.
2. *Mentally retarded*—20.0 percent.
3. *Psychologically disturbed*—4.0 percent.
4. *Orphans*—3.0 percent.
5. *Physically handicapped*—2.5 percent.

• IN UNIFORM. Roughly two million American men and women now serve in one of the four branches of the U.S. military establishment. The proportional breakdown:

1. *Army*—37 percent of uniformed American military personnel.

2. *Air force*—29 percent.
3. *Navy*—25 percent.
4. *Marine corps*—9 percent.
5. *Women*—6 percent.
6. *Officers*—10 percent.
7. *Black enlisted men*—10 percent.
8. *Black recruits in 1977*—33 percent.
9. *GIs stationed overseas*—23 percent (compared with 34 percent in 1970).

• O UT OF U NIFORM . About 30 million American men—41 percent of the adult male population—have served at one time or another in one of the armed services. The breakdown:

1. *World War II veterans*—42 percent of all veterans.
2. *Vietnam War veterans*—28 percent.
3. *Korean War veterans*—19 percent.
4. *Disabled veterans*—7 percent.

• L OCKED U P . About 270,000 Americans are serving time in a federal or state prison, and roughly 100,000 more are locked up in a city or county jail. Some characteristics of the United States prison population:

1. *Males*—97 percent.
2. *Blacks*—40 percent.
3. *Yearly rate of increase since 1970*—10 percent.

• I LLEGAL E NTRIES . Estimates of the number of illegal aliens now living in the United States range from 2 million to 6 million. The largest concentrations are in Southern California, where the estimates range from 500,000 to 1.5 million illegal aliens, and in New York, where the number could be anywhere from 750,000 to 1.5 million. In California the vast majority of illegal aliens are Mexicans, and a good percentage work in garment factories. In New York the bulk of the illegal alien population are either Caribbean blacks or Chinese.

SOURCE

U.S. Bureau of the Census, *Statistical Abstract of the United States: 1978.*

A NOTE ON SOURCES: Sources for the data presented in each section of this book are noted both in the text and at the end of each individual section. A more detailed listing of each source, along with additional information, is found in the back of the book.

HOW OLD WE ARE

The basic story is this: The proportion of younger people in the United States is getting smaller, and the proportion of older people is getting bigger because (a) married people are having fewer babies, and (b) people are living longer. Some sample numbers:

1. *Current birthrate*—about 15 per 1,000 (the rate has remained at this level since the early 1970s).
2. *Current death rate*—about 9 per 1,000 (down from 24 per 1,000 in 1960).
3. *Median age of total American population*—29.0 years.
4. *Median age of black Americans*—24.0 years.
5. *Average life expectancy of American women*—76.5 years.
6. *Average life expectancy of American men*—69.5.
7. *Estimated median age of American population in the year 2000*—37.3 years.
8. *Average life expectancy in the United States compared with that in other countries*—slightly lower than in most Scandinavian countries and Japan but higher than everywhere else.
9. *Proportion of American population under five years old*—7.5 percent (1980 projection).
10. *Between five and 13 years*—13.5 percent.
11. *Between 14 and 21 years*—15 percent.
12. *Between 22 and 34 years*—21 percent.
13. *Between 35 and 44 years*—11.5 percent.
14. *Between 45 and 54*—10 percent.
15. *Between 55 and 64 years*—9.5 percent.
16. *Sixty-five years and older*—11 percent.

SOURCE
U.S. Bureau of the Census, Statistical Abstract of the United States: 1978.

WHERE WE LIVE

The Census Bureau likes to divide the American population into four *main* regions: North East, North Central, West, and South; but the bureau's regional subdivisions give us a more precise picture of population distribution throughout the country. Here is how some of the numbers looked in 1977.

Proportion of Americans who were living in:

1. *New England* (*Maine, New Hampshire, Vermont, Massachusetts, Rhode Island, Connecticut*)—5.5 percent.
2. *Middle Atlantic States* (New York, New Jersey, Pennsylvania)—17.0 percent.
3. *East North Central States* (Ohio, Indiana, Illinois, Michigan, Wisconsin)—19.0 percent.
4. *West North Central States* (Minnesota, Iowa, Missouri, North Dakota, South Dakota, Nebraska, Kansas)—7.5 percent.
5. *South Atlantic States* (Delaware, Maryland, Virginia, West Virginia, North Carolina, South Carolina, Georgia, Florida, District of Columbia)—15.5 percent.
6. *East South Central States* (Kentucky, Tennessee, Alabama, Mississippi)—6.5 percent.
7. *West South Central States* (Arkansas, Louisiana, Oklahoma, Texas)—10.0 percent.
8. *Mountain States* (Montana, Idaho, Wyoming, Colorado, New Mexico, Arizona, Utah, Nevada)—4.5 percent.
9. *Pacific States* (Washington, Oregon, California, Alaska, Hawaii)—13.5 percent.

Trends since 1970? The population in the West, the South, and the Mountain States is rising at nearly twice the rate of growth of the East, the Midwest, and the Middle Atlantic States. The net migration figures—calculated by either adding or subtracting the number of people who move *in* to or from the number of people who move *out*—tell the story. Here are the net total migration figures for the period 1970–77, for selected states:

1. *New York*—down 873,000.
2. *Ohio*—down 464,000.
3. *Pennsylvania*—down 283,000.
4. *Illinois*—down 382,000.
5. *Michigan*—down 247,000.
6. *Florida*—up 1,478,000.
7. *California*—up 817,000.
8. *Texas*—up 760,000.
9. *Arizona*—up 358,000.
10. *Colorado*—up 249,000.

The population, as a whole, rose about 6.5 percent between 1970 and 1977. Here is how the population growth rates for individual states fared in the same period :

1. *Arizona*—up 29.5 percent.
2. *Nevada*—up 29.5 percent.
3. *Florida*—up 24.5 percent.
4. *New Hampshire*—up 15 percent.
5. *Arkansas*—up 11.5 percent.
6. *South Carolina*—up 11 percent.
7. *California*—up 9 percent.
8. *Connecticut*—up 2.5 percent.
9. *District of Columbia*—down 9.0 percent.
10. *New York*—down 1.5 percent.

The fastest-growing metropolitan area in the United States is the Fort Lauderdale–Hollywood area in Florida where the net migration gain between 1970 and 1977 was about 37 percent. New York City had the largest loss in the way of numbers— about 465,000—but the city with the largest rate of loss—5 percent—in this period was Jersey City, New Jersey.

• M o v i n g   O u t . Most Americans, about 54 percent, now live in metropolitan areas with a population of one million or more, but the exodus out of central cities and into suburban and exurban areas was even greater throughout the 1970s than it was throughout the 1960s.

Proportion of Americans who live:

1. *In large metropolitan areas*—40 percent.
2. *In medium-sized metropolitan areas*—34 percent.
3. *In rural areas*—24 percent.
4. *In central cities*—28.5 percent (down from 31.5 percent in 1970).

5. *Outside central cities (suburban areas)*—39 percent
(up from 37 percent in 1970).

Nearly 60 percent of the black population in the United States
live in central cities, as compared with 28 percent of the white
population. And even though in late 1978 the census reported
that for the first time since World War II blacks (chiefly
poor) moving out of northern cities and back to the South
outnumbered those blacks moving from the South to the
North, the major cities of the North and Midwest still show
an inner-city racial makeup that is highly disproportionate to
that found in the rest of the country.

1. *Black population in northern urban centers*—about 28
   percent.
2. *Change since 1960*—up 75 percent.
3. *Rate of population decline in northern cities for whites*
   —25 percent.

• M o v i n g O n . Americans change their addresses more
often during a typical lifetime than probably any other people
in the world, and it has been that way since the early 1800s.
The numbers according to a government report on geographic
mobility:

1. *Proportion of Americans who move in an average year*
   —20 percent.
2. *Number of moves in the lifetime of the typical American*—13.
3. *Of the typical Japanese*—5.
4. *Of the typical Englishman*—8.
5. *Address changes within the same county*—66 percent.
6. *Within the same general neighborhood*—33 percent.

SOURCES

Larry Long, "Geographical Mobility," *Selected Aspects
of Consumer Behavior.*

U.S. Bureau of the Census, *Statistical Abstract of the
United States: 1978.*

WHAT KIND OF HOUSING WE LIVE IN

In early 1979 there were about 80 million housing units in the
United States. The Census Bureau breaks these units down

into two broad categories: one-family houses on ten acres or less, and renter-occupied residences.

• **H O M E S W E E T H O M E** . Roughly two-thirds of Americans live in a one-family house that they "own," or have mortgaged through a bank. The median value of the average house in an urban or suburban area is now around $37,000, compared with $27,000 for houses in rural areas; but these figures are deceptive. In the spring of 1977 the median sale price for new houses was around $43,000; by late 1979 it had risen to around $70,000. What's more, in prestige areas like Beverly Hills, California, Shaker Heights, Ohio, and Fairfield County, Connecticut, the average selling price of a house is upwards of $130,000.

• **S T A N D A R D I S S U E** . The average American home built over the past eight years is a one-story, three-bedroom affair with two baths, a full or partial basement, and a garage. Its area encompasses between 1,600 and 2,400 square feet, and the chances are fifty-fifty that it is centrally air-conditioned.

• **K E E P I N G W A R M** . In the early 1950s nearly 35 percent of all American homes were heated by coal (*cough!*). Here is how the heating picture looks for all households today:

1. *Fuel oil*—22.5 percent.
2. *Electricity*—12.5 percent.
3. *Gas*—56.0 percent.
4. *Coal*—1.0 percent.

• **C L I F F D W E L L E R S** . One out of three Americans lives in an apartment or a rented house. As of early 1979 the median rent paid by renters of apartments and houses was about $190 a month, with urbanites paying 25 percent more than their country cousins.

• **P R I V A T E Q U A R T E R S** . A 1972 Department of Health, Education, and Welfare Health Examination Survey showed more than half the teenagers in the United States have a room to themselves. The chances of this being the case increase, of course, the higher up you go on the socioeconomic ladder; but 17-year-olds as a group are more likely to have private quarters (62 percent) than are 12-year-olds (36 percent), and a slightly higher proportion of boys, as compared with girls, have their own rooms.

SOURCES

U.S. Bureau of the Census, *Statistical Abstract of the United States: 1978.*

U.S. Department of Health, Education, and Welfare, *Parent Ratings of Behavioral Patterns of Youth 12–17.*

WHOM WE LIVE WITH

The average number of people living in the typical American household has been dropping steadily since the 1950s and for a number of reasons, among them the declining birthrate, the soaring divorce rate and the trend among young people to wait longer before tying the knot. Here is a closer look.

• **BY MYSELF.** The number of Americans living alone has more than doubled since 1960 and the number was 50 percent higher in 1977 than it was in 1970. Some representative numbers from the Census Bureau:

1. *Men who live alone*—5.5 percent.
2. *Women*—10 percent.
3. *Men over 65*—14 percent.
4. *Women over 65*—36 percent.
5. *Men 25 to 44*—7 percent (up from 3 percent in 1970).
6. *Women 25 to 44*—10 percent (up from 3 percent in 1970).

• **HOUSEHOLD COUNT.** The proportion of one-person households in the United States rose from 17 percent in 1970 to 21 percent in 1977. Here is a look at the rest of the American household picture as of 1977:

1. *Two-person households*—31 percent (up from 29 percent in 1970).
2. *Three-person households*—17.5 percent (no change since 1970).
3. *Four-person households*—15 percent (no change since 1970).
4. *Five-person households*—8.5 percent (down from 10.5 percent in 1970).
5. *Six-person households*—4 percent (down from 5.5 percent).

6. *Seven-person or more households*—3 percent (down from 5 percent in 1970).

• **F A M I L Y A F F A I R S** . A family household, in the eyes of the Census Bureau, is any group of at least two persons related to one another by either marriage, blood or adoption who live in the same household. And the 1980 census will report a total of about 59 million such households in the United States. Some representative numbers:

1. *Family households in which mother and father are both present*—83 percent.
2. *Family households headed by a female only*—14 percent.
3. *By a male only*—3 percent.
4. *Proportion of black family households headed by a female only*—33 percent.
5. *Children living in single-parent families*—18 percent.
6. *White children younger than 18 living with both parents*—85 percent.
7. *Black children younger than 18 living with both parents*—47 percent.
8. *White children living with mother only*—12 percent.
9. *Black children living with mother only*—42 percent.

Trends? The proportion of female-headed households has gone up some 50 percent since 1960. At the same time, the median age of females who head single-parent households has dropped from 52 to 48 among white women and from 44 to 39 among black women. About 40 percent of all female-headed households are headed by black or Hispanic women.

• **O R P H A N A N N I E S** . About 52,000 Americans younger than 18 have neither a mother nor a father, but the orphan total is well down from the 70,000 figure of 1970. Some other numbers on kids who have either lost a parent or do not live with their natural parents based on Census Bureau figures and a *Newsweek* report on foster children:

1. *Children younger than 18 whose fathers are dead*—3.5 percent of younger-than-18 population.
2. *Whose mothers are dead*—1.5 percent.
3. *Who live in foster homes*—.7 percent, or about 500,000.
4. *Who are adopted*—about 3.0 percent.

5. *Foster children who have no living parents*—3.0 percent.
6. *Whose parents do not want them*—31.0 percent.
7. *Who are handicapped or retarded*—2.0 percent.
8. *Who were taken from homes where one or both parents had a drinking or emotional problem*—50.0 percent.

• ANIMAL HOUSES. According to the Pet Food Institute, an animal of one kind or another lives (as an *invited* party, that is) in one of every two households in the United States. Here is the estimated breakdown:

1. *Dog houses*—40 percent.
2. *Cat houses*—12 percent.
3. *Houses with at least one dog and one cat*—10 percent.
4. *Fish houses*—14 percent.

Slightly more than half the dogs resident in U.S. homes have a pedigree. Only 7 percent of American cats have this social credential.

SOURCES

Newsweek, "Foster Care Fiasco," March 5, 1979.
Pet Food Institute, Washington, D.C.
U.S. Bureau of the Census, *Statistical Abstract of the United States: 1978.*

HOW EDUCATED WE ARE

Forgetting for the moment that the high-school dropout rate is still fairly high (only 80 percent of American schoolchildren now in the sixth grade are expected to graduate from high school), the overall average educational level throughout the country keeps rising every decade. More Americans than ever before are graduating from high school, and more high-school graduates than ever before are going on to college.

• THE BASIC NUMBERS. About 65 percent of Americans 25 years of age and older hold high-school diplomas or better, and somewhere around 15 percent of the older-than-25 population has a college degree. In both cases, the numbers are up. As recently as 1970, only 55 percent of Americans 25 and older had finished high school. And, if you go back to 1950, the proportion of high-school graduates throughout the country was barely over 35 percent, and the proportion of college graduates, only 6 percent. The median number of school years completed by Americans today is 12.4 years, compared with 12.2 years in 1970.

• DEMOGRAPHICS. The two most potent influences on the educational level of Americans are age and race. Americans younger than 35 are twice as likely to have graduated from high school, as compared with Americans 65 and older; and black educational levels lag behind white levels in all age-groups, although the gap is narrowing. Some of the proportional figures are as follows:

1. *Blacks 25 and older with high-school diplomas—44.0 percent (up from 20.0 percent in 1960).*
2. *Blacks 25 to 29 with high-school diplomas—74.0 percent.*
3. *Whites 25 to 29 with high-school diplomas—85.0 percent.*
4. *Blacks 25 to 29 with college degrees—13.0 percent.*
5. *Whites 25 to 29 with college degrees—24.0 percent.*
6. *American adult men with college degrees—18.5 percent.*
7. *American adult women with college degrees—11.0 percent.*

• GOING PRIVATE. Even though the school-age population has been dropping since 1970, the number of students enrolled in the 800 private secular schools throughout the country has risen from 250,000 to 300,000. But overall, the ratio of private and parochial students to public-school students has changed relatively little over the past twenty years. It is still about one to seven.

• HIGHER UPS. Sixty percent of the high-school graduates in the United States now go on to some form of higher education. That is the good news. The bad news is that only about 50 percent of the students who enter college hang in there long enough to collect a degree. Even so, the proportion of college graduates among Americans between the ages of 25 and 29 is nearly 24 percent, which means that about one out of every four American children in school today will probably complete their college education.

• **A D U L T   D I P L O M A C Y .** Nearly 20 million Americans older than 17 are enrolled in some form of formal educational activity apart from high school or college. The largest proportion of this group (around 20 percent) are taking noncredit courses in four-year colleges and universities. And an additional 17 percent are taking similar courses at two-year colleges or technical institutions. Women enrolled in adult-education programs now outnumber men by more than a million and are twice as likely as men to be involved in an adult-education program run by a local community. The actual courses being taken by the 20 million Americans in adult education break down into the following categories:

1. *Occupational training*—49 percent.
2. *General education*—21 percent.
3. *Personal and family living*—15 percent.
4. *Social life and recreation*—12 percent.
5. *Community issues*—10 percent.

SOURCE
U.S. National Center of Education Statistics, *Digest of Educational Statistics,* 1977–78.

WHAT KIND OF FINANCIAL SHAPE WE ARE IN

Inflation notwithstanding, Americans today are earning more money than ever before, although the distribution of wealth throughout the country has stayed pretty much the same over the past 20 years, with a very sizable slice of the American economic pie still in the pantry of a relative handful.

• **T H E   B A S I C   N U M B E R S .** As of early 1979, the average yearly income of an American family headed by a full-time worker was about $18,000, and the median income was just over $16,000. When you figure in *all* households, however, including singles, and the unemployed, the median-income level drops to about $13,500 a year. Generally speaking, average and median-income levels in the United States are 20 percent higher than they were in the mid-1970s.

• THE DEMOGRAPHICS. White families headed by males who have four or more years of college education enjoy the highest median-income level in the United States—around $26,000 in 1978. These families make up less than 10 percent of the population. Next in line are black families headed by college-degreed males, with a 1978 median-income level of $22,000. All told, white families headed by full-time workers enjoy a higher yearly median-income level—about $20,500 in 1978—than do blacks in the same position, whose median income was $15,000 in 1978; and the ratio has remained the same since the late 1960s. When you take *all* households (single and unemployed included) into consideration, the gap widens: about $15,000 for whites against $8,600 for blacks. Demographic gaps also separate men and women, and Americans in various age-groups, but there is a racial component in each situation. Here is a sampling of approximate average yearly income levels as of 1978:

1. *Families headed by a person aged 25 to 34*—$17,400 for whites; $12,000 for blacks.
2. *A person aged 45 to 54*—$24,000 for whites; $15,000 for blacks.
3. *A white-collar worker*—$25,500 for whites; $17,000 for blacks.
4. *A blue-collar worker*—$18,600 for whites; $15,500 for blacks.
5. *A high-school graduate*—$17,600 for whites; $12,200 for blacks.
6. *A divorced person*—$10,900 for whites; $8,700 for blacks.
7. *Families with seven or more persons*—$23,000 for whites; $14,600 for blacks.
8. *Families in which both the husband and wife work*— $18,800 for whites; $15,500 for blacks.
9. *Male-headed families (both races combined)*—$17,600.
10. *Female-headed families (both races combined)*— $7,800.
11. *Suburban families*—$19,300 for whites. $13,100 for blacks.
12. *White central-city families*—$16,300.
13. *Black central-city families*—$9,700.

• **SHARED WEALTH**. The basic distribution curve of wealth in the United States has remained pretty much the same since the 1950s. The wealthiest 20 percent of the population now still take home about 40 percent of all the income that is earned in a given year. As of 1978, the annual picture of income distribution among all American households looks like this:

1. *Under $3,000*—7.0 percent.
2. *Between $3,000 and $4,999*—9.0 percent.
3. *Between $5,000 and $6,999*—8.5 percent.
4. *Between $7,000 and $9,999*—11.5 percent.
5. *Between $10,000 and $14,999*—18 percent.
6. *Between $15,000 and $19,999*—15.5 percent.
7. *Between $20,000 and $24,999*—11.5 percent.
8. *Over $25,000*—18.0 percent.

• **BIG MONEY**. Yearly income exceeds $50,000 in just over 2.5 percent of all American households, but this proportion is deceptive, as the following numbers show. The percentages indicate the proportion controlled by one percent of the population.

1. *All personal wealth*—20 percent.
2. *Real-estate holdings*—39 percent.
3. *Corporate stock*—30 percent.
4. *Bonds*—60 percent.
5. *Cash assets*—13 percent.
6. *Trusts*—90 percent.

The proportion of the country's wealth that the top one percent of the population has held throughout this century has undergone some interesting fluctuations. Examples:

1. *In 1929 (just before the stockmarket crash)*—36 percent.
2. *In 1950*—an average of 24 percent.
3. *Since 1960*—20 percent.

In 1977, the last time somebody counted, there were about 179,000 men and women in the United States with personal assets in excess of $1 million.

• **DOWN-AND-OUTERS**. Based on the U.S. government's own barometer, approximately 12 percent of the country's population live below what is usually referred to as the "poverty level," a sliding scale based not so much on income per se but rather on the family's economic ability to meet basic survival needs. The demographics of poverty in the United States look like this:

1. *White families*—9 percent.
2. *Black families*—30 percent.
3. *Male-headed families*—7 percent.
4. *Female-headed families*—34 percent.

The proportion of Americans living below the poverty level is half what it was in 1959, but has remained at the 11–12 percent figure since 1970.

• **HELP FROM UNCLE.** Some form of government-initiated financial help seeps into the households of 40 percent of Americans. Here is how it comes in:

1. *Social Security*—15.5 percent.
2. *Welfare*—6.0 percent.
3. *Other* (e.g., Medicaid, disability pensions)—78.0 percent.
4. *Public assistance for female-headed families*—20.0 percent for whites; 46.5 percent for blacks.

• **BLACK PROGRESS REPORT.** Even though black Americans, on the whole, are concentrated at the lower levels of the American economic ladder, a slowly increasing proportion have begun to make their presence felt in the upper reaches of the economy. A 1978 report in *Black Enterprise* had this to say on the subject:

1. *Black households with incomes exceeding $50,000*—19,000, or 1.5 percent of total in this category.
2. *Black households with incomes of $25,000 and over*—3.0 percent of all households in this category.

The bulk of the richer black households in the United States are in the South. Virtually all are headed by men.

• **MARKET VALUE.** Roughly one out of three American adults owns either stocks, bonds, mutual funds, or some other security, but the number of Americans actively trading in securities is less than 2 percent. Some related numbers:

1. *Americans who own stock in the company they work for*—16 percent.

2. *Americans who own stock in companies other than their own*—8 percent.
3. *Americans with a portfolio worth more than $20,000*—under 3 percent.

Surprisingly, there are twice as many women stockholders as men stockholders. Not so surprisingly, American stockholders with college degrees double the number of those with high-school diplomas. Finally, half the people in the United States who own stock or other securities live in a metropolitan area in which the population exceeds one million.

• I n H o c k . A Federal Reserve report in 1978, quoted in the *New York Times*, put the average American's ratio of outstanding debt to disposable income at 68 percent—a record high. Most of this figure, however, was tied up in mortgage debt. Some other numbers:

1. *Average amount of installment debts owed by Americans in early 1979*—$3,000 per household.
2. *Estimated number of American families that are "over-extended"* (i.e., have an installment-debt level that is more than 20 percent of their disposable income)—10 percent.
3. *Per capita debt in U.S.*—$3,600.

SOURCES

Andrew Brimmer, "The Upper Crust: High Incomes in the Black Community," *Black Enterprise*, August 1978.

New York Times, "National Economic Survey," January 7, 1979.

U.S. Bureau of the Census, *Statistical Abstract of the United States: 1978*.

HOW WE LEAN POLITICALLY

The political waters through the United States are muddier today than they have ever been, the chief reason being a conflicting jumble of social and political viewpoints throughout the country. Here is a general picture of our schizoid political personality as we inch our way into 1980.

• **PARTY LINES**. The number of Americans who describe themselves as "Democrats" is nearly twice the number who describe themselves as "Republicans," although the margin has been narrowing somewhat over the past several years. What's more, the proportion of Americans who consider themselves "strong Democrats" is declining rapidly, whereas the proportion of "strong Republicans" is on the rise. A general social survey conducted in 1978 by the National Opinion Research Center (NORC) yielded this picture of current party affiliations based on self-descriptions:

1. *Not very strong Democrat*—25.0 percent.
2. *Not very strong Republican*—16.0 percent.
3. *Independent*—14.5 percent.
4. *Strong Democrat*—14.0 percent.
5. *Independent, close to Democrat*—13.0 percent.
6. *Strong Republican*—7.0 percent.

A comparative look at NORC surveys taken throughout the 1970s shows the Republicans hitting rock bottom around the time of Watergate but picking up some support in 1977 and 1978. The Democrats, in the meantime, have been losing numerical strength while the proportion of Americans who describe themselves as "independent" has been on the increase —up 20 percent since 1972.

• **BRING BACK BARRY. MAYBE**. If there were only two specific political options in the United States—one "liberal" and the other "conservative"—the majority of Americans (57 percent according to a 1978 Harris Survey) say they would line up on the "conservative" side. However, when the pollsters add a third option, the "middle of the road," the proportion describing themselves as either "liberal" or "conservative" drops in each instance to about 35 percent. On a scale of one to seven— "one" representing extremely liberal and "seven" representing extremely conservative—here is how a sampling of Americans polled by Harris in 1978 labeled their political leanings:

1. *Extremely liberal*—1 percent.
2. *Liberal*—6 percent.
3. *Slightly liberal*—15 percent.
4. *Moderate, middle-of-the-road*—36 percent.
5. *Slightly conservative*—17 percent.
6. *Conservative*—17 percent.
7. *Extremely conservative*—2 percent.

Trends? Unmistakably conservative, based on the rate of growth or decline each group has experienced since 1974.

1. *Extremely liberal*—no change since 1974.
2. *Liberal*—down by 25 percent.
3. *Slightly liberal*—up by 17 percent.
4. *Moderate, middle-of-the-road*—down by 2 percent.
5. *Slightly conservative*—up by 20 percent.
6. *Conservative*—up by 15 percent.
7. *Extremely conservative*—slightly down.

• W H O ' S W H O . A composite demographic analysis of political labeling shows generally that Democrats are stronger than Republicans among low-income groups, blacks, and all general occupational groups. Some numbers:

College graduates:

1. *Democrat*—37 percent.
2. *Republican*—22 percent.
3. *Independent*—34 percent.

High school graduates:

1. *Democrat*—47 percent.
2. *Republican*—22 percent.
3. *Independent*—31 percent.

Professionals and semi-professionals:

1. *Democrat*—39 percent.
2. *Republican*—27 percent.
3. *Independent*—34 percent.

Business executives and small businessmen:

1. *Democrat*—37 percent.
2. *Republican*—29 percent.
3. *Independent*—34 percent.

White-collar and sales workers:

1. *Democrat*—42 percent.
2. *Republican*—33 percent.
3. *Independent*—33 percent.

Skilled blue-collar workers:

1. *Democrat*—49 percent.
2. *Republican*—17 percent.
3. *Independent*—34 percent.

The figures above are based on 1976 Gallup surveys, so it is reasonable to assume given the trend toward conservatism that the Democrats have been losing some ground in most of the groups mentioned.

• **ISSUE ORIENTED**. Recent voting patterns suggest that Americans are more issue-oriented (as opposed to party-oriented) than ever before, but the traditional liberal/conservative divisions no longer apply to all issues. Here is a brief list of some of the major issues today and the drift in American political thought on those issues, since 1960, based on Gallup polls.

1. *Government power*—more conservative (nearly 70 percent of Americans now think that government is too powerful).
2. *Women's rights*—more liberal, although mixed on the Equal Rights Amendment.
3. *Crime*—more conservative.
4. *Racial issues*—more liberal, except on the issue of busing.
5. *Pornography*—more conservative.
6. *Taxation*—much more conservative.
7. *Sex education*—more liberal.
8. *Gun ownership*—more conservative.
9. *Sex attitudes in general*—more liberal.
10. *Foreign policy*—mixed.
11. *Marijuana smoking*—more liberal.

SOURCES

American Institute for Public Opinion (hereafter cited as "Gallup Poll").

Louis Harris and Associates, Inc. (hereafter cited as "Harris Survey").

National Opinion Research Center (hereafter cited as "NORC").

WHAT OUR WORK FORCE IS LIKE

Some of the numbers relating to the American work experience are presented in some detail in a separate section (see Part XI, "On the Job"). Here is a general overview.

•THE BASIC NUMBERS. As of early 1979 there were about 102 million Americans 16 years old and older working full- or part-time. This represents an increase of about 16 million since 1970. The *percentage* of working people has risen, too, since 1970—from about 61.5 percent to 63.5 percent. Some other numbers:

1. *Women in the work force*—41.5 percent.
2. *White males 16 and older who work*—78.0 percent of all white males 16 and older.
3. *Black males 16 and older who work*—70.0 percent of black male population.
4. *White males 16 to 19 who are unemployed*—15.0 percent.
5. *Black males 16 to 19 who are unemployed*—37.0 percent.
6. *Married men who work*—96.0 percent.
7. *Married women who work*—47.0 percent.
8. *Married women, with one or more children younger than 18, who work*—48.0 percent.
9. *Married women who work full-time*—about 22.0 percent.
10. *Who have children younger than 18 and work full-time*—10.0 percent of all married women and 19.0 percent of married women with children younger than 18.

Trends? The big change since 1970 has been the growing proportion of young mothers in the work force. As of early 1978 the percentages for married women (with the husband present) working either full- or part-time were:

1. *Married women with no children younger than 18*—45.0 percent (up from 42.0 percent in 1970).
2. *With children 6 to 17 only*—55.5 percent (up from 49.0 percent in 1970).
3. *With children younger than 6*—39.5 percent (up from 30.5 percent in 1970).

•COLLAR WAR. In the mid-1970s for the first time in our history the proportion of white-collar workers in the work force exceeded the proportion of uniformed or blue-collar workers, but the division has remained relatively equal since then. As of April 1978 the figures looked like this:

1. *White-collar workers*—51.0 percent.
2. *Blue-collar workers*—33.0 percent.
3. *Service workers*—14.0 percent.
4. *Farm workers*—2.0 percent.
5. *Professional and technical workers*—15.0 percent.
6. *Managers and administrators*—11.0 percent.
7. *Sales workers*—6.0 percent.
8. *Clerical workers*—6.0 percent.
9. *Skilled workers* (e.g., carpenters, electricians, plumbers) —10.0 percent.
10. *Factory workers*—11.0 percent.
11. *Transport workers*—4.0 percent.
12. *Laborers*—4.5 percent.
13. *Owners of businesses* (including partnerships)—about 7.0 percent.

SOURCE

U.S. Department of Labor, *Monthly Labor Review*, April, 1978.

WHAT OUR SOCIAL STRUCTURE IS LIKE

The Census Bureau does not address itself to the matter of social classes in the United States, the official view being that there *are* no social classes in our egalitarian society. Sociologists, on the other hand, contend that although there is far less social stratification in America than exists in most other countries, there are social classes nonetheless. The problem is that nobody seems to know exactly how the society should be divided up.

• **THE WARNER INDEX.** Probably the most widely quoted picture of the class system in the United States is the one proposed in the late 1940s by W. Lloyd Warner and Paul S. Lunt. Warner was one of the first sociologists to minimize the purely financial elements of class standing and to give more emphasis to family background, education, profession, residence, acceptance by members of the "superior class," as measured by club affiliations, etc. Warner's Index of Status Characteristics, and the percentages he assigned to each category, were:

1. *Upper-upper*—1.4 percent.
2. *Lower-upper*—1.6 percent.

3. *Upper-middle*—10.0 percent.
4. *Lower-middle*—28.0 percent.
5. *Upper-lower*—33.0 percent.
6. *Lower-lower*—25.0 percent.

• S E L F - A P P R A I S A L . Shifting social and economic patterns (for instance, the fact that more people from the "lower" strata of society are going to the more prestigious schools and also that persons in traditionally "lower" strata occupations— e.g., plumbers, electricians—now earn more than those in many "upper" strata occupations—e.g., college professors) have pretty much nullified the Warner index, certainly as far as the lower and middle levels are concerned. And when Americans are asked to name the class to which they *think* they belong, the numbers, according to NORC General Social Surveys carried out in the period 1972–73, look pretty much like this:

1. *Upper class*—2 percent.
2. *Middle class*—45 percent.
3. *Working class*—46 percent.
4. *Lower class*—6 percent.

SOURCES
NORC.
W. Lloyd Warner and Paul S. Lunt, *Social Class in America*, 1949.

HOW WE ARE COEXISTING WITH THE ENVIRONMENT

You would not guess it from the bill for the oil we import each year, but the rate of energy consumption in the United States has actually slowed during the 1970s and, in some areas, even declined. Here is an overall look.

• O N T H E R O A D . Some U.S. Environmental Protection Agency numbers on gas usage in the 1970s:

1. *Rate of increase in the period 1973–78*—about 10 percent.
2. *Average increase per year*—2 percent (compared with 5 percent in the 1960s).

3. *Average miles per gallon on cars manufactured in 1978* —19 (up from 14 in 1973).
4. *Proportion of "small cars" bought in 1978*—48 percent (compared with 35 percent in 1973).

• **H O M E   F I R E S** . Energy consumption in the home *decreased* in the period 1973–78, largely because of lower thermostat settings and thicker insulation in the attic. The numbers:

1. *Homes with accessible attics that have six inches or more of insulation*—57 percent (compared with 18 percent in 1973).
2. *Natural-gas consumption 1973–76*—down 13 percent.
3. *Annual growth rate of electricity use in homes*—3 percent between 1973 and 1976 (compared with 6 percent in previous years).

• **T R A S H Y   N E W S** . Americans generate an average of about 3.6 pounds of solid waste a day, which is slightly more than we were generating in 1971. A look inside the average trash can would show the following items in the proportions specified:

1. *Paper*—40–60 percent.
2. *Grass, brush, and garden cuttings*—10–20 percent.
3. *Garbage*—5–15 percent.
4. *Ashes and dirt*—5–20 percent.
5. *Metal cans and tubes*—8 percent.
6. *Glass bottles and jars*—3–9 percent.
7. *Odd bits of plastic*—2–6 percent.

SOURCES

Frederick C. Klein, "Patterns of Energy Use in the U.S. Are Changing Five Years After Crisis," *Wall Street Journal*, September 7, 1978.

Restoring the Quality of Our Environment: Report of the Environmental Pollution Panel of the President's Science Advisory Committee, 1965.

WHERE OUR MONEY GOES

In 1977 (the most recent year for which figures are available) Americans spent approximately 1 trillion 200 million dollars on personal items. Here, in rough figures, is where it went:

1. *Food and tobacco*—21.0 percent.
2. *Clothing, accessories, and jewelry*—8.0 percent.
3. *Personal care*—1.5 percent.
4. *Housing*—15.0 percent.
5. *Household operation*—14.5 percent.
6. *Medical care*—9.5 percent.
7. *Personal business*—5.0 percent.
8. *Transportation*—14.5 percent.
9. *Recreation*—6.5 percent.
10. *Private education*—1.5 percent.
11. *Religious and welfare activities*—1.0 percent.

And here are some representative dollar amounts:

1. *Food (excluding restaurant meals)*—$177.3 billion.
2. *Food in restaurants*—$62.0 billion.
3. *Shoes*—$95.5 billion.
4. *Jewelry and watches*—$7.5 billion.
5. *Telephone calls*—$20.8 billion.
6. *Drugs and sundries*—$11.3 billion.
7. *Legal services*—$3.5 billion.
8. *Funeral and burial expenses*—$3.5 billion.
9. *Life insurance*—$7.9 billion.
10. *New cars*—$46.2 billion.
11. *Auto repair*—$25.8 billion.
12. *Gas and oil*—$46.5 billion.
13. *Airline tickets*—$4.7 billion.
14. *Books and maps*—$4.4 billion.
15. *Movie admission*—$4.0 billion.
16. *Flowers, seeds, and potted plants*—$1.7 billion.
17. *Spectator sports*—$1.9 billion.

SOURCE
U.S. Department of Commerce, *Survey of Current Business*, July, 1978.

HOW WE COPE WITH INFLATION

Numerous surveys over the past year or so have tried to find out exactly how Americans are fighting inflation. Here are the fighting words some of them came up with.

• **E L E C T R I C E Y E S .** A Roper poll conducted in July 1978 found that most Americans were fighting inflation by cutting down on electricity usage. The numbers:

1. *Proportion of Americans fighting inflation by conserving electricity—72 percent.*
2. *Economizing on food—57 percent.*
3. *Economizing on clothing—54 percent.*
4. *Using or repairing things that would normally be replaced—50 percent.*
5. *Driving at lower speeds—47 percent.*
6. *Economizing on recreation and entertainment—46 percent.*
7. *Cutting down on eating out in restaurants—45 percent.*
8. *Spending more time at home—43 percent.*
9. *Using the car less often—34 percent.*
10. *Not doing anything—28 percent.*

• **S T O M A C H P A I N S .** And from a *New York Times*/CBS News poll done in February 1979, this picture of spending cutbacks:

1. *No cutbacks—21 percent.*
2. *Cutback in expenditures for food—45 percent.*
3. *Clothing—22 percent.*
4. *Gasoline and automobile expenses—11 percent.*
5. *Entertainment—7 percent.*
6. *Recreation—5 percent.*

And this is how inflation is affecting our saving patterns:

1. *Saving more—13 percent.*
2. *Saving less—31 percent.*
3. *No change in saving patterns—31 percent.*

• **H E A L T H C U T B A C K S .** From *The General Mills American Family Report* 1978–79, a survey conducted by Yankelovich, Skelly and White, Inc., this view of how inflation is affecting the health expenditures of the average American family, based on proportion of American families cutting back in the following areas:

1. *Buying high quality food—19 percent.*
2. *Having dental work done—16 percent.*
3. *Serving meat at meals every day—14 percent.*
4. *Going to the doctor for annual checkup—13 percent.*

5. *Getting dental checkups*—11 percent.
6. *Getting new eyeglasses*—11 percent.
7. *Serving fresh fruits and vegetables*—8 percent.
8. *Having eyes/ears checked*—6 percent.
9. *Taking the children to the doctor as often as before*— 8 percent.

SOURCES
The General Mills American Family Report 1978–79.
The New York Times, February 1, 1979.
The Roper Organization.

HOW WE APPROACH LIFE

It is common practice in social research to divide the population into so-called demographic groups (age, race, occupation, region), but it has long been apparent to social scientists (not to mention market researchers) that demographic analyses of specific characteristics of the population give us a limited picture, at best. The main problem is that demographic categories keep cutting into one another's territory so that when you are talking, say, about Americans earning $10,000 or less it is hard to tell what proportion of their number is older than 65 or younger than 21.

Not to worry. The new push in demography is a field known as psychographics. What psychographics does is to categorize Americans less on the basis of traditional demographic divisions and more on the basis of attitudes, tastes, and life-styles. True, there are inescapable demographic patterns to psychographic divisions (older people, for instance, tend to be more conservative in outlook and life-style than younger people), but psychographic studies show clearly that many attitudes and life approaches cut noticeably across traditional demographic lines.

• T H E P L A Y B O Y F O U R S O M E . A classic example of psychographics can be seen in the survey Louis Harris and Associates did for Playboy Enterprises, *The Playboy Report on American Men.* Harris divided American men (aged 18 to 49) into four types.

1. *Traditionalists:* defenders of the past who are committed to "time-honored" values and persist in "old allegiances"—23 percent.

2. *Conventionals:* men who (like Traditionalists) prefer what is "established and familiar" but are a little more open to "new alternatives"—27 percent.
3. *Contemporaries:* men who "prefer the new" but still have a concern for "continuity within the established order"—25 percent.
4. *Innovators:* men who are more adventurous than the other three types when it comes to experimenting with new life-styles—25 percent.

Harris found the following demographic characteristics for each group.

1. *Traditionalists:* older, more likely to be married than other types, and more dominated by men of the "lower" and "working" classes, as compared with the other types.
2. *Conventionals:* slightly younger than Traditionalists, a little less likely to be married, and with a somewhat higher proportion of students and "working class" men.
3. *Contemporaries:* similar to Traditionalists, but a little younger, with a larger proportion of single men.
4. *Innovators:* youngest of all groups by far, and with the highest proportion of "upper middle class" men (27 percent); also the only group in which single men outnumber married men.

• **THE WELLS REPORT.** One of the country's best-known and widely respected psychographers is the Chicago psychologist William D. Wells, who has done a good deal of work for the advertising firm Needham, Harper and Steers. Wells has identified six segments of what we normally think of as "middle-class America":

1. *Status quo:* Americans who are highly traditional and conservative in their views on religion, patriotism, and social change—25 percent.
2. *Mean streets:* struggling blue-collar men (and their wives) who married young and for whom the American dream has gone sour—20 percent.
3. *Salt of the earth:* "solid citizen" types who live simple, untangled lives and spend their leisure time in such activities as leading Boy Scout troops, coaching Little League teams—20 percent.
4. *Horatio Algers:* men who started poor but have made it

big financially; a generous and gregarious group that tends to be politically conservative—17 percent.

5. *Cosmopolitans*: upwardly mobile, generally affluent, college-educated Americans who lead active lives (skiing, playing tennis, jogging), travel a good deal, and make up the bulk of the nation's culture consumers— 20 percent.

6. *Sophisticates*: fashionable women who are somewhat older and wealthier than cosmopolitans, though similar in outlook if not in life-style—15 percent.

• **RANDOM PATTERNS**. The key to Wells's psychographic studies is the interest and opinion statements that reflect general outlooks. Here are some of these outlooks and the proportion of Americans who hold them.

American women who:

1. *Consider themselves "somewhat old-fashioned in their tastes and habits"*—86 percent.
2. *Think there is "too much emphasis on sex today"*—87 percent.
3. *Feel their lives have a definite routine*—67 percent.
4. *Consider themselves "homebodies"*—69 percent.
5. *Feel their first obligation is to their husbands, not their children*—69 percent.

In each of the areas above the proportion of women expressing the outlook is smaller among younger women, but the variation between the younger-than-25 age-group and the 55-and-older age-group is not notably great. Indeed, in some of the outlook areas American women show a characteristically liberal bent once they get past age 55.

American men who:

1. *Consider themselves "somewhat old-fashioned in their tastes and habits"*—86 percent.
2. *Think there is "too much emphasis on sex today"*—66 percent.
3. *Feel their days follow a definite routine*—63 percent.
4. *Consider themselves "homebodies"*—72 percent.
5. *Feel that a wife's first obligation is to her husband, not her children*—57 percent.

Here again, as with women, younger men show a more liberal streak than older men. The difference, though, is that the gap between younger men and older men is much greater than the gap between younger women and older women. In other words, men, as they age, tend to become much more conservative in their outlook than do women.

SOURCES

Angus Campbell, Philip E. Converse and Willard L. Rodgers, *The Quality of American Life*, 1976.
NORC.
Needham, Harper and Steers.
The Playboy Report on American Men, 1979.

WHAT IS IMPORTANT TO US

The old standby values—family, motherhood, country, work— are still alive and well in American life, but there has been a noticeable shift in values among younger people, the majority of whom are far more *self*-oriented than were Americans in decades past. The fitness boom, the success of self-help books, the increase in marijuana smoking, the growth of movements like est, the sexual revolution—all these elements of contemporary American life seem to be rooted in a fundamental shift away from outer-directed values to inner-directed values.

• THE GENERAL PICTURE. Probably the two most important values in American life today ("value" being defined as something that a person considers important to his or her happiness) are health and love. The Institute for Social Research study that led to the book *The Quality of American Life* found that health was the value mentioned most often as being "most important to personal happiness," and the Harris survey that led to *The Playboy Report on American Men* turned up the same results.

Next to health, love is mentioned most frequently when Americans talk about values important to their personal happiness. Nearly all American men between the ages of 18 and 49 (99 percent according to the *Playboy* report) consider love important to happiness, and 85 percent consider it very important. Although love per se was not one of the life domains examined in *The Quality of American Life*, it was reported that 94 percent of the people surveyed considered a happy marriage to be either important or extremely important. This was the only life domain mentioned by more than 50 percent of the respondents as one of the two most important life domains.

Family is still a very strong value among all segments of society but shows signs of losing its overall importance among younger people. The work ethic is strong, too, but, among younger people, seems to be taking on a much more self-oriented character. (Younger people are much more concerned than older people about the *nature* of the work they do rather than the financial rewards, etc.). This leaves religion, whose importance is much more evident among older people than among younger people but, in general, ranks well below the values already mentioned.

• VALUE JUDGMENTS. No single study to date has presented us with a definitive picture of American values in the late 1970s, but here is a sampling of what some of the individual surveys have turned up.

Personal values of college students, with proportion of those considering them "very important" (from a Daniel Yankelovich survey conducted in 1975):

1. *Self-fulfillment*—87 percent.
2. *Education*—76 percent.
3. *Family*—68 percent.
4. *Hard work*—43 percent.
5. *Having children*—31 percent.
6. *Religion*—28 percent.
7. *Money*—20 percent.
8. *Patriotism*—19 percent.

Personal values of parents (from *The General Mills American Family Report 1976–77*):

1. *Family*—81 percent.
2. *Education*—71 percent.
3. *Self-fulfillment*—67 percent.
4. *Hard work*—62 percent.
5. *Religion*—52 percent.
6. *Patriotism*—43 percent.
7. *Having children*—43 percent.
8. *Money*—31 percent.

Basic values of men 18 to 49, with proportion of respondents considering them "very important personally for a happy and satisfied life" (from *The Playboy Report on American Men*):

1. *Health*—89 percent.
2. *Love*—85 percent.
3. *Peace of mind*—84 percent.
4. *Family life*—84 percent.
5. *Work*—65 percent.
6. *Friends*—63 percent.
7. *Respect from others*—58 percent.
8. *Education*—57 percent.
9. *Sex*—49 percent.
10. *Religion*—41 percent.
11. *Money*—39 percent.

Traits considered important by American teenagers, with proportion of those considering them "extremely important" (from a U.S. Department of Health, Education, and Welfare survey):

1. *Obeying the law*—72 percent.
2. *Being neat and clean*—68 percent.
3. *Obeying one's parents*—66 percent.
4. *Knowing how to keep in good health*—64 percent.
5. *Having self-control*—63 percent.
6. *Being dependable*—59 percent.
7. *Being considerate of others*—51 percent.
8. *Being happy*—50 percent.
9. *Facing life's problems calmly*—46 percent.
10. *Being ambitious*—34 percent.
11. *Being able to defend oneself*—34 percent.

Attitudes of American parents toward classic American values, with the proportion of parents who go along with them (from *The General Mills American Family Report*):

1. *Duty before pleasure*—90 percent.
2. *"It's not important to win, it's how the game is played"* —89 percent.
3. *Happiness is possible without money*—86 percent.
4. *Any prejudice is morally wrong*—84 percent.
5. *There is life after death*—79 percent.
6. *Everyone should save money even if it means doing without things right now*—78 percent.
7. *My country right or wrong*—75 percent.

8. *People in authority know best*—70 percent.
9. *Sex outside of marriage is morally wrong*—70 percent.

Things that are very important in a happy, satisfied life, with proportions who consider them so (from a Harris survey conducted in 1978):

1. *Good health*—97 percent.
2. *Family life*—92 percent.
3. *Peace of mind*—91 percent.
4. *Respect from others*—76 percent.
5. *Friends*—71 percent.
6. *Education*—69 percent.
7. *Work*—60 percent.
8. *Religion*—58 percent.
9. *Money*—47 percent.
10. *Sex*—38 percent.
11. *Romantic love*—33 percent.

SOURCES

Angus Campbell, *The Quality of American Life.*
The General Mills American Family Report 1976–77.
Harris Survey.
The Playboy Report on American Men.
U.S. Department of Health, Education, and Welfare, *Behavioral Patterns in School of Youths 12–17 Years,* 1972.
Daniel Yankelovich, *The New Morality: A Profile of American Youth in the 1970s,* 1975.

II OUR PHYSICAL CHARACTERISTICS

HOW TALL WE ARE

In short, we're getting taller.

• **T H E   B A S I C   N U M B E R S .** If we use the standard "reference" scale for men and women that serves as the basic measuring stick in the field known as anthropometrics, the average American man turns out to be around five feet eight inches tall and the average American woman about five feet four inches tall. The average goes up in both cases, however, when you consider only Americans younger than 35. The reasons are: (*a*) with each successive generation in the United States, there has ben a slight gain in the average height; and (*b*) as people get older, they tend to, well, shrink. The shrinking process starts at age 30. The most recent U.S. Department of Health, Education, and Welfare survey on height in America puts the median height of 17-year-old boys at about five feet nine inches and the median height of American girls at about five feet three-and-a-half inches.

• **C H A N G E S .** Comparative studies of the height of American females in the early 1960s and American females today show a noticeable increase in the proportion of tall women and a corresponding decrease in the proportion of short women. Here are some of the 1962 estimated proportions, according to age:

1. *Women aged 18 to 24 who were shorter than five feet—* 12 percent.
2. *Women of all ages who were shorter than five feet—*19 percent.
3. *Women aged 18 to 24 who were taller than five feet six inches—*19 percent.
4. *Women of all ages who were taller than five feet six inches—*13 percent.

Finally, one recent survey among female college students suggests that nearly half (46 percent) are five feet six inches or taller.

• **F A M I L Y   T R E E S .** Anthropometric studies carried out throughout the past thirty years have pointed to certain ethnic and racial patterns in the height of Americans. A few highlights:

1. Americans with northern European roots are taller, on average, than Americans with roots in southern and eastern Europe and Asia.
2. Hispanic Americans are shorter, on average, than white and black Americans.
3. Black teenagers are slightly taller than white teenagers except in the case of 14- and 15-year-old boys and 12- and 13-year-old girls, when the reverse is true.

• **HEIGHT ADVANTAGES.** Over the past few years several studies suggest that in the American business world it helps to be tall. Shorter men apparently have a tougher time getting hired by corporations and are not as likely to be offered as high a starting salary ("We pay by the inch here!") as taller men. On the other hand, recent studies, including one done at the University of Minnesota by Ellen Berscheid and Thomas Brothen, show that women are no more attracted to tall men than they are to men of medium height, although men of medium height enjoy a slight edge in sex appeal over shorter men. Most psychological studies on attitudes toward height indicate that men exaggerate the importance women place on the height of the men they are attracted to.

• **TALL ORDERS.** Nearly six out of ten American teenagers interviewed as part of HEW's National Health Survey expressed satisfaction with their present height, but girls were more likely to do so than boys. About half the teenage boys in the United States would like to be taller, and only 2 percent want to be shorter (it's reasonable to assume that this 2 percent do not play basketball). Among girls, the proportion who aspire to greater heights is 20 percent, whereas 13 percent say they would be happier if they were shorter.

SOURCES

William Graziano, Thomas Brothen, and Ellen Berscheid, "Height and Attraction: Do Men and Women See Eye to Eye?" 1978.

Frank I. Katch and William D. McArdle, *Nutrition, Weight Control and Exercise,* 1977.

U.S. Department of Health, Education, and Welfare, *Height and Weight of Youths 12–17 Years,* 1972.

HOW MUCH WE WEIGH

Given the fact that so many people go up and down in their weight, it is hard to be precise when talking about "average weights" in the United States. Even the "ideal" or "typical" weights used by insurance companies as a basic barometer present problems inasmuch as they do not always account for differences in size, age, and body type.

• **THE BASIC NUMBERS.** The Metropolitan Life Insurance Company's chart of "desirable weight" levels, which follows, should give you some idea of average weights in the United States. Approximately 65 percent of Americans fall into, or close to, these weight categories. About 25 percent of Americans are over these categories, and 10 percent or so fall below.

MEN

Height	Small Frame	Medium Frame	Large Frame
5'6"	124–133	130–143	138–156
5'8"	132–141	138–152	147–166
5'10"	140–150	146–160	155–174
6'	148–158	143–170	165–184
6'3"	160–171	167–185	178–199

WOMEN

Height	Small Frame	Medium Frame	Large Frame
5'	96–104	101–113	109–125
5'2"	102–110	107–119	115–131
5'4"	108–116	113–126	121–138
5'6"	114–123	120–135	129–146
5'8"	122–131	128–143	137–154
5'10"	120–140	136–151	145–163
6'	128–148	144–159	152–173

• **BABY FAT.** A newborn baby is considered average if it arrives weighing seven pounds five ounces—a little more if he is a boy, a little less if she is a girl. This average has not changed all that much since 1950, but white babies tend to weigh, on average, around eight ounces more than black babies.

• **F A T C I T Y .** Estimates on the number of Americans who are overweight by present medical standards range anywhere from 25 percent to 40 percent of the population. A lot depends on whose desirable weight levels you use as a measuring stick, but in any event, there seems to be a higher proportion of overweight women than overweight men, as well as a larger proportion of overweight persons in lower-income groups than among high-income earners. Ethnic factors, too, appear to play a role. Americans with northern European ethnic backgrounds are less likely to be overweight than those with eastern and southern European backgrounds. And even geography appears to influence obesity: The hotter the climate, the lower the percentage of obese persons.

• **D E M O G R A P H I C F A T .** A Department of Health, Education, and Welfare study in the early 1970s gave the following picture of weight patterns in the United States, based on age, income, race, and gender.

"Lean" Americans between the ages of 20 and 44:

1. *White males above the poverty level*—12.5 percent.
2. *Black males above the poverty level*—34.0 percent.
3. *White males below the poverty level*—18.5 percent.
4. *Black males below the poverty level*—39.0 percent.
5. *White females above the poverty level*—12.0 percent.
6. *Black females above the poverty level*—17.0 percent.
7. *White females below the poverty level*—17.5 percent.
8. *Black females below the poverty level*—18.0 percent.

"Obese" Americans between the ages of 20 and 44:

1. *White males above the poverty level*—17.0 percent.
2. *Black males above the poverty level*—11.0 percent.
3. *White males below the poverty level*—9.5 percent.
4. *Black males below the poverty level*—11.0 percent.
5. *White females above the poverty level*—17.0 percent.
6. *Black females above the poverty level*—11.5 percent.
7. *White females below the poverty level*—25.0 percent.
8. *Black females below the poverty level*—35.0 percent.

The related numbers for Americans between the ages of 45 and 74 show a smaller proportion of lean people in each demographic group and a larger proportion of obese persons. Racial differences are consistent, except in two categories:

1. White men in the 45–74 age-group are three times as likely as black men to be obese.
2. White women in this age-group are twice as likely as black women to be lean.

•**TEEN IMPRESSIONS.** When American teenagers were asked by Department of Health, Education, and Welfare pollsters in 1972 how they felt about their present weight, here is how they answered:

1. *Satisfied with present weight—66* percent of all teenagers.
2. *Girls who would like to be thinner—50* percent.
3. *Boys who would like to be heavier—25* percent.
4. *Girls who consider themselves overweight—20* percent.
5. *Boys who consider themselves overweight—20* percent.
6. *Boys and girls who consider themselves underweight—* 12 percent.

•**MEAT ON THE HOOF.** The average National Football League lineman now weighs in at about 260 pounds. In 1978 the Detroit Lions had the beefiest line—it averaged 278 pounds. The sveltest crew of linemen in professional football work for the Miami Dolphins, whose average weight is about 230 pounds.

SOURCES

Anne Scott Beller, *Fat and Thin*, 1977.

Metropolitan Life Insurance Company.

Albert J. Stunkard, "The Results of Treatment for Obesity," 1959.

U.S. Bureau of the Census, *Statistical Abstract of the United States: 1978.*

U.S. Department of Health, Education, and Welfare, *Height and Weight of Youths 12–17 Years.*

HOW ATTRACTIVE WE ARE

Since beauty is, after all, in the eye of the beholder, no major survey has ever been conducted to find out just how attractive a people Americans are. But when the Institute for Social Research conducted its interviews for *The Quality of American*

Life, the interviewers were asked to rate the physical attractiveness of the Americans they surveyed.

Proportion of total sample who were rated:

1. *Strikingly handsome or beautiful*—3 percent.
2. *Good-looking (above average for age and sex)*—26 percent.
3. *Of average looks for age and sex*—56 percent.
4. *Quite plain (below average for age and sex)*—13 percent.
5. *Homely*—2 percent.

SOURCE
Angus Campbell, *The Quality of American Life.*

HOW BIG SPECIFIC PARTS OF OUR BODIES ARE

No two body parts hold more fascination, to most people, than penises and breasts. We shall start at the top.

• S T A C K E D   U P . The average bust size in the United States is now about thirty-five inches, compared with thirty-four inches in 1940. But the increase in size is deceiving since the 1940 sampling did not include so high a proportion of older women (who are generally top heavier than younger women). Actually, American women are probably smaller breasted today because they have become proportionally taller, with no companion increase in bust, waist, and hip size. As far as cup size goes, one survey puts 15 percent of American women in the "A" cup category, 44 percent in the "B" cup category, 28 percent in the "C" cup category, and 10 percent in the "D" cup category.

• H U N G   D o w n . The average American penis, in a nonerect state, measures between three and four inches in length and is just under three-and-a half inches in circumference. Erect, it extends about six inches and expands to a circumference of about four-and-a-half inches. Roughly 90 percent of all men have penises that fall somewhere within the five- and seven-inch range in the erect state, but there appears to be no connection—physically, at least—between penis size and sexual prowess, nor is there any definitive relationship between overall body size and penis size. Ethnic and racial differences in penis size remain a delicate subject, with no official proof as yet that any one ethnic or racial group is better hung than any other group, but do not bet on it. Less controversial is the generally accepted fact that the longer a penis is in the flaccid state, the smaller its relative increase in size in the erect state.

•**S T I T C H E D U P .** Approximately 80 percent of American men have been circumcised.

> SOURCES
> *Man's Body,* 1976.
> *Woman's Body,* 1977.

WHAT OUR HAIR IS LIKE

The ethnic and racial heterogeneity of the American population precludes much talk about "typically American" hair characteristics, but there are bits of general information around. Here is some of it.

•**S H A D Y D E A L S .** According to a survey taken by one leading manufacturer of hair products, the distribution of hair color among American women (and, presumably, American men fall into the same general proportions) is as follows:

1. *Brown hair of differing shades*—70 percent.
2. *Blond hair (natural)*—15 percent.
3. *Black hair*—10 percent.
4. *Red hair*—6 percent.

•**M A K I N G W A V E S .** As far as the *nature* of our hair is concerned, the numbers, according to the Breck Shampoo Company, look like this:

1. *Somewhat wavy or curly*—65 percent.
2. *Straight*—14 percent.
3. *Basically straight but with a slight wave*—15 percent.
4. *Curly hair*—10 percent.

•**C O I F F I N G U P .** Hairstyles move in and out of fashion as unpredictably as clothing, but at last look, in early 1979, here is how American women were wearing their hair, according to a Breck survey:

1. *Short enough for the ears to show*—50 percent.
2. *Medium length (mid-neck)*—33 percent.
3. *Long (Farrah Fawcett style)*—20 percent.

The two most popular hairstyles in the United States over the past several years have been:

1. *Medium-length pageboy*—21 percent.
2. *"No frills" short*—18 percent.

Other related patterns:

1. *Proportion of women who wear their hair long and are 34 or younger*—90 percent.
2. *Women who wear their hair short and are 45 or older*—75 percent.
3. *Teenage girls who wore their hair at chin length in 1978*—75 percent.

• **SPLITTING HAIRS.** Approximately 90 percent of teen-age girls, according to a 1975 *Seventeen* magazine hair care survey, have a complaint about their hair. The biggest complaint—voiced by 43 percent of girls—oily hair. About 38 percent complain about split ends, 29 percent about lack of body, and 26 percent about dandruff and flaking.

• **GONE TODAY.** Roughly 60 percent of American men are either partially or fully bald, with the proportion naturally higher among *older* men. According to Edmund Van Deusen one out of three men between 30 and 40 shows some sign of baldness, with 20 percent displaying the so-called horseshoe pattern. Among age-groups, the proportion of bald men increases with age, leveling off at about 65 percent at age 55, then rising again at age 70.

SOURCES
Breck Shampoo Company.
Edmund Van Deusen, *Baldness*, 1978.
Seventeen.

WHAT OUR TEETH ARE LIKE

You guessed it. Our teeth are getting better, but our gums are getting worse. And most of us still hate to go to the dentist.

• THE BASIC NUMBERS. Only 2 percent (if that!) of Americans have *never* in their lives experienced anything in the way of a tooth problem, which helps explain why tooth disease is sometimes called mankind's most universal malady. Some related numbers from a book called *Your Mouth: Oral Care for All Ages*, and the American Dental Association:

1. *Two-year-old American babies who have at least one cavity*—50 percent.
2. *Americans who have at least 18 of their original teeth filled, decayed, missing, or replaced*—40 percent.
3. *Toothless Americans*—12.5 percent.
4. *Average number of cavities (filled or unfilled) in the typical American teenager's mouth*—6.

• CAVITY REPORT. Despite all the clamor against the use of fluoride in the water, the latest findings show that children who drink naturally or artificially fluoridated water have 50 to 60 percent fewer cavities than children with no access to fluoride.

• OPEN WIDE. Bits and pieces from various dental surveys. Americans who:

1. *Believe in the value of semiannual dental checkups*—56 percent.
2. *Went to a dentist at least twice during 1978*—1 percent.
3. *Went to a dentist at least once in 1978*—50 percent.

Average number of:

1. *Times members of high-income families visit a dentist in a typical year*—2.2.
2. *Times members of low-income families visit a dentist in a typical year*—1.1.
3. *Dollars Americans spend on dentists each year*—$22 per person.

• STRAIGHT TALK. As of early 1979 about four million Americans were wearing braces or some similar orthodontic device, and one out of five of them was older than 18.

SOURCES

American Dental Association.

Nguyen, Nguyen Thanh. *Your Mouth: Oral Care for All Ages*, 1978.

U.S. Department of Health, Education, and Welfare. *Health, United States 1976–77.*

WHAT KIND OF SHAPE WE ARE IN

Physical fitness is such a relative concept (relative to age, gender, body weight) that establishing averages is almost as tough as running a four-minute mile. It is obvious, though, that relative to Europeans at least, Americans are in sad physical shape.

• THE BASIC NUMBERS. Based on data supplied by the U.S. military and public-school testing programs, it appears that no more than 10 to 15 percent of Americans younger than 21 are in good physical condition by international standards, and as much as 30 percent or more are probably well below the norm. As far as adults go, most fitness experts, including aerobics pioneer Dr. Kenneth Cooper, estimate that no more than 20 percent are fit in the true sense of the word.

• FLUNKING OUT. A recent study by the Center for Parenting, UCLA Extension, in Palos Verdes, California, showed that 86 percent of first-graders were unable to pass a minimal physical-fitness test. This means that we are falling back even further from the levels we were at in the mid-1950s, when 58 percent of American schoolchildren were failing basic flexibility and strength tests, compared with the less than 10 percent failure rate in Austria, Italy, and Switzerland. On the other hand, a report from the U.S. Department of Defense, issued in the early 1970s, showed that only one-third of high-school students in the United States were failing the President's Council on Physical Fitness test—a relatively simple test of strength, stamina, and agility.

•**HEART MURMURS**. The average American heart beats anywhere between 72 and 80 times a minute. Well-conditioned athletes generally have a much slower pulse rate. Regular joggers tend to have pulse rates in the low sixties and even the high fifties. But pulse rate is only one measure of cardiac fitness. Another is orthostatic heart strength, which is measured by comparing the difference between the pulse rate after a person has been lying down for several moments and the pulse rate after he or she has been standing for a moment or so. A trained athlete will show a difference of no more than six beats per minute. The average difference is about sixteen beats per minute.

SOURCES
Center for Parenting.
Donald I. Katch, *Nutrition, Weight Control and Exercise.*
Donald K. Mathews, *Measurement in Physical Education*, 1973.
Curtis Mitchell, *The Perfect Exercise Book*, 1976.

HOW WE DEVELOP

•**THE BASIC NUMBERS**. The rate at which babies develop sensory, motor, and conceptual skills varies broadly from child to child, but psychologists have established some rough norms. Here are some of the basic skills babies develop and the approximate age at which these skills materialize:

1. *Make a response to a moving face*—6 weeks to 2 months.
2. *React selectively to certain sounds*—3 months.
3. *Recognize mother or father*—3 months.
4. *Stay propped without support*—3 months.
5. *Make primitive attempts to vocalize*—3 months.
6. *Sit with some support*—4 to 6 months.
7. *Respond to name*—6 months.
8. *Vocalize for the purpose of communicating*—7 months.
9. *Sit alone on a floor without support*—9 to 11 months.
10. *Say "Ma Ma" and "Da Da"*—1 year.
11. *Crawl*—10 months to 1 year.
12. *Stand*—1 year.
13. *Use actual words*—14 months.

14. *Walk*—1 year to 18 months.
15. *Inform parents about going to bathroom*—15 months.
16. *Talk in short sentences*—2 years.
17. *Start toilet training*—2 years.
18. *Be toilet trained throughout the day*—2.5 years.
19. *Stay dry through the night*—3 years or so.

• **COMING OF AGE.** For a variety of reasons (chief among them an improved diet), American teenagers are reaching puberty earlier than ever. The best evidence is the fact that American teenage girls are menstruating earlier today than at any other time in our history. The current average, according to a U.S. HEW survey, is about 12 years 5 months (a little younger for black teenage girls), as compared with an average of 14 years 2 months in 1900. American girls, by and large, begin menstruating a year earlier than European girls.

SOURCES
Child's Body, 1978.
Joseph L. Stone and Joseph Church, *Childhood and Adolescence,* 1968.
U.S. Department of Health, Education, and Welfare, *Age at Menarche, United States.*

HOW WE GO TO SEED

Aging is, of course, inevitable and irreversible, but not everybody's body goes to pot at the same rate. Here is a brief glimpse of what the average person can expect to happen as he or she gets older.

• **INSTRUMENT LANDINGS.** The elasticity in the lens of the average person starts to go at about age 15, but vision problems are likely to start a good deal earlier. All of which explains why roughly half the American population over the age of 3 wear glasses. Women (54 percent) are more likely to wear glasses than men (44 percent), and a higher proportion of whites (51 percent) wear glasses than blacks (33 percent).

• **EAR MUFFS.** The hearing capacity of the average person starts to decline at age 20. This fact helps to explain why one out of every ten Amercans has enough of a hearing loss to be considered hard of hearing, although the hearing loss is serious in only about half these cases.

• **SENSELESS AGING**. Yes, even the taste buds start to go. The process generally begins at about age 50 and is joined about ten years later by a decline in the sense of smell.

• **GOLDEN SWINGERS**. If sexual potency is measured purely in terms of sex-gland activity, it can be said that men start to go downhill sexually somewhere in their twenties, while women do not start to slow down until age 40. This process notwithstanding, recent studies show that as long as they are physically healthy, seven out of ten married couples 60 years of age and older can expect to be sexually active.

SOURCES

Albert Ellis and Albert Albarbanel, *The Encyclopedia of Sexual Behavior*, 1973.

William Keeton, *Biological Science*, 1967.

National Health Education Committee, *Killers and Cripplers*, 1976.

HOW MUCH LIQUOR WE CAN HOLD

Liquor tolerance—the amount of booze you can drink without getting potted—is a highly individual capacity, but there are some general tendencies among the population as a whole. The measure usually used in this area of physical capacity is blood-alcohol level.

• **THE BASIC NUMBERS**. Liquor begins to have an effect on the average person's behavior when the blood-alcohol level reaches 0.03 percent. The law in most states says you are drunk when your blood-alcohol level reaches 0.15 percent. A level of 0.60 percent is usually enough to kill you. The average person who weighs, say, 150 pounds can generally metabolize about 0.40 ounce of absolute alcohol an hour. Using this figure as a measuring stick, you can figure that either six glasses of wine, six cans of beer, or three 2-ounce shots of straight liquor downed within the space of an hour will make most people drunk.

• VARIABLES . The more weight you carry, the higher your tolerance for alcohol. Everything else being equal, a 200-pound man can consume 25 percent more alcohol than a 150-pound man before the same effects will take hold. Men, in general, have a slightly higher tolerance for alcohol than do women, and a heavy drinker usually has twice the tolerance for liquor that an abstainer has, and about 30 percent more tolerance than a moderate drinker.

SOURCE
Oakley S. Ray, *Drugs, Society and Human Behavior,* 1972.

III OUR TRAITS

HOW HAPPY WE ARE

Happiness is a state of being that nearly everybody thinks about and hardly anybody understands. So it is no surprise that sociologists and psychologists have had all sorts of trouble over the years trying to find out for certain exactly how happy Americans really are and trying to get a bead on the factors that contribute to, or take away from, personal happiness. What the survey data show, in general, is that (*a*) most Americans are basically satisfied with their lives; but (*b*) fewer people today are ready to describe themselves as "very happy," as compared with the late 1950s; and (*c*) more Americans in the late 1970s expressed their uncertainty about the future than did so at any other time over the past twenty-five years. Here is a closer look.

• **T H E B A S I C N U M B E R S .** Nearly all the data available on happiness levels in the United States come to us by virtue of surveys in which people are asked to comment on how they feel about the present state of their lives—whether they are "very happy," "pretty happy," or "not too happy." (Many surveys word the choices differently.) An overall view of the most recent surveys give us the following picture:

1. *Very happy*—25–30 percent.
2. *Pretty happy*—55–65 percent.
3. *Not too happy*—5–15 percent.

If we compare the figures above with those from periods in recent history, it is clear that changes are taking place. One widely quoted survey on happiness found 35 percent of Americans in 1960 describing themselves as "very happy," and an additional 54 percent describing themselves as "pretty happy." By the early 1970s, though, the proportion of "very happy" Americans had dipped to 22 percent (according to an Institute for Social Research survey), and the proportion of the "pretty happy" had risen to 68 percent. Curiously, the proportion of Americans who describe themselves as "unhappy" or "not too happy" has remained fairly constant since the late 1950s, the only real change occurring in the mid-1960s (around the time of the Kennedy assassination) when some surveys showed about 16 percent of Americans rated themselves unhappy. Some additional numbers:

Proportion of Americans describing themselves as "very happy," for the years 1972 to 1978 (according to NORC surveys):

1. 1972—30 percent.
2. 1973—35 percent.
3. 1974—37 percent.
4. 1975—30 percent.
5. 1976—34 percent.
6. 1977—34 percent.
7. 1978—34 percent.

• **BLESSING COUNT**. It is one thing to describe yourself as "happy" or "unhappy" and something else again to isolate specific areas of your life and measure the satisfaction therein. Here is how Americans responding to NORC surveys reported their satisfaction with specific areas of their lives during the 1970s.

Americans who say they draw a "very great deal of satisfaction" from:

1. *City or place where they live*—16.0 percent (down from 23.0 percent in 1972).
2. *Hobbies and nonwork activities*—23.0 percent (about the same as 1972).
3. *Family life*—38.5 percent (down from 42.5 percent in 1972).
4. *Friendships*—26.0 percent (down from 33.0 percent in 1972).

Americans who say they draw "a great deal" of satisfaction from:

1. *City or place where they live*—30 percent (up from 23 percent in 1972).
2. *Hobbies and nonwork activities*—38 percent (up from 28 percent in 1972).
3. *Family life*—35 percent (up from 31 percent in 1972).

• **THE DEMOGRAPHICS OF JOY**. No demographic segment of the population has cornered the market on happiness, but this is not to discount the importance of certain demographic factors. Money, age, marital status, race, religion—they all have some statistical impact. But the one overriding observation that can be made about happiness in America is that the perception of happiness is relative: People tend to feel happy or unhappy relative to their own needs and aspirations, *regardless* of life-style.

• **MONEY TALKING**. You need a certain minimum income to be happy in the United States, but once you get past a certain point—psychologist Jonathan Freedman suggests $10,000—the proportions of happy people and unhappy people vary relatively little among different income groups. If anything, high-income people are unhappier as a group today than ever before, based on Angus Campbell's finding that the proportion of high-income people who describe themselves as "very happy" had dipped some 33 percent between 1950 and the mid-1970s. On the other hand, Frank M. Andrews and Stephen B. Withey point out that the level of satisfaction expressed by Americans in *specific areas*—health, marriage, job, leisure—is consistently lower among lower-income groups than it is among higher-income groups. The rich may not be happier, but they do seem to have more fun.

• **PASSAGES**. An odd thing happens to most Americans as they grow older. Up to age 65, age does not seem to have any real statistical bearing on happiness levels; but once past 65, two things happen: The proportion of people who describe themselves as "very happy" gets higher, and so does the proportion of people who describe themselves as "unhappy." The explanation generally given for this curious pattern is that as long as the basics are taken care of—that is, you have enough money, good health, a nice place to live—as you get older your happiness levels will rise. Why? Because your expectations drop. But if things do go bad, you do not have the luxury of looking ahead to better days.

• **MARRIED BLISS**. Nearly all the surveys and studies on happiness point to a similar conclusion regarding marriage and happiness: Married people, in general, are happier than single people. There are exceptions. The happiness levels of single men and married men tend to even out past age 40 ("Men," suggests Jonathan Freedman, "get used to being single as they age"), but single women become progressively more miserable as they grow older—much more so than married women. Andrews and Withey found that married people are likely to evaluate life concerns more highly than single people, and Freedman's findings suggest that married people are happier, even, than the estimated 5 percent of American couples who are just keeping house together. Two more marriage notes: Single people who have never married are happier on the whole than singles who have been divorced or separated, and no group shows higher levels of unhappiness than do recently divorced single women.

•LEARNING HOW. If money does not buy you happiness, education does not teach you how to get it. If anything, education appears to interfere with the happiness of some segments of the population. Freedman notes that high-income, college-degreed Americans are less happy than high-income, nondegreed Americans, probably because the expectations of the college-educated are higher to begin with. All told, there appears to be very little difference in the proportion of college graduates who consider themselves happy and the proportion of nongraduates who share the same blessing.

•BLACK MOODS. If we could separate out income, education, health, neighborhood, and other factors from the differences that separate whites and blacks, we could make a guess about whether there is any racial component to happiness. As it stands, there is no reason in the world to think that blacks are any happier than whites, and plenty of reasons to think the opposite. For example, when Andrews and Withey compared black evaluations of specific life concerns with those of whites, it turned out that of the 24 different life concerns listed (including health, family life, community, job satisfaction) the average level of black satisfaction was substantially lower than the average level of white satisfaction in only one area—entertainment. What is more, the difference in the mean level of satisfaction expressed was particularly high in the areas of marriage, neighborhood safety, security from theft, amount of pressure.

•SEX APPEAL. Nine out of ten Americans, according to one of the surveys used by Freedman, say that sex is important to their happiness. It is obvious that people who are frustrated and dissatisfied with their sex life are not going to be as happy as people who are fulfilled. But all things considered, only a small percentage of Americans list sex as one of the "crucial things missing" from their lives, and there seems to be no correlation at all between happiness and the frequency of sexual experience, or variety of sexual partners.

•HOORAY FOR LOVE. Whereas sex is only marginally related to happiness, love seems to be the whole ball of wax. Indeed, again according to Freedman, love is the single most important element in personal happiness for most people. Single men who took part in a *Psychology Today* survey used by Freedman ranked being in love as the third most important "pillar of happiness" (behind friends and social life, and job); single women ranked it second, behind friends and social life; married men ranked it second, behind personal growth. And married women ranked being in love as the most important pillar.

•FRINGE BENEFITS. The more you like what you do for a living, the more likely you are to be satisfied with the rest of your life. One of Freedman's surveys found that 70 percent of Americans who considered themselves happy liked their jobs, whereas only 14 percent of those who did not like their jobs described themselves as being happy. And Angus Campbell found that job satisfaction was a more reliable barometer of overall life satisfaction than marriage, friendship, education, health, and religion.

•HEAVEN CAN WAIT. Logic would dictate that religious Americans are happier than nonreligious Americans, but no survey to date proves the point. Angus Campbell found that religion, of all the major domains in life, had the least bearing on personal happiness; and Jonathan Freedman was unable even to find a correlation between belief in an afterlife, as expressed by old people, and happiness in old age. Freedman did find, though, that followers of the more liberal religious doctrines were more likely to be happy than followers of stricter, more conservative doctrines. Quakers and liberal Protestants, for instance, were more likely to be happy than Catholics, conservative Protestants, and Jews.

•MINORITY REPORT. Some of the surveys designed to measure how *happy* we Americans are have also tried to determine how *unhappy* we are, and the results, by and large, have not conflicted too much. Studies of the amount of psychological stress Americans experience are discussed in a separate section (see Part XII, "Our Problems"). Here are some of the findings Angus Campbell came up with when he gave respondents a chance to comment on *negative* feelings.

Women who said they:

1. *Felt life is hard*—24 percent.
2. *Felt tied down*—15 percent.
3. *Always felt rushed*—23 percent.
4. *Worried some about bills*—36 percent.
5. *Felt frightened*—47 percent.
6. *Worried about a nervous breakdown*—15 percent.

Men who said they:

1. *Felt life is hard*—28 percent.
2. *Felt tied down*—15 percent.
3. *Always felt rushed*—21 percent.
4. *Worried some about bills*—35 percent.
5. *Felt frightened*—38 percent.
6. *Worried about a nervous breakdown*—10 percent.

The proportion of Americans who express these negative feelings varies, of course, according to age, marital status, income, and other factors. Campbell's results do not necessarily refute survey findings that show that more than 75 percent of Americans are happy, they do suggest that even happy people are not without their unhappy sides.

•THE LAST WORD. Surveys taken in the latter part of 1978 and early 1979 show that most Americans feel they are better off today, as 1980 approaches, than they were ten years ago; but inflation is beginning to take its toll on this optimistic outlook. From an NBC/Associated Press survey in 1978:

1. Americans who *felt better off in 1978 than in 1968*—58 percent.
2. *Felt worse off*—14 percent.

From a Gallup poll in early 1979:

1. Americans who *think the future is going to get worse*—55 percent (compared with 21 percent in 1972).
2. *Expect economic difficulty in the future*—69 percent (up from 52 percent in 1978, but down from 85 percent in 1974).

SOURCES

Frank M. Andrews and Stephen B. Withey, *Social Indicators of Well-Being,* 1976.

N. M. Bradburn and D. Caplovitz, *Reports on Happiness,* 1965.

Angus Campbell, *The Quality of American Life.*

Jonathan Freedman, *Happy People,* 1979.

Gallup Poll.

Harris Survey.

NBC News.

NORC.

HOW MUCH SELF-ESTEEM WE HAVE

Studies that could indicate the number of Americans who have a genuine sense of self-confidence (as measured by an individual's perception of his ability to control his own life) are limited, but here is what two studies have come up with in this tricky to measure area.

• CONFIDENCE SCALE. Angus Campbell and his Institute for Social Research colleagues divided the respondents in *The Quality of American Life* study into five categories of confidence. The numbers.

For whites:

1. *Lowest*—7 percent.
2. *Next to lowest*—19 percent.
3. *Middle*—26 percent.
4. *Next to highest*—29 percent.
5. *Highest*—21 percent.

For blacks:

1. *Lowest*—17 percent.
2. *Next to lowest*—25 percent.
3. *Middle*—26 percent.
4. *Next to highest*—21 percent.
5. *Highest*—11 percent.

• I'M OKAY. As part of their study that produced the book *Social Indicators of Well-Being,* Frank Andrews and Stephen Withey asked their respondents some direct questions about

self-feelings. Here are some of the questions and the proportion
of people answering in different ways:
"How do you feel about yourself?"

1. *Delighted*—8 percent.
2. *Pleased*—30 percent.
3. *Mostly satisfied*—41 percent.
4. *Mixed*—17 percent.
5. *Mostly dissatisfied*—2 percent.
6. *Unhappy*—2 percent.
7. *Terrible*—1 percent.

"How do you feel about what you are accomplishing in your
life?"

1. *Delighted*—6 percent.
2. *Pleased*—32 percent.
3. *Mostly satisfied*—38 percent.
4. *Mixed*—17 percent.
5. *Mostly dissatisfied*—5 percent.
6. *Unhappy*—1 percent.
7. *Terrible*—1 percent.

"How do you feel about the extent to which you are achiev-
ing success and getting ahead?"

1. *Delighted*—7 percent.
2. *Pleased*—22 percent.
3. *Mostly satisfied*—35 percent.
4. *Mixed*—21 percent.
5. *Mostly dissatisfied*—9 percent.
6. *Unhappy*—4 percent.
7. *Terrible*—2 percent.

SOURCES
Frank M. Andrews and Stephen B. Withey, *Social In-
dicators of Well-Being*, 1976.
Angust Campbell et al., *The Quality of American Life*.

HOW HONEST WE ARE

Honesty has been a fundamental American value since as far
back as, well, George Washington's time, but some social scientists are lamenting the fact that we may not be as forthright

as we were, say, thirty years ago. Here is a look at both sides of the coin.

• **HONEST OPINION.** When Americans are asked to name the qualities they consider the "most desirable for a child to have," honesty is mentioned as one of the three most desirable qualities in three out of four instances; and it is listed as the most desirable quality nearly 45 percent of the time, according to NORC surveys. In surveys of this type, honesty outdistances every other trait, even judgment, obedience, and self-control.

• **COPY CATS.** An elaborately designed series of experiments conducted in the 1920's by the psychologist H. Hartshorne showed that most children, under certain circumstances, would cheat on tests. But the experiments also showed that only 3 percent of American school kids would cheat "whenever they had the chance," and that 7 percent would not cheat at all, regardless of the circumstances. Here's what a Gallup poll in October 1978 turned up in the way of numbers relating to the cheating practices in high schools and junior high schools today.

1. *Teenagers (boys and girls) who've ever cheated in school—*62 percent.
2. *Who've been caught—*20 percent.
3. *Boys who've cheated—*62 percent.
4. *Girls who've cheated—*58 percent.
5. *Above average students who've cheated—*58 percent.
6. *Below average students who've cheated—*66 percent.

In general, older teenagers are more likely to cheat than younger teenagers, and teenagers in the west are more likely to cheat than teens in the other parts of the country. Finally, 30 percent of American teens admit they cheat "a great deal."

• **WHO DO YOU TRUST?** Asked to rate the "honesty" and "ethical standards" of people in various fields, here's how a Gallup poll sampling in 1977 responded.
Americans who rate honesty and ethical standards high for:

1. *Clergymen—*62 percent.
2. *Medical doctors—*51 percent.
3. *Engineers—*46 percent.
4. *College teachers—*43 percent.
5. *Bankers—*39 percent.

6. *Policemen*—37 percent.
7. *Journalists*—34 percent.
8. *Lawyers*—26 percent.
9. *Undertakers*—26 percent.
10. *Senators*—19 percent.
11. *Businessmen and executives*—15 percent.

Who rate honesty and ethical standards "low" for:

1. *Car salesmen*—48 percent.
2. *Labor union leaders*—47 percent.
3. *Advertising practitioners*—43 percent.
4. *State office holders*—41 percent.
5. *Local political officeholders*—36 percent.
6. *Congressmen*—35 percent.
7. *Realtors*—31 percent.
8. *Insurance salesmen*—27 percent.
9. *Lawyers*—27 percent.
10. *Senators*—26 percent.

• **HONOR SYSTEM.** It may or may not mean much, but a circulation executive of the *New York Times* reports that the proportion of newspaper-vending-machine customers who remove more newspapers than they pay for (once you deposit the appropriate number of coins in one of those machines, you can remove as many papers as you want) is only about 2 to 3 percent. Theft rates vary according to neighborhood, and not according to the headline on any particular day.

• **RING AROUND THE WHITE COLLAR.** A U.S. Department of Commerce report in 1974 claimed that white-collar crime (bribery, pilferage, etc.) exceeds by *several billion dollars* the losses sustained as a result of all robberies and burglaries combined. It is estimated, for example, that about 10 percent of both personal-loss and automobile-insurance claims are deliberately fraudulent. Worse, some federal officials now estimate that half the people who work in plants or offices steal or pilfer to some extent (for instance, using the office stamp machine for personal mail) and as many as 5 to 8 percent of the work force may now be stealing "in volume."

• **TAX DODGERS.** It could be paranoia, but the general feeling among Internal Revenue Service investigators (based on a random sampling of ten IRS workers who operate out of the

Northeast) is that 90 percent of Americans, knowingly or unknowingly, file deceitful tax returns. One knowledgeable Florida CPA, who handles the taxes for more than 500 professionals and executives, estimates that no more than 5 percent of his clients insist that every deduction be absolutely legal.

• T R I C K Y   D I C K S . When a group of social psychologists, headed by S. G. West, trumped up a situation designed to parallel the circumstances surrounding the Watergate break-in, nearly 55 percent of a random sampling of unsuspecting subjects expressed a willingness to commit burglary when they were given the impression that (*a*) the job was being done for the U.S. government and (*b*) immunity was guaranteed. What really surprised the psychologists, though, was that 20 percent of the subjects expressed interest in doing the burglary on a strictly cash basis, with no political implications.

SOURCES
Gallup Poll.
M. A. Hartshorne, *Studies in the Nature of Character,* 1930.
S. G. West et al., "Ubiquitous Watergate: An Attributional Analysis," 1975.

HOW SMART WE ARE

There are so many different ways of measuring mental capacity (IQ being just one) that social scientists have been chary of making observations that reflect on the intelligence of Americans on the whole. There is a good deal of data in the field but quite a bit of trepidation when it comes to interpreting these data and drawing conclusions from them. Here goes, anyway.

• T H E   B A S I C   N U M B E R S . The first thing that comes to the mind of most people when you talk about intelligence is IQ (intelligence quotient). However, IQ is not so much an index of how much you *know*; rather it is the rate of intellectual development you had when you were younger. To determine IQ, you take a test designed to measure mental age, the result of which is divided by your actual age and then multiplied by 100. Mental age, according to IQ specialists, stops developing by age 15. This does not mean that you start getting dumber from this point on. It only means that your rate of intellectual development stops increasing at a regular rate at this age. Enough said. Most of the data on intelligence testing skirt the issue of "average" IQ, except to say that approximately half the population of the United States have IQs over 100 and half have IQs below 100. Here is one estimate of how the American population breaks down according to IQ level:

1. *140 or over*—2 percent.
2. *120 to 139*—12 percent.
3. *110 to 119*—36 percent.
4. *90 to 100*—25 percent.
5. *Below 90*—25 percent.

•IQ DEMOGRAPHICS. Few subjects in education are more controversial than the question of whether intelligence is an inherited or acquired trait. It is a fact that Jews and northern Europeans score higher on average than southern Europeans and blacks, and that blacks, on average, score fifteen points lower on IQ tests than whites; but the argument concerns whether these differences reflect genetic differences or environmental differences. Supporting the genetic argument is the fact that children tend to have the same approximate IQs as their parents. Supporting the environmental view is the fact that many individual blacks score higher on IQ tests than individual whites. The jury is still out.

•BASIC SMARTS. Forget IQ for a moment. How do Americans shape up when it comes to basic mental-coping skills—that is, the mental capacity needed to function with competency in various areas of everyday life. A University of Texas at Austin study, published in 1975, tried to find out. Tests were given to measure basic competency in nine areas, and on the basis of the results, the sampling was divided into three categories: people who functioned with difficulty; people who were functional; and people who functioned proficiently. The results were as follows.

Proportion of American adults who *"function with difficulty"* in key life areas:

1. *Occupational knowledge*—19.0 percent.
2. *Consumer economics*—30.0 percent.

3. *Government and law*—26.0 percent.
4. *Health*—21.3 percent.
5. *Utilizing community resources*—22.5 percent.
6. *Reading*—22.0 percent.
7. *Problem solving*—28.0 percent.
8. *Computation*—33.0 percent.
9. *Writing*—16.5 percent.

Proportion of American adults who are *"functional"* in key life areas:

1. *Occupational knowledge*—32.0 percent.
2. *Consumer economics*—33.0 percent.
3. *Government and law*—26.0 percent.
4. *Health*—30.5 percent.
5. *Community resources*—26.0 percent.
6. *Reading*—32.5 percent.
7. *Problem solving*—23.5 percent.
8. *Computation*—26.5 percent.
9. *Writing*—25.5 percent.

Proportion of Americans who *"function proficiently"* in key life areas:

1. *Occupational knowledge*—49.0 percent.
2. *Consumer economics*—37.5 percent.
3. *Government and law*—48.0 percent.
4. *Health*—48.0 percent.
5. *Community resources*—51.5 percent.
6. *Reading*—46.5 percent.
7. *Problem solving*—41.0 percent.
8. *Computation*—41.0 percent.
9. *Writing*—58.0 percent.

Generally speaking, the functional-competency level of whites is significantly higher than that of blacks and Hispanics, based on findings of the University of Texas study. The proportion of whites whose test scores indicate they function with difficulty is 16 percent of whites, compared with 44 percent for blacks and 56 percent for Hispanics. The proportion of whites who test out to be functional is 34 percent, compared with 39 percent of blacks and 26 percent of Hispanics. The proportion of whites who test out to be proficient is 50 percent, compared with 17 percent for blacks and 18 percent for Hispanics.

But the differences are just as varied when you compare test results on the basis of education. For instance:

1. *Proportion of college graduates who function proficiently*—80 percent.
2. *College graduates who function with difficulty*—2 percent.
3. *High-school graduates who function proficiently*—52 percent.
4. *High-school graduates who function with difficulty*—11 percent.
5. *Adults with 8 to 11 years of schooling who function proficiently*—27 percent.
6. *Adults with 8 to 11 years of schooling who function with difficulty*—18 percent.

• **RATING GAME**. One possible way of finding out how smart a person is, is to ask someone who knows or has dealings with him or her. When HEW pollsters asked a large sampling of American teachers to rate their junior-high and high-school students on the basis of intellectual ability, the results were as follows:

1. *Boys rated above average*—25 percent.
2. *Girls rated above average*—30 percent.
3. *Boys rated average*—50 percent.
4. *Girls rated average*—52 percent.
5. *Boys rated below average*—25 percent.
6. *Girls rated below average*—18 percent.

Yet another subjective glimpse of American intelligence comes from the ratings that Institute for Social Research interviewers assigned to respondents in the sampling on which *The Quality of American Life* was based.

Proportion of respondents whose "apparent intelligence" was rated as:

1. *Very high*—6 percent.
2. *Above average*—30 percent.
3. *Average*—54 percent.
4. *Below average*—9 percent.
5. *Very low*—1 percent.

• **WORDS OF WISDOM**. Below is a random list of twenty words taken from a typical vocabulary test. If you can define at least eighteen of them, your vocabulary is equal to that of a highly verbal college graduate (about 10 percent of the population). If you know fifteen, your vocabulary is on the level of the average college sophomore (about 15 percent of the population). Knowing ten to fifteen puts you in the average category (about 50 percent of the population). Five to ten is below average (about 15 percent of the population). And zero to five is well below average.

1. *Aberration.*
2. *Abject.*
3. *Acumen.*
4. *Cavil.*
5. *Diffidence.*
6. *Effervescence.*
7. *Fulminate.*
8. *Histrionic.*
9. *Incompatible.*
10. *Loquacious.*
11. *Mordant.*
12. *Meretricious.*
13. *Palliate.*
14. *Redolent.*
15. *Sanguine.*
16. *Sobriquet.*
17. *Surfeit.*
18. *Tenuous.*
19. *Ubiquitous.*
20. *Voluble.*

• DOWN THE TUBE. Tests that have long been used to measure scholastic achievement in American schoolchildren indicate a slight decline in the intellectual ability of the average American student. Average verbal scores on the Scholastic Aptitude Test (normally given to college-bound high-school seniors) have dipped to 429 in 1977, from 466 in 1966, and average math scores have dropped to 470, from 492, during the same period. Then again, there are proportionally more high-school students taking these tests, which raises the possibility that the drop may simply reflect the presence of a larger sampling base. Other studies show a gradual increase in the reading proficiency of the average American high-school student but a slight decline in the area of science achievement.

• **AMERICA VERSUS THE WORLD.** How do American students stack up against their counterparts in foreign countries when it comes to performance in mathematics, science, reading comprehension, and literature? Well, test scores in 1970 showed that American 14-year-old students compared favorably with 14-year-olds from France, Germany, Italy, the Netherlands, Sweden, and the United Kingdom in science and reading comprehension, but did not demonstrate nearly so high an aptitude for science or mathematics as did Japanese 14-year-olds. American high-school graduates, on the other hand, were on the lowest end of the comparative scale in three categories—mathematics, science, and reading comprehension— and next to last (ahead of Italy) in literature. On the surface these statistics do not speak very well of the American education system, but it is instructive to remember that the proportion of American teenagers who were enrolled in a full-time education program at the time these tests were administered (84 percent) was higher than the proportion of teenagers enrolled in schools in any of the other countries, including even Japan (67 percent), Sweden (68 percent), and Germany (50 percent).

SOURCES

Angus Campbell, *The Quality of American Life.*

J. P. Guilford, *The Nature of Human Intelligence,* 1967.

Norvell Northcutt, *Adult Functional Competency,* 1975.

U.S. Department of Health, Education, and Welfare, *The Condition of Education: 1976.*

U.S. Department of Health, Education, and Welfare, *Intellectual Development and School Achievement of Youths 12–17.*

HOW WELL INFORMED WE ARE

Even though Americans are graduating from high school, and going on to college, in unprecedented numbers, a high—and, some might say, alarming—proportion of the adult and young-adult population lacks a clear understanding of some of the most basic subjects that most of us have to deal with on a day-to-day basis. Some examples.

•**WITHHOLDING KNOWLEDGE.** A Roper Organization survey, done in 1978 for H & R Block, showed that only a relative handful of Americans fully understand how the federal income-tax system works, with many people not even aware of how much they themselves pay in taxes. Some representative numbers:

1. *Americans who understand the graduated-tax system— less than 10 percent.*
2. *Who understand how the earned-income tax credit works—33 percent.*
3. *Who underestimate what people earning $25,000 and over pay in taxes—about 95 percent.*
4. *Who think that a tax deductible contribution is something that doesn't cost you anything because you can take it off your income tax—26 percent.*
5. *Who, less than a month after April 15, did not know how much they had paid in taxes the previous year—33 percent.*

•**LITERACY ILLS.** Christopher Lasch, in *The Culture of Narcissism*, argues that the public education system in the United States fails to teach most students a basic knowledge of how the American political system works. To back up his argument, Lasch cites these survey findings:

1. *Seventeen-year-olds who do not know how many senators each state sends to Congress—47 percent.*
2. *Who believe the president has a constitutional right to break the law—12 percent.*
3. *Who think members of Congress are appointed by the president—50 percent.*
4. *Thirteen-year-olds who think our laws forbid the starting of a new political party—50 percent.*
5. *Who do not know the significance of the Fifth Amendment, i.e., protection against self-incrimination—75 percent.*
6. *University of California students who have to take remedial English—40–60 percent each year.*

•**ANWAR WHO?** In 1978 the center for Family Research conducted a survey for the Newspaper Advertising Bureau designed to measure how familiar American children aged 6 to 17 were with public figures. The findings.

Percentage of 6- to 8-year-olds who could correctly identify:

1. *Jimmy Carter*—61 percent.
2. *Donny and Marie Osmond*—70 percent.
3. *Martin Luther King, Jr.*—4 percent.
4. *Anwar el-Sadat*—1 percent.

Nine- to 11-year-olds who could correctly identify:

1. *Jimmy Carter*—83 percent.
2. *Donny and Marie Osmond*—78 percent.
3. *Martin Luther King, Jr.*—22 percent.
4. *Anwar el-Sadat*—8 percent.

Twelve- to 14-year-olds who could correctly identify:

1. *Jimmy Carter*—90 percent.
2. *Donny and Marie Osmond*—87 percent.
3. *Martin Luther King, Jr.*—36 percent.
4. *Anwar el-Sadat*—16 percent.

Fifteen- to 17-year-olds who could correctly identify:

1. *Jimmy Carter*—92 percent.
2. *Donny and Marie Osmond*—84 percent.
3. *Martin Luther King, Jr.*—46 percent.
4. *Anwar el-Sadat*—26 percent.

•PICASSO? DIDN'T HE WORK WITH PETER FRAMPTON? Gallup pollsters queried American teens in 1978 to find out how familiar they were with names of famous people in the arts and famous people in world history. The results, based on the proportion of teens who knew who the person was, what he or she did and, in the case of world leaders, what nation he or she was associated with:

1. *Adolf Hitler*—79 percent.
2. *Winston Churchill*—50 percent.
3. *Indira Gandhi*—31 percent.
4. *Pablo Picasso*—60 percent.
5. *Robert Frost*—48 percent.
6. *Helen Hayes*—38 percent.
7. *Alexander Calder*—6 percent.

In general, boys turned out to be more informed about these people than girls, and teens whose fathers had been to college did much better than teens whose fathers had less formal education.

• **M u s c l e b o u n d** . From *The Perrier Study of Fitness in America*, a glimpse of how much Americans know about basic fitness:

1. *Americans who understand the importance of cardiovascular fitness as a prime goal in exercise*—75 percent.
2. *Who overestimate the fitness benefits of tennis*—59 percent.
3. *Of baseball*—47 percent.
4. *Of bowling*—35 percent.
5. *Of golf*—33 percent.

• **S a v o i r F a i r e** . Estimates of how much Americans know about wine range anywhere from 2–3 percent of wine drinkers to 10 percent, depending on whom you ask, but here is what a *Ladies' Home Journal* survey, done in 1977, turned up in the way of problems cited most often by women who buy wine.
Women who say they have problems:

1. *Pronouncing the names of wines*—58 percent.
2. *Knowing how the wine will taste*—57 percent.
3. *Knowing whether their guests will like the wine*—43 percent.
4. *Knowing what to buy*—39 percent.
5. *Knowing how to serve it*—26 percent.

• **C l o s e E n c o u n t e r s** . It was called "The National Love, Sex and Marriage Test," and it was broadcast by NBC-TV in 1978. The idea was to find out how American views on love, sex and marriage compared with those of the "experts." The final score, based on the proportion of the national sampling who gave correct answers:

1. *On love*—70 percent.
2. *Sex*—78 percent.
3. *Roles*—64 percent.
4. *Fighting*—80 percent.
5. *Feelings*—82 percent.
6. *Trust*—86 percent.

Some of the questions that drew the highest proportion of *incorrect* answers:

1. *Jealousy is natural if you really love your mate*—53.5 percent said true.

2. *People are often less satisfied with their marriages if they have children*—83 percent said false.

3. *There is no way to know for sure what your mate feels unless he or she tells you*—42 percent said true.

4. *Fighting can actually lead to a better relationship*—35 percent said false.

SOURCES

The American Public and the Income Tax System, 1978.

Rubin Carson, *The National Love, Sex & Marriage Test*, 1978.

Ladies' Home Journal.

Christopher Lasch, *The Culture of Narcissism*.

Newspaper Advertising Bureau, *Children, Mothers and Newspapers*, 1978.

The Perrier Study of Fitness in America, 1979.

HOW RELIGIOUS WE ARE

It is hard to say exactly *how* religious a people Americans really are. The surveys on the subject, and the relatively high level of church participation, both suggest a level of religiosity that is unsurpassed among the industrialized countries of the world. The problem, though, is that sociological studies designed to measure the degree to which religion plays a meaningful part in the life of the average American suggest an inconsistency between the spirituality that *should* be here and the spirituality that really *is* here.

• **THE BASIC NUMBERS.** Here is what the most recent Gallup surveys tell us about religious beliefs and involvement in the United States.

Proportion of American adults who:

1. *Say they believe in God*—95 percent.

2. *Say they believe in an afterlife*—70 percent.

3. *Describe themselves as "born-again Christians"*—33 percent.

4. *Belong to one of the 250 religious orders or groups in the country*—61 percent.

5. *Consider religion an important influence in their lives*—84 percent.

6. *Attend church or synagogue at least once a week*—40 percent.
7. *Believe the Bible is to be taken literally, word for word* —38 percent.
8. *Say they've had a moment of sudden religious insight or awakening*—31 percent.

• THE DEMOGRAPHICS. Americans who describe religion as being very important to them fall into these demographic categories:

1. *Men and women older than 30*—63 percent.
2. *Men and women younger than 30*—45 percent.
3. *Blacks and Hispanics*—72 percent.
4. *Whites*—54 percent.
5. *Women*—66 percent.
6. *Men*—47 percent.
7. *Have been to college*—49 percent.
8. *Have an eighth-grade education or less*—70 percent.
9. *Housewives*—68 percent.
10. *Blue-collar workers*—47 percent.
11. *White-collar workers*—54 percent.

• CHURCHGOERS. The demographics of churchgoing, by proportion of each group who attend church or synagogue on a regular basis:

1. *Catholics*—56 percent.
2. *Protestants*—37 percent.
3. *Jews*—19 percent.
4. *Women*—43 percent.
5. *Men*—35 percent.
6. *Southerners and midwesterners*—43 percent.
7. *Easterners*—28 percent.
8. *Westerners*—29 percent.
9. *Men and women older than 50*—46 percent.
10. *Eighteen- to 29-years-old*—23 percent.

Trends? Tricky to discern. Church attendance is down in general since the 1950s but seems to have bottomed out among Catholics and Protestants in the late 1970s and appears to be on the rise again. In the meantime, the proportion of Americans involved in what the Gallup organization calls the "experiential religions" (faith healing, mysticism, etc.) continues to grow each year and is now between 10 and 15 percent of the adult population.

• **GOING EAST**. From a late 1978 Gallup poll, this view of how many Americans are looking eastward for their spiritual needs:

1. *Adult Americans who are currently involved with an Eastern religion*—2 million (less than .2 percent of the adult population).
2. *Who practice meditation*—3 percent.
3. *Who practice yoga*—5 million.

• **CULTITIS**. Estimates from Flo Conway and Jim Siegelman, the authors of *Snapping*, offer this picture of religious cultism in the United States:

1. *Number of cults in the country*—1,000–3,000.
2. *Number of Americans involved with cults*—about 3 million.
3. *Unification Church members (Moonies)*—3,500–7,000.
4. *Hare Krishna members*—about 9,000.
5. *Scientologists*—3.2 million according to the Church of Scientology; about 25,000 according to Conway and Siegelman.

• **HEAVENLY KNOWLEDGE**. The results of a Gallup poll taken in the early 1970s suggest that most Americans lack even a rudimentary knowledge of the Bible. Only 21 percent of respondents, for instance, could name any of the Old Testament prophets, and only 33 percent of respondents were able to name the fairly well-known fellow who delivered the Sermon on the Mount. (*Hint:* He is believed to be the son of an even more Famous Person.) The poll, incidentally, shows that 54 percent of Americans say that religion affects in no way the manner in which they conduct their business affairs.

• **AMERICA VERSUS THE WORLD**. Forgetting for the moment the possible gap between what Americans say they believe in and how religious Americans actually are, surveys show that Americans consider religion more important than do the residents of any other major industrialized country, including such bastions of Catholicism as Italy and France. The United States is the only major industrialized country in which the proportion of people who say religion is not important is less than 15 percent, as well as being the only country in which the proportion of people who say religion is very important is more than 50 percent.

SOURCES
Flo Conway and Jim Siegelman, *Snapping*, 1978.
Gallup Poll.
NORC.

HOW PATRIOTIC WE ARE

Inasmuch as different people have different ideas of what, exactly, patriotism means (witness the debate over the patriotic merits of *serving* or *not serving* in the Vietnam War), patriotism is one of the toughest traits to measure. It is clear, of course, that the overwhelming majority of Americans—maybe 98 percent—have no desire to live in any other country, but our patriotic feelings in general took something of a beating during the Vietnam War and then again during the Watergate mess. The most recent surveys suggest a slight upturn in strongly patriotic sentiments—but nothing to measure the levels that prevailed in the 1940s and 1950s.

• THE GENERAL PICTURE. One of the few recent surveys that has made it a point to question respondents directly about their patriotic attitudes is *The General Mills American Family Report*, which found that in 1976, 43 percent of American parents felt patriotism was a very important value but nonetheless ranked it sixth in order of importance, behind:

1. *Family.*
2. *Education.*
3. *Self-fulfillment.*
4. *Hard work.*
5. *Religion.*

When Daniel Yankelovich, Inc. surveyed college students in 1974, only one-third described patriotism as being a very important value.

• FLAG WAVERS. A National Family Opinion, Inc., survey taken in 1960 showed that at the time about one out of five

American families owned an American flag and that about 60 percent of flag owners (about 12 percent of the family population) displayed the flag on special occasions. Industry spokesmen today say the proportion of American flag owners has not changed much since 1960 (the Bicentennial did marvels for flag sales), but the proportion of Americans who display the flag with any regularity is probably no more than 5 percent of the population. The demographic patterns of flag waving are not especially striking. Families with children are somewhat more likely to own and display flags than families without children, and higher-income families are more likely to fly the flag than lower-income families. In each instance, though, the statistical differences are minor. According to the 1960 survey, Memorial Day is the day that the largest proportion of flag displayers (86 percent) are likely to show the flag, followed closely by Independence Day (82 percent). The survey also showed, surprisingly, that the smallest proportion of flag owners (less than 10 percent) live in the Midwest and the highest proportion (28 percent), in the East.

SOURCES
Angus Campbell, *Quality of American Life*.
The General Mills American Family Report 1967–77.
National Family Opinion, Inc.

HOW PREJUDICED WE ARE

Prejudice, like patriotism, is a tricky trait to measure, but the numbers are at least encouraging. Most of the survey data over the past twenty years show a *decrease* in the proportion of Americans holding what are normally thought of as prejudiced views, and this is particularly true for the 1970s. Less encouraging is the fact that when pollsters manipulate questions in a way that subterfuges the attempt to measure prejudice, the answers show that we still have a long way to go.

• BASIC BLACK NUMBERS. Even granting the possibility that not all the most recent survey data are true reflections of racial attitudes in the United States, it is safe to say that white attitudes toward blacks have undergone some dramatic changes over the past twenty-five years. Here are some of the attitudes that have been surveyed, with the proportion of Americans who expressed them in 1978 and at other times.

Proportion of white Americans who said:

1. *They would vote for a qualified black for president—*84.0 percent in 1978 (up from 42.0 percent in 1952).
2. *Blacks have a right to live anywhere—*93.0 percent in 1978 (up from 71.0 percent in 1958).
3. *They would favor laws prohibiting interracial marriages*—28.0 percent in 1978 (down from 51.0 percent in 1965).
4. *They would object to sending their children to a school where a few of the children were black*—4.5 percent in 1978 (down from 6.0 percent in 1972).
5. *They would object strongly if a family member wanted to bring a black friend home to dinner—*11.0 percent (down from 12.0 percent in 1972).

• S t a t u s   Q u o. There are still a number of racial issues on which a sizable percentage of white Americans still hold views that some people would consider racist. Some examples based on NORC surveys.

Proportion of white Americans who say:

1. *Blacks should not push themselves where they are not wanted—*43.0 percent.
2. *White people have a right to keep blacks out of their neighborhoods if they want to, and blacks should respect that right—*28.5 percent.
3. *They oppose programs designed to encourage black people to buy houses in white suburbs—*54.5 percent.
4. *Differences between white and black income, jobs, and housing exist because most blacks have less in-born ability to learn—*25.0 percent.
5. *Most blacks just don't have the motivation or willpower to pull themselves up out of poverty—*64.0 percent.

• T h e   D a t i n g   G a m e. Less than half of American teenage girls (white and black alike) say they either approve or strongly approve of interracial dating according to a *Seventeen* magazine survey of teen trends, but the proportion who say they disapprove or strongly disapprove is now less than 30 percent and dropping. Here are some other numbers from a March 1979 *Seventeen* survey.

Proportion of teenage girls who:

1. *Have dated a boy of another race*—25.0 percent.
2. *Are black and have dated a boy of another race*—47.0 percent.
3. *Are white and have done so*—20.0 percent.
4. *Live away from home and have dated a boy of another race*—30.5 percent.
5. *Live at home and have done so*—20.0 percent.
6. *Have dated a boy of a different faith*—86 percent.
7. *Say they would definitely not date a boy of another faith*—2.5 percent.
8. *Say they would definitely not date a boy of another race*—47 percent (higher in the South than anywhere else).

• CLOSET RACISTS. Some social psychologists argue that even people who consider themselves free of prejudice often harbor latent racist sentiments, and to prove the point the psychologist Gary I. Schulman staged an elaborate—and controversial—experiment designed to measure the attitudes of white males toward black males who date white females. The subjects taking part in the experiment, which took place in 1974, had the option of either cheating at a task that had been assigned by the experimenter or *not* cheating at the task. By cheating, the subject had the power to prevent another person from being given an electric shock (the shock was faked, but the subject did not know that). What Schulman did was to vary the race of the "victim." In some cases the victim was white. In others the victim was black. The victims themselves were divided into two categories: those who were dating women from a different race and those who were not. All of the subjects in Schulman's experiment were white college students who were not known to have any openly racist attitudes. But Schulman discovered nonetheless that his subjects tended to allow black victims to receive more pain than white victims and tended to show the least compassion to black males who were known to be involved with white females.

• SOME OF MY BEST FRIENDS . . . Although the proportion of Americans who are anti-Jewish appears to be on the decline, the proportion who harbor classic anti-Semitic attitudes is still substantial. A study done in the late 1960s by G. J. Selznick determined that 50 percent of Americans, regardless of educational level, agreed with the statement: "Jews always like to head things," which is a polite way of saying that Jews are pushy; and 25 percent of the population believed that "Jews control international banking." All in all, though, anti-Semitic attitudes are dominant mainly among Americans with the lowest educational levels. The proportion of Americans with less than a high-school education who agree with the statement "Jews use shady practices to get ahead" is better than 50 percent, but among college graduates the proportion accepting that statement drops to 22 percent.

SOURCES

Alan Elembemp, "Race and Physical Attractiveness as Critera for White Subjects Dating Choices," 1976.

Gallup Poll.

Harris Survey.

NORC.

New York Times, February 19, 1978.

Gary I. Schulman, "Race, Sex and Violence," 1974.

G. J. Selznick and S. Steinberg, The Tenacity of Prejudice, 1969.

Seventeen.

Daniel Yankelovich, The New Morality.

HOW VIOLENT WE ARE

The statistics (which tell us, among other things, that a violent crime is committed once every 31 seconds), paint a scary picture of violence in the United States. But just how violent *is* the average American? Which is to say, how many Americans have had a firsthand experience with violence? This was one of the questions pursued by the researchers who put together the report to the National Commission on the Causes and Prevention of Violence, which came out in the late 1960s and is still considered the definitive work on violence in the United States.

• THE GENERAL PICTURE. It is virtually impossible to say how many Americans can be described as "violent" (the proportion, though, is probably very small), but close to one out of five adult Americans knows what it is like to be on either the giving or receiving end of violence. When the researchers for the National Commission report queried Americans on their own personal experience with violence as adults, they learned the following.

Proportion of Americans who say they have:

1. *Kicked or slapped another person (other than spanking) in their adult lives*—12 percent.
2. *Punched or beaten another person in their adult lives*—12 percent.
3. *Been kicked or slapped*—13 percent.
4. *Been punched or beaten*—12 percent.
5. *Been threatened with a gun, or shot at*—6 percent (excluding combat veterans).
6. *Had to defend themselves with a knife or gun at least once*—6 percent.

• THE DEMOGRAPHICS. No demographic factor figures more prominently in the American violence picture than race. According to the National Commission findings, the average black American is 40 percent more likely to be a victim of violence than the average white American and is three times as likely to have to defend himself with a knife or gun. In virtually every category of violence—as victim or perpetrator—the proportion of blacks concerned is anywhere from 25 percent to 40 percent higher than among whites. The statistics also show that men are five times more likely to experience a violent incident as an adult than are women, and the most violent section of the country is the wild West, where 20 percent of the residents say they have punched or beaten somebody, compared with only 7 percent in the South.

• ALL IN THE FAMILY. Most of the violence Americans do unto each other takes place in the home, but nobody is sure exactly how much of it takes place and how severe the problem really is. One 1975 survey suggests that child beatings serious enough to cause injury occur in about 3 percent of American family households each year. Four percent of American parents admit that they beat up their kids from time to time. Even worse, 3 percent admit to using a gun or knife to threaten their children. If these estimates are valid, it means that each year close to two million American children are victims of violence inside the home.

• **S L A P   H A P P Y .** One out of five Americans (according to the National Commission study) do not see anything wrong with slapping a spouse on "appropriate" occasions. But what surprised the researchers was that a higher proportion of college graduates would condone spouse slapping on appropriate occasions (25 percent) than would Americans with eight years of schooling or less.

• **B O Y S   W I L L   B E   B O Y S .** Most Americans (70 percent according to the National Commission findings) believe that it is "good" for a boy to have a few fistfights as he grows up, with lower-income and lower-education level groups tending to buy this philosophy more than richer and better-educated parents. The macho view holds more sway in the West and Midwest than it does in the South and East and is more likely to be supported by parents younger than 30 and older than 65 than among parents in the age-groups in-between.

• **H A N G   ' E M   H I G H .** The spirit of vigilantism still runs high, with nearly 50 percent of Americans polled by the National Commission researchers allowing as how, while justice may have been a little "rough-and-ready" in the days of the Old West, things still "worked better than they do now with all the legal red tape." Males (51 percent) are only slightly more likely than females (49 percent) to harbor traces of lynch-mob fever, and lower-income and less well educated groups are more likely to condone vigilantism than higher-income and better-educated groups. Blacks, on the other hand (having been the victims of lynch-mob fever), are less inclined toward the vigilante state of mind than whites.

• **A N I M A L   C R A C K E R S .** The majority of Americans (58 percent according to most surveys) are convinced that human nature being what it is, there must always be war and conflict, and nearly three out of four American adults during the late 1960s were willing to accept civilian casualties in Vietnam as an "unfortunate" but "unavoidable" fact of life. Southerners, by and large, appear more willing to accept the inevitability of war than Americans from other regions, and men tend to be more philosophical about war and its by-products than women.

The difference in attitude among various age-groups, however, is quite small, as is the variation in opinion among economic and education groups.

•EXTENUATING CIRCUMSTANCES. Ever since 1972 NORC interviewers have been asking respondents to name those situations in which they would approve of a man's punching an adult male stranger. The percentages have been fairly consistent throughout the yearly surveys, the only exception being a growing acceptance of violence against bad guys.

Proportion of Americans who would approve of a man's punching a stranger when the stranger:

1. *Was beating up a woman*—79 percent.
2. *Had broken into the man's house*—80 percent.
3. *Had hit the man's child after the child had accidentally damaged the stranger's car*—51 percent.
4. *Was drunk and bumped into the man and his wife on the street*—9 percent.
5. *Was in a march protesting against the man's views*—3 percent.

Proportion of Americans who would approve of a policeman's hitting a stranger when the stranger:

1. *Was being questioned as a suspect in a murder case*—9 percent.
2. *Was attempting to escape from custody*—74 percent.
3. *Was attacking the policeman with his fists*—97 percent.

SOURCES

U.S., *Mass Media and Violence: A Staff Report to the National Commission on the Causes and Prevention of Violence*, 1969.

NORC.

U.S. Department of Health, Education, and Welfare, 1977 *Analysis of Child Abuse and Neglect Research*, 1978.

HOW PUBLIC-SPIRITED WE ARE

It is a basic axiom of sociology that the more self-oriented a society becomes, the less its involvement with political and civic matters, and the numbers relating to public spirit in the United States throughout the 1970s do nothing to suggest anything different.

• **POLL SITTING**. Although more Americans than ever before—around 82 million—voted in the 1976 presidential election, the proportion of eligible voters who actually went to the polls was the lowest it has ever been since 1948. The numbers:

1. *Americans who voted for president in 1976*—54.5 percent.
2. *In 1968*—61.0 percent.
3. *In 1972*—55.5 percent.
4. *White voter participation in the 1976 election*—61.0 percent.
5. *Black participation*—49.0 percent.
6. *Hispanic participation*—32.0 percent.
7. *Eighteen- to 20-year-olds who voted in 1976*—47.0 percent.
8. *In 1972*—58.0 percent.

Voter turnout since 1976 has been averaging less than 40 percent in most places except in elections involving a local tax issue. Demographic studies on voting patterns suggest that (*a*) older people are more likely to vote than younger people, (*b*) southerners vote more religiously than residents of any other section of the country, and (*c*) voting participation level increases with level of education.

• **NO-SHOWS**. So much for the bad news. The not-so-bad news is that a 1976 U.S. Department of Commerce study found that voter apathy was *not* the main reason for not voting in in 1974.

Proportion of nonvoters who:

1. *Could not leave work to get to polls*—13.5 percent.
2. *Were sick or had a family emergency*—17.5 percent.
3. *Were out of town*—13.5 percent.
4. *Were not interested*—18.5 percent.
5. *Did not like any of the candidates*—8.5 percent.

No striking demographic pattern distinguishes these findings. Men and women, generally speaking, give the same reasons for not voting, except that men are more likely to cite work as a reason; and no major differences in reasons separate blacks and whites, except that blacks are a little more likely to say they did not know of the election.

• TAKING PART. The proportion of Americans who get actively involved in political matters has never been notably high, and throughout the 1970s it was a good deal lower than in the 1960s. When the NORC asked about political participation in 1973, it got these numbers.

Proportion of Americans who, as of 1973, had ever taken part in:

1. *A civil-rights demonstration*—4 percent.
2. *An antiwar demonstration*—4 percent.
3. *A prowar demonstration*—less than .01 percent.
4. *A school-related demonstration*—4 percent.

NORC surveys also show a drop in the proportion of Americans who belong to political clubs—from 4 percent in 1966 to 3 percent in 1978, representing a decline of around 1.6 million persons. And 1978 figures from W. R. Simmons give the following picture of political participation.

Proportion of American adults who, as of 1978, had ever:

1. *Written to the editor of a publication*—1.0 percent.
2. *Addressed a public meeting*—13.5 percent.
3. *Taken an active part in a civic issue*—11 percent.
4. *Written to an elected official*—11 percent.
5. *Actively worked for a political party*—8 percent.

SOURCES
NORC.
Newspaper Advertising Bureau.
W. R. Simmons.
U.S. Bureau of the Census, *Statistical Abstract of the United States: 1978*.

HOW GENEROUS WE ARE

If we measure generosity purely in terms of the amount of money spent on charity and gifts, Americans rank, hands down, as the most generous people on earth. But the latest figures on individual charity donations suggest that inflation may be squelching some of our generous instincts.

•**THE BASIC NUMBERS**. According to figures from the American Association of Fund-Raising Counsel Inc., charitable donations in the United States in 1977 totaled about $35 billion, with 83 percent of it coming from individual donations. The average American now spends about 2.25 percent of his or her disposable income on charity—the same proportion spent on liquor, cosmetics, and movies. Roughly half the money we donate to charity goes to religious organizations. About 12 percent goes to hospitals, and another 12 percent, to social-welfare groups. Educational institutions get about one out of every ten charity dollars, and arts and humanities groups fare the worst, receiving less than 4 percent of all the charity dollars Americans dispense.

•**TIME EXPENDITURES**. About one out every four Americans older than 18 is generous with his or her time, which is to say, does volunteer work of one kind or another. The proportion of Americans involved in volunteer work is up about 25 percent since the mid-1960s, with the biggest jump showing up in the 14–24 age-group. The reasons Americans give for doing volunteer work differ among individual age-groups, with enjoyment cited most often by persons older than 65 and personal reasons (having a child in a program, for instance) most often cited by volunteers in the 25–44 age-group.

Proportion of all volunteers motivated:
1. *By desire to help people*—53 percent.
2. *By enjoyment*—36 percent.
3. *By sense of duty*—32 percent.
4. *Because their child is in program*—22 percent.
5. *Because they could not refuse when asked*—15 percent.
6. *Had nothing else to do*—4 percent.
7. *Hoped it would lead to job*—3 percent.

The proportions listed above reflect attitudes surveyed in 1974. They are similar to the findings of a 1965 survey except in the area of "desire to help people." In 1965 the proportion of volunteers giving this reason was only 38 percent.

•**SANTA'S HELPERS**. Gift giving is another good barometer of generosity, and a *Seventeen* magazine survey on teenage girls Christmas gift spending patterns shows that teenage girls alone generate about $1.8 billion dollars in gifts received and given for Christmas. Here is what the average American teenage girl spends on Christmas gifts for the people in her life:

1. *Boyfriend—$34.*
2. *Mother—$27.*
3. *Father—$21.*
4. *Girl friends—$18.*
5. *Older brothers and sisters—$16.*
6. *Younger brothers and sisters—$14.*

• **TIPSTERS.** Tipping is an American institution, and the proportion of Americans who *do not* tip in restaurants is estimated to be less than 2 percent. Virtually all residents of luxury apartments in New York City tip their doorman. About 70 percent of American homeowners (according to a random survey of mailmen in Fairfield County, Connecticut) give Christmas gifts to their mailmen. Bartenders are tipped about 50 percent of the time, hairdressers about 90 percent of the time, and bellboys nearly all the time. Finally, Frank Valenza, owner of the Palace Restaurant in New York—one of the most expensive restaurants in the world—estimates that 80 percent of his guests tip *beyond* the suggested 23 percent.

SOURCES
American Association of Fund-Raising Counsel, Inc.
Palace Restaurant.
Seventeen.
U.S. Department of Labor, ACTION, *Americans Volunteer*, April 1969 and February 1975.

HOW THRIFTY WE ARE

Even though inflation is beginning to change some of our traditional attitudes on saving, thrift is still a central value in the American way of life. Even people who do not save any money still believe, for the most part, that it is a good idea to save.

• **THE BASIC NUMBERS.** About one out of two American families (based on findings in *The General Mills American Family Report 1974–75*) manages somehow to put money in a savings bank, but only one out of four families saves on a regular basis. In early 1979 Americans had about $142 billion on deposit in savings accounts throughout the country according to the National Association of Mutual Savings Banks. This averages out to about $645 per person, or nearly $1,900 per household. The most recent figures show that Americans save an average of 6.7 percent of their disposable income.

• **FINANCIAL STATEMENTS.** Some of the views expressed in the Needham, Harper and Steers studies of life-style, give some insight into how men and women in America feel about certain financial matters.

Proportion of total sample (male or female) agreeing with the statement:

1. *"I like to pay cash for everything I buy"*—75 percent for males; 77 percent for females.
2. *"I pretty much spend for today and let tomorrow bring what it will"*—26 percent for males; 22 percent for females.
3. *"I like to save and redeem savings stamps"*—43 percent for males; 75 percent for females.
4. *"I find myself checking prices even on small items"*—79 percent for males; 90 percent for females.
5. *"I shop a lot of specials"*—60 percent for males; 84 percent for females.

Attitudes toward the statements above vary according to age-group, but the patterns are different for men and women. As women age, they tend to get *less* thrifty. As men age, they tend to get *more* thrifty.

• **AMERICA VERSUS THE WORLD.** Thrifty as Americans are, we are less prone toward saving money than people in most other industrialized countries. The Japanese, for instance, save about 24.0 percent of their disposable income (nearly four times the percentage saved by Americans). The French save an average of 17.0 percent. The West Germans save an average of 15.0 percent. Even the Canadian percentage, 10.5, is higher than ours.

• **WHO SAVES.** Most Americans tend to describe themselves as being either "savers" or "spenders." *The General Mills American Family Report* presents a demographic comparison based on this self-description. Spenders, in general, tend to be younger, more urban, and more likely to have children younger than 18. Yet, there appears to be no relationship between family income and the proportion of income that gets set aside for savings. And, for what it is worth, people who describe themselves as "arguers" are more likely to be spenders than people who describe themselves as "nonarguers."

• HERE'S THAT RAINY DAY. Most people (70 percent according to *The General Mills American Family Report*) cite emergencies as their principal reason for saving. Here are some other widely cited reasons:

1. *Protection against bad times*—38 percent.
2. *Looking ahead to old age*—37 percent.
3. *Saving for something special*—25 percent.
4. *The kids' college education*—17 percent.

• FAMILY ACCOUNTING. In most American families (68 percent) the various members agree in their description of the family's spending patterns. The General Mills report also tells us that in only 12 percent of the families in which dual interviews were conducted did the husband and wife differ in their descriptions, and in most cases (63 percent) the perceptions of the teenage children were consistent with those of their parents.

SOURCES

The General Mills American Family Report 1974–75.
National Association of Mutual Savings Banks.
Needham, Harper and Steers.

HOW NEAT WE ARE

Neatness *does* count in America. Our concern with being neat and organized shows up in attitude surveys, in our housekeeping habits (see page 199) and in the prodigious amount of money—nearly $5 billion annually—that is spent on cleaning and bathroom items.

• THE BASIC FIGURES. Psychographic studies by Needham, Harper and Steers show that roughly seven out of ten American women, and five out of ten American men, are sufficiently concerned with neatness so as to feel uncomfortable when they are in a house that is not completely clean. The same proportion also feel an impulse to empty immediately a full ashtray or wastebasket. Still, the importance we attach to neatness varies according to age. The proportion of women who say they are uncomfortable in an atmosphere of disarray is a good third higher than the proportion of men who share the same trait, but men tend to grow fussier as they age, whereas women become less fussy. Among men and women older than 65, for instance, the proportion who visibly care about neatness is the same for both sexes—64 percent.

• NEAT JOBS. Roughly half the office workers in the United States (according to *The Steelcase National Study of Office Environments*) consider a neat and well-organized look one of the two or three characteristics that are most important for a personal work space. This makes neatness the number-one office priority for most American office workers—higher in importance than the second choice, privacy. Here is how various segments of the office population compare with one another, on the basis of the proportion who consider neatness an important priority:

1. *Women*—55 percent.
2. *Men*—44 percent.
3. *Secretaries*—66 percent.
4. *Executives*—55 percent.
5. *Professionals*—42 percent.
6. *Clerical workers*—55 percent.

• STARTING YOUNG. No basic value, apart from obeying the law, is perceived by American teenagers (according to a 1972 Dept. of Health, Education, and Welfare study) as more important than being neat and clean. Three out of every four teenage American girls consider neatness and cleanliness "extremely important," and six out of ten American boys in the same age-group share this view. Indeed, most American teenagers consider neatness a more important value than self-control, dependability, obeying one's parents, and ambition. The importance of neatness and cleanliness as a personal value tends to increase as teenage girls get older but loses its importance among boys as they move into their late teens.

• FAMILY PLANNING. About 40 percent of American parents (according to *The General Mills American Family Report 1976–77*) say that neatness and cleanliness are among the most important characteristics they want to see their sons and daughters develop. Neatness is thus in the upper-middle portion of the hierarchy of desired characteristics—less important than being responsible, having good manners, and showing respect for elders, but more important than being a good student, having interests and talents, and being good at sports. The majority of parents who see neatness as an important personal value stress it more for daughters than for sons, and "Traditional" parents place more value on this trait than do "New Breed" parents.

•LITTER BUGGED. Of all the various problems that have to do with an unsightly environment—auto junkyards, unattractive construction, billboards—nothing bugs Americans more than trash and litter on the streets. Nearly 70 percent of Americans, according to a 1975 Harris survey done for the Associated Councils of the Arts, feel that litter and trash on the streets is either a serious problem or a very serious problem. City dwellers (83 percent) are more sensitive to the problem than suburbanites (64 percent). And lower-income people (who have to look at the litter every day) find it more irritating than do higher-income people.

SOURCES

Associated Councils of the Arts, *Americans and the Arts,* 1975.

General Mills American Family Report 1976–77.

The Steelcase National Study of Office Environments, 1978.

U.S. Department of Health, Education, and Welfare, *Behavioral Patterns of Youths* 12–17.

HOW CULTURED WE ARE

In the eyes of some Europeans, America has always been a land of Philistines, but surveys—particularly the 1975 Associated Councils of the Arts Survey by Louis Harris—suggests an involvement with, and enthusiasm for, culture that goes far beyond what most people think. It could be argued, of course, that *attending* cultural events is hardly the only measure of cultural sensibility, but the figures are impressive all the same.

• **T h e G e n e r a l P i c t u r e** . On the basis of his 1975 findings, Harris divided the American population into four general groups:

1. *Cultural nonattenders* (those who never go to museums, concerts, the theatre)—29 percent.
2. *Infrequent attenders*—41 percent.
3. *Moderately frequent attenders*—20 percent.
4. *Frequent attenders*—10 percent.

Harris also analyzed specific cultural categories on the basis of frequency of attendance:

1. *Theatregoers* (people who see at least four live theatre performances a year)—11 percent.
2. *Concertgoers* (at least four concerts a year)—10 percent.
3. *Dancegoers* (at least two ballets a year)—4 percent.
4. *Museumgoers* (at least three visits a year)—22 percent.
5. *Art-museum goers* (at least three visits a year)—12 percent.

• **T h e D e m o g r a p h i c s** . In almost every category relating to culture, the frequent attenders are most likely to be found among white, affluent, 35- to 49-year-olds. Women are slightly more cultural-minded than men, and Americans in urban and suburban areas are understandably more likely to attend cultural events than their country cousins.

• **U n d e r e x p o s e d** . Most Americans who are nonattenders or infrequent attenders of cultural events were not exposed to teachers or to people with artistic interests when they were younger. Nor did they have teachers who helped develop their interest in artistic or creative things. Here is a sampling of the findings that emerged from this aspect of the study.

Proportions in each category who had teachers who helped develop their interest in artistic or creative things:

1. *Americans in general*—44 percent.
2. *Americans aged 16 to 20*—54 percent.
3. *College-degreed Americans*—57 percent.
4. *High-school graduates*—42 percent.
5. *Americans earning $15,000 or over*—50 percent.
6. *Frequent cultural attenders*—71 percent.
7. *Cultural nonattenders*—23 percent.

Proportions in each category who had friends or family involved in creative or artistic activities:

1. *Americans in general*—55 percent.
2. *White Americans*—55 percent.
3. *Black Americans*—48 percent.

•CREATIVE RESPECT. One good way to measure the cultural sensibility of a people is to find out how much respect they accord to specific occupations that relate to the arts. Here is how Americans responded when asked, again in the Harris survey, to name various artistic fields for which they had a "great deal of respect":

1. *Professional musicians*—55 percent.
2. *Painters and sculptors*—46 percent.
3. *Architects or city planners*—45 percent.
4. *Professional photographers*—36 percent.
5. *Poets*—35 percent.
6. *Professional actors*—33 percent.
7. *Ballet dancers*—33 percent.
8. *Film or play directors*—29 percent.
9. *Art or theatre critics*—20 percent.

Several demographic variables enter into these choices. Women, for instance, have a higher regard for creative people than do men, especially in the fields of painting and ballet. And in only one artistic occupation, acting, do men exceed women in the amount of respect shown. People with higher educational levels tend to show more respect for the creative professions than lesser-educated Americans. Regional patterns are mixed, but blacks, generally speaking, indicate *more* respect for creative types than do whites in every area. So much for the good news. The bad news is that creative occupations, as a group, do not fare especially well when compared with other occupations and professions.

Proportion of Americans who say they have a great deal of respect for:

1. *Doctors*—82 percent.
2. *Scientists*—75 percent.
3. *Schoolteachers*—71 percent.
4. *Policemen*—69 percent.
5. *Master carpenters*—60 percent.
6. *Lawyers*—59 percent.
7. *Electrical engineers*—57 percent.

8. *Professional musicians*—55 percent.
9. *Bankers*—46 percent.
10. *Painters or sculptors*—46 percent.
11. *Businessmen*—45 percent.
12. *Architects*—45 percent.
13. *Bus drivers*—38 percent.
14. *Professional photographers*—36 percent.
15. *Major-league baseball players*—36 percent.
17. *Poets*—35 percent.
18. *Sanitation workers*—34 percent.
19. *Professional actors*—33 percent.
20. *Ballet dancers*—33 percent.
21. *Gas-station attendants*—29 percent.
22. *Directors of films or plays*—29 percent.
23. *Art or theatre critics*—20 percent.

One final note: Of the ten occupations for which the highest proportion of Americans say they have not much respect, seven are related to the arts.

• C U L T U R E D   A T T I T U D E S . Whatever their feelings of respect toward specific creative professions, Americans are strongly in favor of exposing their children to as much culture as possible and see a direct connection between the availability of cultural attractions and the quality of life in their communities. Some sample views.

Proportion of Americans who:

1. *Think their kids are not getting* enough *exposure to the arts*—45 percent.
2. *Feel it is either important or somewhat important to go to art museums*—89 percent; *plays*—81 percent; *the opera*—70 percent.
3. *Think art appreciation should be offered in schools for credit*—70 percent.
4. *Think acting should be offered in schools for credit*—46 percent.
5. *Think cultural facilities are important to the business and economy of the community*—80 percent.
6. *Feel there are not enough places for cultural events in the communities where they live*—50 percent.
7. *Would be willing to pay an additional $5 a year in taxes to stimulate cultural activities*—64 percent; *$25 a year*—47 percent; *$50 a year*—36 percent.

8. *Who say they are more interested in the arts than their parents were*—45 percent.

SOURCE

Associated Councils of the Arts, *Americans and the Arts*, 1975.

WHAT'S QUIRKY ABOUT US

So many different forces shape personality that it is ridiculous to even suggest that Americans can be lumped into tidy personality groups. Still and all, a number of studies have turned up some interesting facets of our personalities, and the proportion of people who exhibit them.

• BLUSHING VIOLETS. How shy is the average American? From psychologist Philip Zimbardo, author of *Shyness*, these numbers:

1. *Americans who, based on Zimbardo's findings, are shy* —70 percent.
2. *Who describe themselves as "chronically shy"*—40 percent.
3. *Shy all the time, in all situations, with all people*—2 percent.
4. *Shy the first time they meet a new person*—50 percent.

Zimbardo found that shyness is more common among schoolchildren than among adults and that certain ethnic groups— Jewish Americans, for instance—are *less* shy than other ethnic groups, and some ethnic groups—Asian Americans, for instance—are notably shyer than average.

• TYPE CAST. In their best-selling book *Type A Behavior and Your Heart*, Dr. Meyer Friedman and Dr. Ray H. Rosenman divided the American population into two broad categories: Type A's and Type B's. They defined Type A's as people "aggressively involved in a chronic, incessant struggle to achieve more and more in less and less time." Type B's, on the other hand, are the exact opposite: laid back, cool, not interested in ever entering, let alone winning, the rat race. Their estimates for urban Americans are:

1. *Type A's*—50 percent.
2. *Type B's*—40 percent.
3. *Mixtures of the two*—10 percent.

• E M B R A C E A B L E   Y O U ' S . Based on a sampling of 1,400 Cleveland families, the Project on Human Sexual Development estimates that only three out of ten American men ever hug their male friends. Some hugging percentages, based on the same survey:

1. *Women who hug their friends very often*—60 percent.
2. *Girls who hug their girl friends "usually"*—60 percent.
3. *Sons who* never *hug their friends* (*according to parents*) —60 percent.

• T R O U B L E M A K E R S . About one out of four American junior and senior high school students needs "frequent disciplinary action" according to the teachers surveyed in a 1972 U.S. Department of Health, Education, and Welfare survey. Girls tend to be less of a disciplinary problem than boys, and teachers say that they are less likely to discipline academically accomplished students than low achievers.

• T H E   N A K E D   T R U T H . Only about 2 percent of Americans, according to California sociologist Jack Douglas, can get undressed in public and not feel initially uncomfortable and embarrassed. Douglas bases this raw conclusion on a study he conducted among nude bathers at Eden Beach in San Diego. Douglas's study, reported in *Human Behavior,* suggests that women are less inhibited about going topless on a beach than they are about going *bottomless,* and men, although quicker to undress at a nude beach than women, are also quicker to run into the water for cover. In any event, it is the rare first-time nude bather who parades around in the all-together. Most remain prudently seated.

• R O M A N T I C   P L A C E S . Most Americans consider themselves romantic, but self-perceptions about romantic tendencies vary among different segments of the population. Some representative numbers from a 1977 Roper poll:

1. *Men who say they tend to be romantic*—61 percent.
2. *Women who say the same thing*—65 percent.

3. *Men and women younger than 30 who profess to be romantic*—75 percent.
4. *Men and women who think* men *are more romantic than women*—19 percent (with men somewhat more likely to think this way than women).
5. *Who think* women *are more romantic than men*—45 percent (with women more inclined to think this way than men).
6. *Who earn $18,000 a year or more and describe themselves as romantic*—75 percent.
7. *Who make $6,000 or less and describe themselves the same way*—55 percent.

• BREATHING SPACE. A study of New York City pedestrians, reported by psychologist John Nicholson, suggests that the average pedestrian usually keeps a distance of at least fifteen feet between himself and the pedestrian walking in front. A companion study showed that when two strangers are walking toward one another in the same "traffic lane," one of them will give way to the oncoming person at a distance of anywhere from five feet to seven feet, depending on how crowded the sidewalk is. What these studies tell us is that the concept of territoriality, popularized by writers like Robert Ardrey, applies at least in part to humans, and most of us need some personal space in order to feel comfortable.

SOURCES

Meyer Friedman and Ray H. Rosenman, *Type A Behavior and Your Heart,* 1974.

John Nicholson, *Habits,* 1977.

The Roper Organization.

U.S. Department of Health, Education, and Welfare, *Behavioral Patterns of Youths 12–17.*

Philip Zimbardo, *Shyness,* 1978.

IV OUR GENERAL ATTITUDES

ON WHAT THE COUNTRY'S PRIORITIES SHOULD BE

Since the Vietnam War ended, American concerns on a national scale have focused mainly on two issues: money and crime. Money—that is, inflation—has been the chief worry. Here is what several 1978 surveys turned up when Americans were asked to name the things that the government should either pay more attention to or spend more money on to improve.

• THE BASIC NUMBERS. From *The American Public and the Income Tax System.* (The percentages indicate the proportion of Americans who name each issue as "one of the two most important things to be done now.")

1. *Controlling inflation*—38 percent.
2. *Lowering the crime rate*—36 percent.
3. *Making the tax system fair*—23 percent.
4. *Improving the educational system*—18 percent.
5. *Improving the nation's defense capabilities*—13 percent.
6. *Setting up a program to provide national health insurance for everyone*—13 percent.
7. *Lowering unemployment*—12 percent.
8. *Improving and protecting the environment*—6 percent.
9. *Lowering Social Security taxes*—4 percent.
10. *Simplifying income-tax forms*—3 percent.
11. *Improving public transportation*—2 percent.

From a survey conducted by *Public Research.* (The percentages indicate the proportion of Americans naming each issue as one of the two or three problems facing the country that they themselves are most concerned or worried about.)

1. *Inflation*—61 percent.
2. *Crime and lawlessness*—46 percent.
3. *The tax burden of working Americans*—38 percent.
4. *Rising costs of hospital and health care*—29 percent.
5. *Unemployment*—27 percent.
6. *Energy*—22 percent.
7. *Condition of older people*—20 percent.
8. *Declining quality of education*—19 percent.

9. *Water and air pollution*—12 percent.
10. *Condition of blacks and other minorities*—9 percent.

From *The Playboy Report on American Men*. (The percentages indicate the proportion of American men 18 to 49 years of age who define each issue as "very important.")

1. *Reducing crime*—90 percent.
2. *Eliminating corruption in government*—81 percent.
3. *Reducing inflation*—78 percent.
4. *Reducing unemployment*—76 percent.
5. *Promoting world peace*—76 percent.
6. *Eliminating energy shortages*—75 percent.
7. *Reducing environmental pollution*—63 percent.
8. *Lowering taxes*—55 percent.
9. *Improving consumer protection*—50 percent.
10. *Securing equal rights for minorities*—50 percent.
11. *Helping revitalize the cities*—43 percent.
12. *Providing health insurance for all*—40 percent.
13. *Helping our allies around the world*—23 percent.

From *NORC 1978 General Social Survey*. (The percentages indicate the proportion of Americans who feel the government is spending "too little" on each issue.)

1. *Halting the rising crime rate*—64 percent.
2. *Dealing with drug addiction*—55 percent.
3. *Improving and protecting the nation's health*—55 percent.
4. *Improving and protecting the environment*—52 percent.
5. *Improving the nation's education system*—51 percent.
6. *Solving the problems of the big cities*—38 percent.
7. *The military, armaments, and defense*—27 percent.
8. *Improving the condition of blacks*—24 percent.
9. *The Space Exploration Program*—11 percent.
10. *Welfare*—7 percent.
11. *Foreign aid*—3 percent.

Trends? A comparison of the NORC survey findings for 1978 and the early 1970s gives some indication of the drift of national concern on certain issues. (Note that inflation is not included here because it was not asked about in the surveys.)

1. *Crime*—slightly more concern.
2. *Drug addiction*—slightly less concern.

3. *Education*—slightly more concern.
4. *The environment*—less concern.
5. *Health*—less concern.
6. *Urban problems*—considerably less concern.
7. *Improving the condition of blacks*—considerably less concern.
8. *Military and defense*—much more concern.
9. *Space exploration*—more concern.
10. *Welfare*—less concern.
11. *Foreign aid*—about the same.

• **THE DEMOGRAPHICS.** Here is a glimpse of our national priorities as perceived by various demographic segments of the society. (The percentages indicate the proportion of Americans in each group who show concern for each issue, based on findings of a 1978 Public Research survey.)

Inflation (Total adult population—61 percent.)
1. *All age-groups*—about 61 percent.
2. *Whites*—63 percent.
3. *Blacks*—41 percent.
4. *Northeasterners*—58 percent.
5. *Southerners*—58 percent.
6. *Midwesterners*—63 percent.
7. *Westerners*—66 percent.
8. *College graduates*—67 percent.
9. *High-school graduates*—59 percent.
10. *Non-high-school graduates*—57 percent.
11. *Under $7,000 a year earners*—51 percent.
12. *$7,000 to $14,999 earners*—62 percent.
13. *$15,000 to $24,999 earners*—63 percent.
14. *$25,000 and over earners*—67 percent.
15. *Executives and professionals*—72 percent.
16. *White-collar workers*—62 percent.
17. *Blue-collar workers*—57 percent.

Crime and lawlessness:
1. *Total population*—46 percent.
2. *Americans younger than 30*—41 percent.
3. *Aged 30 to 44*—47 percent.
4. *Aged 45 to 59*—44 percent.
5. *Sixty and older*—54 percent.
6. *Whites*—44 percent.
7. *Blacks*—59 percent.

8. *Northeasterners*—45 percent.
9. *Midwesterners*—46 percent.
10. *Southerners*—61 percent.
11. *Westerners*—37 percent.
12. *College graduates*—40 percent.
13. *High-school graduates*—47 percent.
14. *Non-high-school graduates*—52 percent.
15. *Under $7,000 a year earners*—51 percent.
16. *$7,000 to $14,999 earners*—62 percent.
17. *$15,000 to $24,999 earners*—35 percent.
18. *$25,000 and over earners*—67 percent.
19. *Executives and professionals*—44 percent.
20. *White-collar workers*—43 percent.
21. *Blue-collar workers*—46 percent.

Tax burden on working Americans:

1. *Total population*—38 percent.
2. *Americans younger than 30*—32 percent.
3. *Aged 30 to 44*—42 percent.
4. *Aged 45 to 59*—45 percent.
5. *Sixty and older*—35 percent.
6. *Whites*—41 percent.
7. *Blacks*—20 percent.
8. *Northeasterners*—38 percent.
9. *Midwesterners*—44 percent.
10. *Southerners*—34 percent.
11. *Westerners*—39 percent.
12. *College graduates*—41 percent.
13. *High-school graduates*—40 percent.
14. *Non-high-school graduates*—32 percent.
15. *Under $7,000 a year earners*—23 percent.
16. *$7,000 to $14,999 earners*—37 percent.
17. *$15,000 to $24,999 earners*—42 percent.
18. *$25,000 and over earners*—48 percent.
19. *Executives and professionals*—47 percent.
20. *White-collar workers*—44 percent.
21. *Blue-collar workers*—38 percent.

SOURCES

Albert H. Cantril and Susan Davis Cantril, *Unemployment, Government and the American People*, 1978.
NORC.
The Playboy Report on American Men.

ON THE WOMEN'S MOVEMENT

All things considered, advocates for the women's movement in the United States had a lot to smile about throughout the 1970s, for even though American attitudes toward some women's issues—namely, the Equal Rights Amendment—began to stiffen toward the end of the decade, the overall drift in public opinion since the early 1970s has been consistently pro-woman.

• **THE BASIC NUMBERS.** A comparison of survey data from the late 1970s and the early 1970s reveals that the proportion of Americans who *no longer hold* conventional male-chauvinist attitudes is down by about 10 percent, which is to say that there are probably 16 to 18 million *fewer* male chauvinists around today than there were in the early 1970s. Some related numbers.

Americans who say they:

1. *Would vote for a qualified woman if their party nominated her for president*—81 percent (up from 50 percent in 1949, 57 percent in 1963, and 76 percent in 1976).
2. *Approve of a married woman earning money in business and industry, even though she may have a husband capable of supporting her*—75 percent (up from 67 percent in 1972).
3. *Go along with the statement, "Women should take care of running their homes and leave running the country to men"*—25 percent (down from 35 percent in 1974).

• **TIME MARCHING ON.** A 1978 survey done for *Time* by Yankelovich, Skelly, and White, Inc., produced these numbers for American attitudes on the role that women should play in the family.

"A wife should put her husband and children ahead of her career":

1. *No longer believe*—22 percent.
2. *Completely believe*—39 percent.
3. *Partially believe*—39 percent.

"It is still the wife's responsibility to make sure the house is clean and neat even if she works as hard as her husband":

1. *No longer believe*—22 percent.
2. *Completely believe*—22 percent.
3. *Partially believe*—30 percent.

"Marriages are stronger when the wife stays at home and doesn't go out to work":

1. *No longer believe*—47 percent.
2. *Completely believe*—27 percent.
3. *Partially believe*—26 percent.

"Children suffer when the mother goes to work":

1. *No longer believe*—31 percent.
2. *Completely believe*—32 percent.
3. *Partially believe*—37 percent.

•**Ms. America.** A 1977 Roper Organization poll produced the following numbers on the question of women being addressed as "Miss," Mrs." or "Ms.":

1. *Americans who prefer women to be addressed as "Miss" and "Mrs."*—69 percent (down from 75 percent in 1973).
2. *To be addressed as "Ms."*—18 percent (up from 11 percent in 1973).
3. *Women who prefer the "Ms." title*—19 percent.
4. *Men who prefer the "Ms." title*—19 percent.
5. *Men who are not sure of their preference*—19 percent.

•**The ERA Muddle.** The shift in public attitudes notwithstanding, support for the Equal Rights Amendment is not as solid as amendment supporters would like. A Harris survey taken in the summer of 1978 showed that only 55 percent of Americans are in favor of the amendment, representing a loss of 10 percentage points since 1976.

•**Latent Chauvinists.** A 1978 study by Mirra Komarovsky, designed to find out how college men *really* feel about women's rights, turned up the following categories:

1. *College men who are openly chauvinistic*—25 percent.
2. *College men who are trying to become more supportive but not doing a good job of it*—50 percent.

3. *College men who talk a good game but have not changed their chauvinistic ways*—16 percent.
4. *Genuinely liberated college men*—9 percent.

• DEMOGRAPHICS. The degree to which American women individually subscribe to the various battle cries of the women's movement vary noticeably according to age, income bracket, social background, and education, and the demographic patterns are fairly consistent. Older women, for instance, are more likely than younger women to hold traditional views about women in the home, and college women are less likely than noncollege women to stress the importance of a man being a good provider.

As far as American teenage girls are concerned, there are only three areas of the women's movement in which more than half the girls surveyed in a 1978 *Seventeen* magazine teen trends survey describe themselves as "very interested." They are:

1. *Equal training and education.*
2. *Reform of the rape laws.*
3. *Equal employment.*

The percentages on other issues look like this:

1. *Very interested in the Equal Rights Amendment*—33 percent of teen girls.
2. *Have little or no interest in abortion reform*—33 percent.
3. *Somewhat or very interested in seeing an end to stereotyping of women*—75 percent.
4. *Somewhat or very interested in equal credit and mortgage privileges*—80 percent.

SOURCES
Gallup Poll.
Harris Survey.
Mirra Komarovsky, "Cultural Contradictions and Sex Roles," 1978.
NORC.
The Roper Organization.
Time.

ON INFLATION

Inflation inspired more questions from pollsters in the 1970s than probably any other topic. Here is a sampling of what the surveys revealed.

• **THE BASIC NUMBERS.** Most of the surveys done in the late 1970s showed inflation to be the number-one problem in the United States in the minds of about 60 percent of the adult population. Some related numbers from a 1978 Roper poll.

Americans who feel that:

1. *Inflation is pretty much here to stay*—88 percent.
2. *Inflation can be halted at the one- or two-percent level* —12 percent (down from 65 percent in 1975).
3. *1978 was a good time to buy a "big ticket" item*—65 percent.

• **CHOOSING SIDES.** You would not guess it from how gun-shy everybody seems to be when it comes to taking decisive measures against inflation, but the overwhelming majority of Americans, when asked, say they would be willing to modify their life-style in the interests of holding down inflation. Here is a little of what a 1975 Harris survey turned up on this question.

Proportion of Americans willing to:

1. *Have one meatless day a week*—91 percent.
2. *Stop feeding all-beef products to pets*—78 percent.
3. *Eliminate annual model changes in automobiles*—92 percent.
4. *Accept a sharp cut in the use of plastic bags and packaging that most products are sold in*—90 percent.
5. *Wear old clothes until they wear out*—73 percent.
6. *Do away with changing clothing fashions every year*— 90 percent.
7. *Drive cars to 100,000 miles before junking them*—79 percent.

• **WAR CRIES.** When asked to choose between controlling inflation and a number of other alternatives, Americans in early 1979 had these preferences.

Proportion who would favor:

1. *Controlling inflation rather than a tax cut*—91 percent.
2. *Controlling inflation rather than a large pay hike*—54 percent.
3. *Wage and price controls*—53 percent.
4. *A substantial spending cut*—63 percent.
5. *A balanced budget requirement*—85 percent.
6. *Slower economic growth with less inflation*—87 percent.

SOURCES
Gallup Poll.
Harris Survey.
The Roper Organization.

ON TAXES

Complaining about taxes is, historically, as American as the Boston Tea Party, and today is no exception. Most Americans, according to a Roper survey done in 1978 for H & R Block, Inc., see taxation as a necessary evil but also feel that our present system of taxation leaves much to be desired. Here is a closer look.

• **THE BASIC NUMBERS.** Only one out of three Americans considers the present income-tax system fair. And only four of every hundred Americans are enthusiastic enough about the system to describe it as "quite" fair. On the other hand, about one out of three Americans considers the income tax "somewhat" unfair, and a similar proportion take the more extreme view that it is "quite" unfair. These sentiments are shared equally by Americans in all demographic groups, but the loudest beefs come from folks who earn $15,000 to $25,000 a year, from union members, and from white-collar workers.

• **SELF-CRITICISM.** When Americans are asked to comment on the relative fairness of their *own* income-tax burden, here is how they reply.

Proportion of Americans who consider:

1. *Their taxes in general to be excessively high*—51 percent.

2. *Their income taxes to be too high*—53 percent.
3. *Their property taxes to be excessively high*—32 percent.
4. *Their income taxes just about right*—26 percent.
5. *The amount of taxes they pay to be very reasonable*— 7 percent.

• H o w   M a d   A r e   Y o u ? On a scale of 1 to 10—"1" representing complete satisfaction and "10" blind fury—the median anger level of taxpayers in the United States today is 6.35. Here is a look at those who are angriest:

1. *Blacks*—7.15.
2. *Northeasterners*—7.07.
3. *Americans earning $25,000 or more*—6.95.
4. *White-collar workers*—6.94.
5. *Americans earning $15,000 to $25,000*—6.48.

• L o g i c a l   D e d u c t i o n s . One man's deduction is another man's loophole. Here is the proportion of American taxpayers who describe as "loopholes" current legal deductions:

1. *Charitable contributions*—30 percent.
2. *Interest on home mortgage*—7 percent.
3. *Interest income on municipal bonds*—40 percent think it should be taxed.
4. *Business lunches*—90 percent (65 percent of Americans would favor a 50-percent deductible allowance for business meals).

• S o a k i n g   t h e   R i c h . Most Americans are under the impression that the rich do not contribute their fair share when it comes to paying taxes. More than half the population agree with the statement, "More than half the people who make more than a half million dollars a year or more pay no income taxes at all" (the statement has no basis in fact). And when asked to name the one thing that bothers them the most about the income-tax system, 17 percent of respondents answer: "The rich pay too little or none at all."

SOURCE
The American Public and the Income Tax System, 1978.

ON CRIME

If there is one issue on which Americans agree unanimously it is the need to reduce crime. Next to inflation, crime is the issue cited most often when Americans are asked to list national priorities. And among certain segments of the population —the poor urban segments, in particular—crime is far and away the burning issue of our time.

• S E M I - T O U G H . The overwhelming majority of Americans would like to see the criminal-justice system get a lot tougher with criminals, as the NORC numbers that follow amply demonstrate:

1. *Do not feel our criminal justice system deals harshly enough with criminals*—84 percent (compared with 66 percent in 1972).
2. *Feel our courts deal too harshly with criminals*—2 percent (compared with 6 percent in 1972).
3. *Feel the way our courts deal with criminals is just about right*—7 percent.

• F E D E R A L   A I D . Most Americans (nearly 70 percent according to NORC surveys) would like to see the federal government spend *more* money to halt the rising crime rate, and 90 percent of American men between the ages of 18 and 49 (according to *The Playboy Report on American Men*) consider the reduction of crime the most important priority we face. Concern for crime shows up strongly in all demographic segments but is especially high among men in the lower-middle class (of whom 94 percent consider it "very" important that we reduce crime).

• D E A T H   R O W . If it ever came down to a national referendum on the subject, Americans would vote overwhelmingly in favor of the death penalty for persons convicted of murder. Roughly two-thirds of American adults (according to NORC surveys) now favor the death penalty for convicted murderers, and 68 percent of the men queried in *The Playboy Report on American Men* felt the same way. Support for the death penalty appears to be picking up steam. In 1972 only 57 percent of Americans were in favor of it, with 43 percent opposed. To-day only about 27 percent of Americans say they oppose capi-tal punishment, and another 6 percent are not sure.

SOURCES
NORC.
Playboy Report on American Men.

ON UNEMPLOYMENT

Unemployment is currently an $11-billion industry in the United States, if you figure the money the government spends on jobs, job-training programs, and unemployment benefits. So to get a fix on public attitudes toward the unemployment situation, the U.S. Department of Labor commissioned Albert and Susan Cantril of Public Research to do a study. Here is a little of what they found out.

• THE GENERAL PICTURE. More than half the Ameri-can adult population (57 percent) say they are moderately con-cerned about unemployment; but in terms of national priori-ties, unemployment ranks anywhere from third to eighth, de-pending on how pollsters phrase their questions on priorities. Most Americans are more concerned about inflation, crime, the cost of health care, and taxes than about unemployment. About 45 percent of Americans think that the unemployment problem is getting worse in the United States (as compared with only 20 percent who see it getting better). Meanwhile 80 percent of the population seem resigned to accepting unem-ployment as a fact of American life that will always be with us.

• THE DEMOGRAPHICS OF CONCERN. Not surpris-ingly, the Americans who register the most concern for unem-ployment are those who are getting burned by it. Of the 16 percent of Americans who consider unemployment a "primary" concern, nearly one out of four is younger than 30 and nearly one out of three is black. Concern for unemployment runs deeper among central-city residents than among suburbanites; and small-town and rural Americans show more concern than the nation as a whole. For obvious reasons, too, Americans who are not high-school graduates are more worried about unem-ployment than are college graduates.

• **MAKING CONNECTIONS**. When Americans are asked to give their views on the *consequences* of unemployment, five answers turn up most frequently. They are:

1. A *rise in the crime rate*—77 percent.
2. A *rise in the cost of welfare programs*—69 percent.
3. A *rise in the drug and narcotics problem*—48 percent.
4. An *increase in family breakups*—43 percent.
5. A *rise in unrest throughout the country*—30 percent.

One curious aspect of these findings is that in terms of the way the consequences of unemployment are viewed by (*a*) the consequences of those Americans who *are not* concerned about unemployment and (*b*) those who *are*, there is almost no difference. So what it means is that people tend to respond to unemployment more on an emotional level than on an intellectual level.

• **FIXING BLAME**. The reasons Americans offer to explain the unemployment situation vary according to the direct experience the individual has had with unemployment. About 60 percent of Americans who have had no *direct* experience with unemployment blame the unemployment situation on the largesse of existing welfare and unemployment programs, but this view is echoed by only 46 percent of Americans who have ever been out of work themselves. Similarly, while "laziness" is cited as a reason for unemployment by about one out of four Americans who have never been out of work themselves, only about 10 percent of Americans who know unemployment firsthand share the same opinion. By the same token, Americans who are either out of work now or have been out of work recently are much more likely to blame the unemployment problem on the failure of business to create jobs rather than on working Americans. Here are the reasons cited most frequently, by *all* Americans, as being among the chief causes for unemployment:

1. "*Welfare and unemployment benefits are so good, people don't have to work*"—57 percent.
2. "*Even though jobs exist, people don't have the basic skills they need to get jobs*"—35 percent.
3. "*Foreign competition reduces the number of jobs in this country*"—30 percent.
4. "*More women are looking for jobs now than before*" —28 percent.

5. *"More young people are looking for jobs now than ever before"*—28 percent.
6. *"Illegal aliens are taking away jobs"*—20 percent.
7. *"Some people have it too easy in their youth and feel no need to work"*—19 percent.
8. *"Business isn't creating enough jobs"*—17 percent.
9. *"The jobs that are available aren't very desirable"*—15 percent.
10. *Discrimination against blacks and other minorities*—8 percent.

• SUGGESTION BOX. When Americans in this poll were asked to suggest solutions to the unemployment problem, here is what was proposed:

1. *The federal government should provide training and jobs for people out of work*—33 percent.
2. *Should give incentives to business as a means of increasing employment*—28 percent.
3. *Should stimulate the economy by cutting taxes*—20 percent.
4. *Should let things take their course*—2 percent.

SOURCE
Albert and Susan Cantril, *Unemployment, Government and the American People.*

ON FOREIGN AFFAIRS

The mood of isolationism that arose just after the Vietnam War ended shows signs of easing, and most recent surveys show an increasing number of Americans either resigned to, or actively supporting, the idea of the United States taking more initiative in world affairs.

Proportion of Americans who, according to NORC surveys:

1. *Want the United States to stay in the UN*—80 percent.
2. *Would not commit troops to fight overseas for any reason other than a direct attack on the United States*—63 percent.
3. *Might consider sending U.S. troops overseas if Middle East oil sources were jeopardized*—52 percent (men

and younger Americans tend to be more hawkish when it comes to oil; and women, generally, are less hawkish regardless of the circumstances).

4. *Feel friendly to China*—51 percent.
5. *Felt friendly to China in 1977*—23 percent.
6. *Feel friendly to Israel*—75 percent.
7. *Feel friendly to England*—83 percent.
8. *Feel friendly to Russia*—24 percent.
9. *Felt friendly to Egypt in 1977*—52 percent.

• T HE R U S S I A N S A RE C O M I N G . In late 1978 an ABC-Harris survey polled Americans to find out whether they felt the U.S. military defense system was stronger or weaker than that of the Soviet Union. The results:

1. *U.S. military defense system is stronger*—14 percent.
2. *Weaker*—40 percent.
3. *About as strong*—39 percent.

When compared with the findings of a December 1976 survey, the results show also that in 1978 fewer Americans felt that U.S. military might was equivalent to or stronger than that of the Russians than did so in the mid-1970s.

SOURCES
Gallup Poll.
Harris Survey.
NORC.

ON EDUCATION

Relative to other institutions, education as a whole is holding its own in the minds of most Americans, but our confidence in the ability of public schools to deliver quality education is on the wane.

• R E P O R T C A R D . From a 1976 Roper poll, this picture of how Americans view the performance of their local schools:

1. *Consider their local schools either excellent or good—* 47 percent.
2. *Consider their local schools either fair or good*—36 percent.

3. *Think the government is doing too little to improve the nation's education system*—50 percent.

On the other hand, only 15 percent of the American parents cited in a 1972 Gallup poll cited mental stimulation as the chief reason they wanted their children to go to college. The most frequent answer (44 percent) had to do with getting a better job.

• **HARD-LINERS**. Survey results throughout the 1970s consistently showed that American parents would like to see their public schools toe the line more on discipline and academics. Some of the numbers from a 1975 Gallup poll:

1. *Public-school parents who do not think elementary school children are made to work hard enough*—53 percent.
2. *Who think that kids are made to work too hard*—5 percent.
3. *Who think high-school students should be made to work harder*—54 percent.
4. *Who think high-school students are made to work too hard*—2 percent.

SOURCES
Gallup Poll.
Playboy 1977 Survey of the College Market.
The Roper Organization.
Seventeen.

ON SEX

Few areas of American life have undergone such a major shift in attitudes, in so short a time, as sex, although most surveys point to a slackening of strongly libertine attitudes. A detailed look at the sex habits of Americans follows in Part VIII, "Sex," but here are some general attitude perspectives.

• **UNHOLY WEDLOCK**. Probably the most significant attitude change regarding sex in America revolves around the question of whether it is okay for a man and woman to bed down together without the sanction of a marriage contract.

Some representative attitudes based on composite survey findings:

1. *American men who, in 1940, considered it "wicked" or "unfortunate" for young girls to have sexual relations before marriage*—80 percent.
2. *Americans believing that sex before marriage is "always wrong" or "almost always is wrong"*—40 percent today (48 percent in 1972).
3. *Americans believing that sex before marriage is "not wrong at all" or "wrong only sometimes"*—36 percent today (up from 27 percent in 1972).
4. *Teenage girls who approve of premarital sex (according to a* Seventeen *Survey)*—33 percent.
5. *Who disapprove of premarital sex*—33 percent.
6. *Who would like to be virgins when they get married*—41 percent.
7. *Who say they're not sure*—20.5 percent.
8. *Who would like to marry virgins*—20 percent.
9. *Who would not like to marry virgins*—56 percent.
10. *Who would like to live with the men they marry before their marriage*—42 percent.

• **CAMPUS REVOLT.** A comparison of results from two studies done at the University of Georgia (and reported in the *Journal of Marriage and the Family*) suggests that the so-called double standard is gradually disappearing on college campuses.

Proportions who considered it "sinful" for a woman to have sexual intercourse with a great many men:

1. *Female students*—70 percent in 1965; 37 percent in 1975.
2. *Male students*—58 percent in 1965; 20 percent in 1975.

• **SELF-HELP.** Most recent sex surveys show that a more tolerant attitude toward masturbation prevails throughout the country, but a 1975 study by Ibtihaj Arafat suggests that some curiously outdated attitudes still remain.

1. *College males who masturbate*—90 percent of college population.
2. *College females who masturbate*—61 percent.
3. *Male masturbators who feel guilty about it*—13 percent.

4. *Female masturbators who feel guilty about it*—10 percent.

5. *Male masturbators who worry about "going insane" from it*—4 percent.

6. *Female masturbators who worry about "going insane" from it*—7 percent.

• STATUTORY LIBERTY. Most Americans (63 percent according to a 1977 Yankelovich poll for *Time*) think it is morally wrong for unmarried teenagers to have intercourse. Attitudes differ according to age-group, however:

1. *Americans younger than 25 who think teenage intercourse is immoral*—34 percent.

2. *Americans older than 50 who share this view*—80 percent.

• ROOMMATES. A slight majority of Americans (52 percent according to the *Time* survey) now approve of men and women living together without getting married, but 70 percent disapprove of having children out of wedlock.

• X-RATED VIEWS. Some representative American opinions on pornography based on NORC numbers.
Proportion of Americans who:

1. *Would favor government action to eliminate pornography in movies, books, and nightclubs*—74 percent.

2. *Believe that pornographic materials lead people to commit rape*—60 percent.

3. *Believe pornography leads to a breakdown of morals*—60 percent.

• PARENTAL GUIDANCE. From a recently published study of 600 Cleveland families by the Project on Human Sexual Development:

1. *Mothers who feel that premarital sex is okay for their daughters*—30 percent; *for their sons*—60 percent.

2. *Parents who approve of premarital intercourse for their sons*—64 percent.

3. *Who approve of masturbation for their sons*—43 percent.

4. *Who accept the idea of masturbation for their daughters*—35 percent.

5. *Who accept the idea of premarital sex for their daughters*—30 percent.
6. *Single mothers who want their daughters to grow up thinking that premarital sexual activity is acceptable*— 50 percent.

Most parents would like their children to wait until they are 18 to 21 before they have their first intercourse.

In virtually all the areas mentioned above, college-educated parents take a much more liberal stance than do parents with less education.

• G a y   S e n t i m e n t s . From a Gallup poll taken in the summer of 1977, these views on homosexuality.

Proportion of Americans who:

1. *Think homosexuality is more prevalent today than 25 years ago*—66 percent.
2. *Think that more than 20 percent of women today are homosexuals*—26 percent.
3. *Feel that homosexuality is the result of upbringing and environment*—56 percent.
4. *Think that homosexual relations between consenting adults should be illegal*—43 percent.
5. *Should be legal*—43 percent.
6. *Do not think homosexuals should teach in elementary schools*—65 percent.

• C l o s e t   J o b s . The gay-rights movement appears to be making at least some dent in the antipathy that Americans have historically shown against homosexuality, but the change of heart is more related to the rights of homosexuals and not to the idea of homosexuality itself.

Proportion of Americans who, according to NORC surveys:

1. *Consider homosexuality always wrong*—68 percent (down from 70 percent in 1973).
2. *Almost always wrong*—5 percent.
3. *Wrong only sometimes*—7 percent.
4. *Not wrong at all*—14 percent (up from 10 percent in 1973).
5. *Favor legislation that would guarantee the rights of homosexuals*—56 percent.
6. *Would not want to see an admitted homosexual teaching at a college or university*—50 percent.

SOURCES

Ibtihaj Arafat and Wayne Cotton, "Masturbation Practices of Males and Females," 1974.

Karl King et al., "The Continuing Premarital Sexual Revolution Among College Females," 1977.

Gallup Poll.

Harris Survey.

NORC.

Daniel Yankelovich, "A Second Look at the Sexual Revolution," *Reader's Digest*, June 1978.

ON ABORTION

Abortion could be *the* most divisive issue in the United States today—more so, even, than race. What has been happening to American attitudes is that a higher proportion of people now favor allowing a woman to get an abortion if she chooses, but opposition to government participation in the process is stiffening. Here are some representative views.

Proportion of Americans who:

1. *Consider abortion morally wrong*—64 percent (according to a 1977 Yankelovich poll); 58 percent of all Catholics.
2. *Favor abortion if there is a strong chance of serious defect in the baby*—85 percent (according to NORC surveys).
3. *If mother's health is endangered*—90 percent.
4. *If woman is married and simply does not want to have children*—40 percent.
5. *If family has a low income and cannot afford any more children*—44 percent.
6. *Oppose the idea of using government funds to finance abortions*—60 percent.

SOURCES

NORC.

Daniel Yankelovich, "A Second Look at the Sexual Revolution."

ON DEATH AND DYING

Death—how much we think about it, what we think about it, and how we prepare for it—has become an increasingly popular subject among poll-takers in recent years. Here is a sampling of what some of the surveys have uncovered.

• **THINKING ABOUT IT.** From a 1975 Institute of Life Insurance survey, these numbers on what Americans think about death.

Americans who say they think about death:

1. *Often*—32 percent.
2. *Occasionally*—38 percent.
3. *Hardly ever*—25 percent.
4. *Never*—4 percent.

Who agree with the following statements:

1. *"Each person has the right to die with dignity"*—97 percent.
2. *"Death is sometimes a blessing"*—94 percent.
3. *"Death itself is not to be feared, only the manner of dying"*—87 percent.
4. *"Death is not tragic for the person who dies, only for the survivors"*—83 percent.
5. *"If a person is dying, a doctor ought to tell him"*—78 percent.
6. *"Death is like a long sleep"*—55 percent.

• **SAY ''GOOD-BYE'' NOW.** Euthanasia—mercy killing —is now favored by a majority of Americans, but only when both the family and the patient who is dying request it.

From a 1973 Gallup poll, Americans who think doctors should be allowed by law to end the life of a patient with an incurable disease if the patient and the family request it:

1. *Total population*—53 percent.
2. *Men*—53 percent.
3. *Women*—53 percent.
4. *College-educated*—61 percent.
5. *High-school-educated*—54 percent.

6. *Younger than 30*—67 percent.
7. *50 and older*—44 percent.

And from a 1978 NORC survey:

1. *Americans who would favor euthanasia under the circumstances described above*—57 percent.
2. *Who would favor the ending of a person's life if a board of doctors appointed by the court agreed the patient could not be cured*—3 percent.

• G O I N G   T O   M E E T   T H E   M A N . In 1973 the *Minneapolis Star* asked a sampling of its readers what they would do if they had only six months to live. Their answers:

1. *Take care of responsibilities, make sure family is provided for*—26 percent.
2. *"Everything I've always wanted": travel, quit work, undertake special projects*—22 percent.
3. *Continue to live in the same way*—21 percent.
4. *Live each day to the fullest, make the best of it*—17 percent.
5. *"Take a look at myself" and the meaning life had*—9 percent.

SOURCES
Gallup Poll.
Institute of Life Insurance.
The *Minneapolis Star*.
NORC.

ON GOVERNMENT

Historically, American attitudes toward government fluctuate according to how good or bad things are going at home and abroad. But generally speaking, Americans have been losing confidence in basic government institutions over the past twenty years.

• F E D E R A L   C A S E S . The confidence Americans have in the ability of Washington to solve our problems was at its lowest in 1978, as the following findings of a Harris survey well indicate.

Percentage of Americans who:

1. *Express high confidence in the White House*—14 percent (down from 26 percent in 1977).
2. *Express high confidence in Congress*—10 percent (an all-time low).
3. *Blame the federal government for rising costs*—51 percent.
4. *Believe the U.S. government is "almost wholly free of corruption and payoffs"*—51 percent.
5. *Believe public life attracts the best people*—12 percent.
6. *Believe politicians put special interests ahead of the good of the country*—75 percent.

• LOCAL CONTROL. American attitudes toward state and local government institutions have gone the way of attitudes toward the federal government. The proportion of Americans who say they have a great deal of confidence in state government is now 15 percent, and the proportion who say they have a great deal of confidence in local government is 19 percent.

• LOOKING UP. Current disenchantment notwithstanding, most Americans still think it is possible for an American government to work for the needs of the people. Some representative opinions from a 1978 Harris survey on the subject:

1. *Americans who think it is possible to have a government that is almost wholly free of corruption*—48 percent.
2. *See no way that we can have a government that is almost wholly free of corruption*—45 percent.
3. *See the possibility of one day having a corps of public officials who "really care about what happens to people"*—81 percent.
4. *College students who, according to a Playboy survey of college students in 1977, say they would consider a career in government*—27 percent.
5. *Who believe a career in government might be financially rewarding*—21 percent.

SOURCES
Gallup Poll.
Harris Survey.
The Playboy Report on American Men.
The Roper Organization.

ON THE ENERGY CRISIS

Energy barreled its way into the American consciousness in 1973, during the Arab oil boycott, and then again in early 1979, when Iran overthrew the Shah and the Three Mile Island nuclear reactor went on the fritz. Still at no time during the 1970s was it ever perceived by Americans as being one of the three or four biggest problems. Some sample views.

• **No More Nukes.** Just as nuclear-energy officials figured, the accident at Three Mile Island in March 1979 soured public opinion against the idea of nuclear power plants. Here is what a *New York Times*/CBS News poll found out in April 1979:

1. *Americans who would approve building more nuclear power plants*—69 percent in 1977; 46 percent after the Three Mile Island accident.
2. *Americans who would approve the building of a nuclear plant in their community*—55 percent in 1977; 38 percent in 1979.
3. *Men who would favor the building of more nuclear plants*—56 percent.
4. *Women who would favor the idea*—36 percent.
5. *Americans who think a nuclear power plant accident could cause a Hiroshima-like atomic explosion*—36 percent.
6. *Who believe that public officials were honest in telling the public all they knew about the danger from the accident*—20 percent.
7. *Who think there was more danger than was actually disclosed*—55 percent.

• **Alternatives.** Some related energy views, based on the same survey.
   Americans who:

1. *Think that higher prices for oil will lead companies to discover more oil*—56 percent.
2. *Think solar energy is the solution to the energy crisis*—42 percent.

3. *Would prefer coal to nuclear generating power*—66 percent.
4. *Who say they would drive less if gasoline went up to one dollar a gallon*—56 percent.

SOURCE
New York Times, April 10, 1979.

• **Boiled in Oil**. The latest oil shortage, in the summer of 1979, hit so quickly and had such a devastating effect on gas lines that not all pollsters are ready to accept as truly representative of the American view the survey results obtained during the middle of the crisis. In any event, here is what the *New York Times*/CBS Poll turned up in the way of public feeling about some of the issues related to the situation.

1. *Americans who favored gas rationing in June, 1979*—62 percent.
2. *Who favored it in mid-July when the limit being talked about was 10 gallons a week*—52 percent.
3. *Who favor a 78 degree limit on air conditioning in public buildings*—77 percent.
4. *Who are opposed to decontrol of gasoline prices*—77 percent.
5. *Who had trouble getting gas in July*—38 percent.
6. *Who said they expected to change vacation plans because of gas shortage*—29 percent.
7. *Who believe the oil shortage is real*—26 percent.
8. *Who approved of the way President Carter was dealing with the situation*—16 percent.

ON TELEVISION

Given the amount of television we watch (not to mention the fact that virtually every U.S. household has at least one television set), it is hardly surprising that American attitudes toward television are notably favorable, with the only pocket of negativism showing up in the area of children's programming.

• **The Basic Numbers**. A sampling of attitudes, based on a Roper Organization poll done for the Television Information Office.

1. *American who see commercials as a fair price to pay for free entertainment*—74 percent.
2. *Who don't mind commercials on children's television shows*—63 percent.
3. *Who feel the quality of children's shows has improved over the years*—30 percent.
4. *Gotten worse over the years*—21 percent.
5. *Who feel that television presents a classically sexist view of women*—12 percent.
6. *Portrays women as being even more liberated than women are in real life*—44 percent.

• **F I R E D   U P** . Most Americans see a relationship between TV violence and the rising crime rate; and if a sizable proportion of the population had its way, shows with violence would be taken off television entirely. The numbers:

1. *Americans who connect TV violence with the rising crime rate*—70 percent.
2. *Parents who feel this way*—67 percent.
3. *Americans who would like to see all television programs that show violence taken off television entirely* —35 percent.
3. *Parents who feel this way*—29 percent.
4. *Nonparents, and parents with grown children, who feel this way*—41 percent.

SOURCE
Television Information Office.

ON DRUGS

Despite the fact that more marijuana is being smoked, and more cocaine sniffed, in the United States than at any other time in our history, the majority of the American public takes a dim view of drug-taking in general and is against the notion of legalizing pot—at least for now. Here are some of the feelings Americans have about drugs and how these attitudes have changed throughout the 1970s.

• **U P   I N   S M O K E** . The most recent NORC surveys show that in 1978 about 34 percent of American adults favored the legalization of marijuana, as compared with 12 percent in 1969 and 28 percent in 1977 (the latter according to a Gallup poll). The demographics are fairly predictable. Younger people are much more gung ho on the idea of legalizing marijuana than are older people (50 percent of college freshmen in 1979 favored legalization), and college-educated Americans take a more liberal stance than do high-school- or grade-school-educated Americans. Some other views based on Gallup findings:

1. *Americans who think marijuana is physically harmful* —55 percent.
2. *Women who feel this way*—61 percent.
3. *Men who feel this way*—48 percent.
4. *Southerners who feel this way*—61 percent.
5. *Westerners who feel this way*—50 percent.
6. *Americans who think that marijuana is physically addictive*—59 percent.
7. *Who have tried marijuana and think this way*—23 percent.
8. *Who have never tried it and think this way*—70 percent.
9. *Who think marijuana leads to hard drugs*—59 percent (down from 75 percent in 1972).
10. *Who think possession of marijuana should be treated as a criminal offense*—41 percent.
11. *Who do not think possession of small amounts of marijuana should be treated as a criminal offense*—53 percent.

• **M A L E   B A G .** *The Playboy Report on American Men* devotes an entire section to attitudes toward drug use. Some of the key findings.

American men (18 to 49) who approve the use, by the general public of:

1. *Tranquilizers*—38 percent.
2. *Sleeping pills*—33 percent.
3. *Marijuana*—31 percent.
4. *Amphetamines*—11 percent.
5. *Barbiturates*—9 percent.
6. *Cocaine*—8 percent.
7. *Hallucinogens*—4 percent.
8. *Heroin*—2 percent.

In all instances younger men (the "Innovators") are much more favorably disposed to drugs than older, more conventional men; and married men tend to be more conservative on the issue than single men.

SOURCES
Gallup Poll.
NORC.
Playboy Report on American Men.
The Roper Organization.

ON ASTROLOGY AND THE OCCULT

Interest in astrology, the occult, and UFOs and the like reached an all-time high in the United States during the 1970s and appeared to gather more steam as the decade came to an end. Here are some of the results of two Gallup polls taken in 1975 and 1978.

•STAR STRUCK. Roughly 22 percent of American adults polled in 1975 said they believed their lives were governed, in part at least, by the stars, and by 1978 the number had risen to 29 percent. Some related numbers from the two polls.

1. *Americans who know their astrological sign*—75 percent.
2. *Who read an astrology column regularly*—23 percent.
3. *Women who believe in astrology*—32 percent.
4. *Men who believe in it*—26 percent.
5. *Americans who do not believe in astrology but say they read the columns anyway*—17 percent.

Generally speaking, astrology plays a bigger part in the lives of Americans who are young, poor, and of limited education and has a stronger hold on blacks and single people than on whites and married people. Curiously, though, nonchurchgoers are only slightly more likely to believe in astrology than regular churchgoers.

•ONE STEP BEYOND. Here are some additional and related survey findings from a 1978 Gallup poll:

1. *Americans who say they believe in UFOs*—57 percent.
2. *Who believe in "Bigfoot"*—13 percent.
3. *Who believe in ghosts*—11 percent.

4. *Who say they have had a "close encounter" with a UFO*—9 percent.

• **TEEN BELIEFS**. A look at teen-age beliefs in the paranormal, from a 1978 Gallup Youth Survey.

American teens who believe in:

1. *ESP*—67 percent.
2. *Angels*—64 percent.
3. *Sasquatch*—40 percent.
4. *The Loch Ness monster*—31 percent.
5. *Witchcraft*—25 percent.
6. *Clairvoyance*—25 percent.
7. *Ghosts*—20 percent.

In general, teen boys and teen girls are similar in their psychic beliefs, although boys (39 percent) are much more likely to buy the existence of the Loch Ness monster than girls (23 percent). Above average students, curiously enough, are more likely to believe in the supernatural than students of average or below average academic standing. And western teen-agers are more outer-world oriented than teen-agers from any other part of the country.

SOURCE
Gallup Poll.

ON OTHER INSTITUTIONS

All told, the confidence Americans have in major institutions not already mentioned has been plunging throughout the 1970s, but some institutions are taking a tougher beating than others. Here is a comparative look based on 1978 NORC survey findings.

Proportion of Americans who have a great deal of confidence in:

1. *Banks and other financial institutions*—33 percent (up from 31 percent in 1975).
2. *Organized labor*—11 percent (down from 15 percent in 1972).
3. *The press*—20 percent (down from 23 percent in 1972).

4. *Medicine*—46 percent (down from 54 percent in 1972).

5. *Television*—13.5 percent (down from 18.5 percent in 1972).

6. *Supreme Court*—28 percent (down from 31 percent in 1973 and 35 percent in 1976).

7. *Scientific community*—36 percent (no change from 1972 on but down from 44 percent in 1974).

8. *The military*—30 percent (no change since 1972 but down from 39 percent in 1976).

Americans who have hardly any confidence in:

1. *Banks and other financial institutions*—11.5 percent (no change since 1972).

2. *Organized labor*—37.5 percent (up from 25 percent in 1973).

3. *The press*—19.5 percent (up from 14 percent in 1973).

4. *Medicine*—9 percent (up from 5.7 percent in 1973).

5. *Television*—31 percent (up from 21 percent in 1973).

6. *Supreme Court*—14.5 percent (no change since 1972 but up 9 percent in 1977).

7. *Scientific community*—7 percent (no change since 1972).

8. *The military*—12.5 percent (down from 16 percent in 1973).

SOURCE
NORC.

ON SPORTS AND ATHLETICS

Over the past ten years there have been two noteworthy changes in the attitudes Americans bring to sports and athletics. First of all, Americans are more interested in participatory sports than ever before and not quite as wrapped up in spectator sports. A bigger change, though, has been the new attitude toward women in sports, with many parents feeling the same about their daughters' involvement in sports as they do about their sons'.

•FAMILY PLANNING. The vast majority of American parents (93 percent according to *The Perrier Study of Fitness in America*) now consider it either "very" or "somewhat" important for their sons or daughters to grow up with a "deep concern" for staying in top physical shape. Some related attitudes and the proportion of parents who share them:

1. *It is important for sons to be active in sports and athletics*—89 percent.
2. *It is important for daughters to be active in sports and athletics*—82 percent.
3. *Parents who favor some form of competitive sports activity for their sons*—70 percent.
4. *Parents who favor some form of competitive sports activity for their daughters*—50 percent.
5. *Parents who think it is either "very important" or "somewhat important" for their sons to become sports stars*—25 percent.
6. *Parents who feel the same way about their daughters* —25 percent.

• **PICKING SIDES**. American parents have some rather definite views on *which* sports they would like to see their children get involved in. If the parents with sons had their way, the following sports would get the preferential nod:

1. *Baseball*—53 percent.
2. *Swimming*—48 percent.
3. *Basketball*—46 percent.
4. *Football*—30 percent.
5. *Bicycling*—27 percent.
6. *Running*—24 percent.
7. *Tennis*—24 percent.
8. *Track and field*—20 percent.

And for daughters:

1. *Swimming*—60 percent.
2. *Tennis*—34 percent.
3. *Bicycling*—34 percent.
4. *Gymnastics*—32 percent.
5. *Dancercise*—28 percent.
6. *Ice-skating*—23 percent.
7. *Bowling*—19 percent.
8. *Softball*—19 percent.

• **FOOTBALL HEROES**. A 1961 study by James S. Coleman determined that high-school jocks in the five California high schools enjoyed more status than boys who were known to be either scholars or ladies' men. High-school athletes, Coleman found, had more friends, enjoyed the affection of more students, and were more likely than scholars or ladies' men to hang out with the "leading crowd of the school."

• TAKING THE GLOVES OFF. American parents are *least* enthusiastic about their sons' participation in the following sporting activities:

1. *Boxing*—33 percent cite it as the least preferred sport.
2. *Football*—25 percent.
3. *Wrestling*—23 percent.
4. *Mountain climbing*—22 percent.
5. *Karate*—14 percent.
6. *Hockey*—14 percent.

And for their daughters:

1. *Wrestling*—48 percent.
2. *Football*—39 percent.
3. *Boxing*—38 percent.
4. *Weight lifting*—34 percent.
5. *Mountain climbing*—22 percent.

SOURCES
James S. Coleman, *The Adolescent Society*, 1961.
The Perrier Study of Fitness in America.

ON FITNESS AND NUTRITION

Interest in fitness and nutrition is at an all-time high in the U.S., but so is confusion. Two recent surveys, *The Perrier Study of Fitness in America*, conducted by Louis Harris and Associates, and a *Woman's Day* nutrition study conducted by Yankelovich, Skelly and White, have produced numbers to support both sides of the picture. Here are some of them.

• THE BASIC NUMBERS. From the *Woman's Day* study:

1. *Americans who say they are more interested in nutrition today than they were a few years ago*—77 percent.
2. *Who feel well informed about nutrition*—25 percent.

3. *Who believe "there's too much talk about what's good and what's bad for you when it comes to food*—71 percent.

4. *Who are convinced that any food on sale is safe*— 34 percent.

5. *Who support the idea of taking vitamins even without a doctor's blessing*—41 percent.

6. *Who consider naural foods healthier than processed foods*—68 percent.

7. *Who are concerned about vitamins in foods*—76 percent.

8. *About pesticides being used*—71 percent.

9. *About sugar*—64 percent.

10. *About additives*—62 percent.

11. *About cholesterol*—64 percent.

From the Perrier study:

1. *Americans who believe that exercise is good for health and at least "one way to reduce the threat of heart attack and coronary disease"*—90 percent.

2. *Who cite physical fitness as a major reason for their interest in nutrition*—40 percent.

• **SPLIT VIEWS.** The Harris pollsters who gathered data for the Perrier study found sizeable differences in attitudes toward fitness expressed by Americans actively involved in a fitness activity and those who had no such involvement. Some examples.

Active exercisers who agree with the following statements:

1. *"I get enough exercise without doing any sports or athletics"*—15 percent.

2. *"Too much exercise can enlarge the heart, and this is bad when you stop exercising"*—44 percent.

3. *"Middle-aged and older people don't really need exercise other than walking"*—10 percent.

4. *"The key to staying fit is not exercise but controlling how much you eat"*—21 percent.

Non-active exercisers who agree with the following statements:

1. *"I get enough exercise without doing any sports or athletics"*—50 percent.

2. *"Too much exercise can enlarge the heart, and this is bad when you stop exercising"*—64 percent.

3. *"Middle-aged and older people don't really need exercise other than walking"*—39 percent.

4. *"The key to staying fit is not exercise but controlling how much you eat*—50 percent.

• **FINE PRINT**. From the *Woman's Day* study, these numbers on how carefully we read labels:

1. *Americans who pay a lot of attention to nutritional labeling*—25 percent.

2. *Who pay no attention to nutritional labeling*—27 percent.

3. *Label-readers who are looking for "nutrition for dollar"*—59 percent.

4. *Who think the nutritional data on labels is too technical*—42 percent.

5. *Americans who want to see more information about ingredients on labels*—78 percent.

SOURCES
The Perrier Study of Fitness in America.
Woman's Day, Nutrition.

ON FAMILY MATTERS

Reports on the death of the American family are both exaggerated and premature, but it is obvious from numerous surveys that attitudes toward most family matters have been changing throughout the country, and among all segments of the population. Probably the biggest change is that marriage and family is no longer seen by so many people as the value *most* important to personal happiness.

• **VEILED ATTITUDES**. Most Americans still view marriage as an important part of life, but attitudes regarding *when* it should happen, and what it should be like, are different today from what they were fifteen years ago. Some of the numbers:

1. *Men (18 to 49) who believe that family life is very important*—84 percent (according to *The Playboy Report on American Men*).

2. *Who believe that husbands and wives should give one another room to develop as individuals*—66 percent (a stronger attitude among younger men than older men).

3. *Teenage girls who (according to a* Seventeen *survey) disagree with the statement, "Marriage and family should be the primary goal of a woman"*—25 percent.

4. *Men who regard "before 25" as the "best time to marry"*—33 percent.

• S I N G L E   F I L E . Americans today are more tolerant toward people who *choose* to remain single than they were in the late 1950s. A 1976 survey by the Institute for Social Research of the University of Michigan elicited the following responses on the question of staying single versus getting married.

Proportion of Americans who:

1. *Feel a person who does not want to get married is either "sick," "immoral," "selfish," or "neurotic"*—25 percent in 1976; 80 percent in 1957.

2. *Are neutral on the subject of single versus married*—66 percent in 1976; 20 percent in 1957.

• T o   H a v e   o r   H a v e   N o t . The proportion of married couples who say they do not intend to have children is higher today than at any time in our history, but it still represents a relatively small percentage of married couples in general. A 1978 survey by the Institute for Social Research drew the following responses from a sampling of childless married couples:

1. *Childless couples who say they "definitely" do not want children*—8 percent.

2. *Who are not sure*—7 percent.

3. *Who express concern about "having someone to carry on after you've gone"*—33 percent.

4. *Who do not think a one-child family is a good idea*—77 percent.

5. *Who, given a hypothetical option of having either "six children or no children at all," would opt for six children*—58 percent.

Of the more than 70 percent of childless couples who say they "definitely" intend to have children, most couples prefer a family mixture of boys and girls; boys, however, are the preferred sex when parents are forced to limit the gender choice to one. Couples who do not want kids most often cite money as the reason, although women are showing more ambivalence than ever on the question of having children or pursuing a career.

• OLD FOLKS AT HOME. It is obvious from the shifting population patterns (older people are moving to such places as Florida and Arizona) that the number of extended-family households (that is, households in which grandparents and other relatives live together with the basic family) is on the decline. Recent Gallup polls, on the other hand, show an increasing number of Americans who *like* the idea of extended-family households. The numbers:

1. *Americans who think it is a good idea for older people to share a home with grown children*—35 percent today; 31 percent in 1973.
2. *Who think it is a bad idea*—49 percent today; 57 percent in 1973.

• SPLIT VIEWS. American attitudes toward divorce are not as lenient as you might think given the number of marriages that have been dissolved since 1970. If anything, the majority of Americans would like to see steps taken to make it *harder* for people to get a divorce. The numbers, according to NORC surveys:

1. *Americans who believe that divorce should be easier to obtain*—26.5 percent in 1978 (down from 31 percent in 1974).
2. *Who think divorce should be more difficult to obtain*— 41 percent (no change from 1974).
3. *American parents who believe that even though they are not getting along, they should hang in there for the kid's sake*—31 percent.

SOURCES
Gallup Poll.
Institute for Social Research.
NORC.
The Playboy Report on American Men.

ON ASSORTED EVENTS, ISSUES, AND QUESTIONS

Here is a look at how Americans in early 1979 were thinking about issues and questions that do not fit conveniently into any of the categories already listed.

• CONSPIRACY THEORIES. A Harris survey published in late 1978 shows that only a minority of Americans are willing to accept the notion that a single assassin was involved in the deaths of John F. Kennedy, Robert Kennedy, and Martin Luther King, Jr. The numbers.

Americans who feel that these assassinations were part of a broader plot:

1. *John F. Kennedy*—75 percent.
2. *Robert Kennedy*—55 percent.
3. *Martin Luther King, Jr.*—69 percent.

Who feel these assassinations were the work of one man:

1. *John F. Kennedy*—18 percent.
2. *Robert Kennedy*—34 percent.
3. *Martin Luther King, Jr.*—19 percent.

• BAN THE BAN. A 1977 Harris survey canvassed American sentiments on the controversial cancer drug laetrile. The findings:

1. *Americans who have heard of the drug*—78 percent.
2. *Who oppose the FDA ban on its usage*—53 percent.
3. *Who favor the ban*—23 percent.
4. *Who feel it is cruel to raise the hopes of cancer victims by allowing them to use a possibly ineffective drug*—47 percent.
5. *Who would favor laws allowing laetrile to be sold in their state*—68 percent.

Despite the absence of scientific evidence that laetrile does anything to help cancer victims, college graduates are more likely to favor the lifting of the ban on its usage than are noncollege graduates.

• **No Butts.** Americans are more antismoking than ever in their attitudes, but what is surprising is that even a high proportion of smokers have a dim view of the habit. Some of the views that emerged from a 1976 study by the U.S. Public Health Service, and the proportion of Americans who share them:

1. *Smoking should be allowed in fewer public places*— 81 percent of nonsmokers; 51 percent of smokers.
2. *Smoking is enough of a health hazard for something to be done*—90 percent of nonsmokers; 72 percent of smokers.
3. *Smoking advertising should be dropped entirely*—62 percent of nonsmokers; 43 percent of smokers.
4. *It's annoying to be near a person who is smoking*—80 percent of nonsmokers; 30 percent of smokers.

• **Holiday Meanings.** Christmas has more personal meaning to Americans than any other holiday, and here is what an ABC News-Harris survey turned up, in late 1979, on the question of what exactly the holiday means to Americans.

Proportion of Americans who find personal meaning in each of the following aspects of Christmas:

1. *It is time when families can enjoy a joyous holiday together*—97 percent.
2. *When people can take a few days off and renew the spirit of peace on earth and goodwill to men*—90 percent.
3. *A special time for young children who believe in Santa Claus*—88 percent.
4. *A time when the depth of feeling about religion is renewed*—76 percent.
5. *When people spend too much money and celebrate more than is good for them*—68 percent.
6. *When people look forward to giving and receiving nice gifts*—62 percent.
7. *A chance to let it all out in parties around Christmas and New Year's*—31 percent.

• **You're Okay.** NORC surveys designed to measure how Americans view their fellow men and women have shown a general increase in the degree of trust we have in others; yet the majority of Americans take the position that "you can't be too careful" in dealing with people. The numbers from a 1978 survey.

Americans who believe that:

1. *Most of the time people try to be helpful*—59 percent (up from 46 percent in 1972).
2. *People are mostly just looking out for themselves*—34 percent (down from 46 percent in 1972).
3. *Most people will try to take advantage of you*—29 percent (down from 33 percent in 1972).
4. *Most people try to be fair*—64 percent (up from 59 percent in 1972).
5. *Most people can be trusted*—38 percent (down from 45 percent in 1972).
6. *"You can't be too careful" in dealing with people*—56 percent (up from 49 percent in 1972).

• **W H O D O Y O U T R U S T .** Given four versions of the same news story—one from television, one from radio, one from a newspaper, and one from a magazine—most Americans (according to a Roper poll commissioned by the Television Information Office) find the television version the most credible. Here is how the media rate in terms of proportion of Americans who choose each source as most believable:

1. *Television*—50 percent.
2. *Newspapers*—22 percent.
3. *Magazines*—9 percent.
4. *Radio*—7 percent.

• **G U I L T Y A S C H A R G E D .** The public esteem enjoyed by lawyers in the United States started to drop in the early 1970s and reached a low ebb in 1977. Here is a sampling of public attitudes based on an NORC survey for the American Bar Association.

Americans who think that lawyers:

1. *Charge more for their services than they are worth*—68 percent.
2. *Do not work as hard for poor clients as they do for clients who are rich and important*—60 percent.
3. *Are not prompt about getting things done*—59 percent.

The survey also found that only 27 percent of Americans would rate the honesty and ethical standards of lawyers "very high" or "high," and that the proportion of Americans who have a great deal of confidence in lawyers dropped from 24 percent in 1973 to 14 percent in 1977.

SOURCES
American Bar Association.
Harris Survey.
NORC.
U.S. Public Health Service.

THE BLACK VIEWPOINT

A 1973 survey done by Daniel Yankelovich, Inc., for *Ebony* magazine divided black Americans into two broad attitudinal groups: blacks who maintain at least moderate faith in the American system, and those who view the plight of black Americans with despair. These attitudinal differences account for sharply divided opinions among blacks on virtually every racial issue. Here is a look at black attitudes.

Percentage of black Americans who:

1. *Think of themselves as black first and American second*—25 percent.
2. *Think of themselves as American first and black second*—12 percent.
3. *Think of themselves as equally black and American*—63 percent.
4. *Are against the idea of violence to instigate change*—60 percent.
5. *Feel that violence is justified only when all else fails*—30 percent.
6. *Feel that violence is necessary to instigate change*—8 percent.
7. *Feel that the traditional concept of integration is the best method for resolving the racial problem in the United States*—47 percent.
8. *Believe in a separatist approach to racial problems*—16 percent.
9. *Believe in a modified approach to integration, starting with equalizing opportunities in housing and education and then going into other areas of American life*—36 percent.

• **DEMOGRAPHICS**. Generally speaking, the younger and more educated a black American is, the more likely it is that he or she will take a more aggressive stand on racial issues. For instance, of the 8 percent of blacks who believe violence is the only means of instigating change, 52 percent are younger than 30.

SOURCES
Ebony Magazine, Black Americans in the Seventies.

HOW KIDS FEEL ABOUT THINGS

When Yankelovich, Skelly, and White, Inc., interviewed families for *The General Mills Family Report 1976–1977,* they also talked to kids between the ages of 6 and 12. The idea was to get a reading on the values of the children of the children of the 1960s.

• **WHAT KIDS LIKE A LOT**. Given a list of some of the more common activities and areas in their lives, and asked to indicate which of these areas they "liked a lot," the kids gave these responses:

1. *Their homes*—79 percent.
2. *Visits to relatives*—76 percent.
3. *Their teachers*—65 percent.
4. *Children in their classes*—65 percent.
5. *Their neighborhoods*—65 percent.
6. *Their school principals*—52 percent.
7. *Going to church or synagogue*—48 percent.
8. *Playing with older children*—46 percent.
9. *Playing with children of different races*—32 percent.
10. *Playing with younger children*—32 percent.
11. *Helping around the house*—31 percent.

• **BOYS' LIFE**. In all these activities but one—"playing with older children"—a higher proportion of girls than boys said they liked the activity a lot. The average difference was six percentage points. The biggest differences were in "visits to relatives," "teachers," "playing with younger children," and "working around the house," and the smallest differences, in "neighborhoods" and "playing with children of different races."

• **Bringing up Daddy.** Most American kids have fairly traditional views on how they should be raised, but there are some differences in attitude between children of "Traditional" parents and children of "New Breed" parents.

Proportion of all kids ("New Breed" and "Traditional" alike) who agree that:

1. *It's all right for mothers to smoke cigarettes*—24 percent.
2. *It's all right for fathers to smoke*—36 percent.
3. *It's all right for parents to vacation without children*— 44 percent.
4. *Parents should separate if they are not happy*—49 percent.
5. *It's the mother's job, not father's, to cook and clean*— 63 percent.
6. *It's all right for parents to spank their children*—75 percent.
7. *Mothers should go to work if they want to*—76 percent.

• **Parental Beefs.** Parents complain about their kids and kids complain about parents. Some of the more commonly voiced complaints and the proportion of kids who voice them:

1. *Being forced to eat foods they don't like*—59 percent.
2. *Being forced to turn off the television*—56 percent.
3. *Not being allowed to eat snacks*—38 percent.
4. *Being punished unfairly*—36 percent.
5. *Hearing their parents criticize their playmates*—35 percent.
6. *Not being bought what they see advertised on television*—34 percent.
7. *Being made fun of in front of other people*—25 percent.
8. *Having their allowances taken away*—21 percent.
9. *Not being able to spend enough time with their parents*—21 percent.
10. *Hearing their parents argue about money*—19 percent.

SOURCE
General Mills American Family Report 1976–1977.

V OUR TASTES

IN FOOD

Americans are essentially conservative when it comes to food preferences, and as most food specialists estimate, no more than 10 percent of the population have anything approaching an adventurous palate. We shall take a closer look at American eating habits in the section on our everyday habits. Here, in the meantime, are some bits and pieces about our food tastes.

• RESTAURANT FAVORITES. From a survey by the trade publication *Institutions/Volume Feeding*, the items in various categories that sell best in American restaurants:

1. *Appetizer*—shrimp cocktail.
2. *Soup*—vegetable.
3. *Sandwich*—hamburger.
4. *Entrée, meat*—roast beef.
5. *Entrée, nonmeat,* spaghetti.
6. *Entrée, fish*—fried shrimp.
7. *Side dish*—green beans.
8. *Dessert*—apple pie.
9. *Juice*—orange.
10. *Breakfast entrée*—bacon.
11. *Salad dressing*—French.

When families eat out they order these items most frequently. At breakfast:

1. *Coffee*—ordered 59 percent of time.
2. *Eggs*—44 percent.
3. *Sausage or bacon*—31 percent.
4. *Doughnuts*—22 percent.
5. *Pancakes*—16 percent.

At lunch:

1. *Soft drinks*—37 percent.
2. *Hamburgers*—34 percent.
3. *French fries*—33 percent.
4. *Coffee*—20 percent.
5. *Salad as a side dish*—14 percent.

At dinner:

1. *French fries*—34 percent.
2. *Hamburgers*—26 percent.

3. *Soft drinks*—26 percent.
4. *Salad as a side dish*—26 percent.
5. *Coffee*—16 percent.

• **TEEN CHOICES.** From a 1978 Gallup Youth Survey, these "best" and "worst" food picks from American teenagers. Favorite foods:

1. *Italian food*—47 percent.
2. *Steak*—36 percent.
3. *Hamburgers*—25 percent.
4. *Chicken/turkey*—21 percent.
5. *Seafood*—14 percent.
6. *Vegetables*—13 percent.
7. *Potatoes*—13 percent.
8. *Mexican food*—10 percent.
9. *Fish*—10 percent.

Least favorite foods:

1. *Spinach*—20 percent.
2. *Liver*—19 percent.
3. *Broccoli*—8 percent.
4. *Vegetables in general*—8 percent.
5. *Beans*—7 percent.
6. *Peas*—7 percent.
7. *Fish*—7 percent.

Teen boys and teen girls tend to be similar in their food tastes, although girls harbor a stronger distaste for spinach and liver than boys do and are fonder of Italian food.

• **CULTURED TASTES.** About one out of three Americans (according to Dannon Yogurt market studies) describes himself as a regular yogurt eater, and one out of two Americans eats yogurt on occasion. Women prefer yogurt more than men do, and younger people like it more than older people. Regular yogurt eaters are more likely to be found in the East, among higher-income families, and among health-conscious families rather than in other sections of the country, among lower-income families, and among families for whom nutrition is not a principal concern.

• **IN THE PINK.** The vast majority of Americans (about 70 percent according to most estimates) prefer their beef products served medium with perhaps a hint of pink. Preferences, though, vary according to age, region, gender, and socioeconomic status. About 30 percent of the people who order roast beef or steak at the "21" Club in New York order it "blood rare," with only 10 percent specifying "well done." The less fancy the restaurant, the smaller the proportion of bloodthirsty diners. Women, in general, do not order their beef as rare as men do, and older people are more likely to specify "medium well" to "well" than younger people. Finally, easterners and westerners are more likely than southerners to prefer their beef rare.

• L o v e   I t   o r   L e a v e   I t . A Roper Organization poll taken in the fall of 1978 provided this picture of the American palate, based on responses to the question, "Which one or two of the foods on this card do you particularly like?"

1. *American food*—61 percent.
2. *Italian food*—44 percent.
3. *Chinese food*—30 percent.
4. *Mexican food*—23 percent.
5. *French food*—9 percent.
6. *German food*—9 percent.
7. *Soul food*—9 percent.
8. *Japanese food*—4 percent.
9. *Greek or Middle Eastern food*—3 percent.

SOURCES
Jerry Berns, "21" Club.
Dannon Milk Products.
Gallup Poll.
Institutions/Volume Feeding, "10th Annual Menu Census," April 1, 1978.
The Roper Organization.

IN LIQUOR

American preferences in liquor have been undergoing a steady change since the 1960s (see "Drinking" in the section on our everyday habits). We are moving away from the hard stuff—Scotch, bourbon—and drinking more vodka and gin. The differences between the drinking tastes of men and women are still substantial.

• **THE GENERAL PICTURE**. On the assumption that the proportion of the population who drink a certain type of alcoholic beverage reflects tastes, the most preferred beverages in the United States (according to W. R. Simmons' numbers) are as follows.

Proportion of American men who drink:

1. *Vodka*—12.0 percent.
2. *Bourbon*—12.0 percent.
3. *Scotch*—11.0 percent.
4. *Gin*—8.0 percent.
5. *Canadian whiskey*—7.0 percent.
6. *Blended whiskey or rye*—6.0 percent.
7. *Brandy or cognac*—5.0 percent.
8. *Cordial or liqueur*—4.0 percent.
9. *Tequila*—3.0 percent.

Proportion of American women who drink:

1. *Vodka*—11.0 percent.
2. *Bourbon*—6.0 percent.
3. *Gin*—6.0 percent.
4. *Scotch*—5.0 percent.
5. *Rum*—5.0 percent.
6. *Canadian whiskey*—5.0 percent.
7. *Cordial or liqueur*—4.0 percent.
8. *Brandy or cognac*—4.0 percent.
9. *Blended whiskey or rye*—4.0 percent.
10. *Tequila*—3.0 percent.

• **EDUCATED TASTES**. The preferences among American college students (according to the Survey of the College Market), based on proportion of students who drink each type:

1. *Vodka*—53.5 percent.
2. *Rum*—48.0 percent.
3. *Gin*—41.0 percent.
4. *Bourbon*—39.0 percent.
5. *Tequila*—38.0 percent.
6. *Canadian whiskey*—35.0 percent.
7. *Cordials and liqueurs*—35.0 percent.
8. *Blended whiskey or rye*—34.0 percent.
9. *Scotch*—31.0 percent.

• **C o l l e g e F a v o r i t e s** . From the same college survey, here is a glimpse of the specific brands drunk most often by college-age Americans:

1. *Favorite blended or rye whiskey*—Seagram's Seven.
2. *Favorite bourbon*—Jack Daniel's.
3. *Favorite Canadian whiskey*—Canadian Club.
4. *Favorite scotch*—Chivas Regal.
5. *Favorite gin*—Beefeater.
6. *Favorite vodka*—Smirnoff.
7. *Favorite rum*—Bacardi.
8. *Favorite tequila*—Jose Cuervo.
9. *Favorite cordial or liqueur*—Kahlua.

SOURCES
Survey of the College Market, 1971.
W. R. Simmons.

IN MUSIC

It is the rare American who does not listen to—and enjoy—music, and the rare nation in which there are as many different types of music to listen to as there are in the United States. This look at American musical tastes is based on sales patterns in 1978 and on a 1975 Harris survey of musical preferences.

• **T h e H i t P a r a d e** . It is one thing to enjoy a certain kind of music. It is another thing to call that kind of music your favorite.

Proportion of Americans who say they "enjoy" listening to:

1. *Popular music*—65 percent.
2. *Country and western*—53 percent.
3. *Folk*—50 percent.
4. *Religious*—47 percent.
5. *Broadway-show*—41 percent.
6. *Classical*—40 percent.
7. *Rock*—37 percent.
8. *Jazz*—33 percent.
9. *Opera*—20 percent.

Proportion of Americans who say their "favorite" kind of music is:

1. *Popular*—20 percent.
2. *Country and western*—20 percent.
3. *Religious*—14 percent.
4. *Rock*—13 percent.
5. *Classical*—11 percent.
6. *Broadway-show*—6 percent.
7. *Jazz*—5 percent.
8. *Folk*—5 percent.
9. *Opera*—2 percent.

• DEMOGRAPHIC NOTES. Fairly predictable. Younger people like rock and popular music better than older age-groups do. Country and western is obviously bigger in the South than in other regions but is more popular among whites than blacks, and among grammar-school graduates than college graduates. Religious music has its biggest following among lower-income Americans in rural areas and is much more popular among older folks (70 percent) than among Americans younger than 20 (20 percent). Folk music is big with younger college graduates and Broadway-show music is more popular with urbanites and suburbanites than with rural Americans and much more popular among whites than among blacks. Jazz is the only form of music in which the proportion of blacks who enjoy it is higher than the proportion of whites. And classical music and opera are both listened to mostly by older, wealthier, and better-educated segments of the population. Opera, in particular, enjoys its biggest following among suburbanites in the age-group 50–64, and its smallest following among the younger-than-21 crowd.

• TEEN SCENE. Among American teenage girls in 1978 the two most popular American singers were Barry Manilow and Linda Ronstadt (according to a *Seventeen* teen trends survey), and the most popular singing group, by a landslide, was the Bee Gees. The list of the top ten, in different musical categories, is as follows:

Proportion of teenage girls whose favorite male singer in 1978 was:

1. *Barry Manilow*—20.0 percent.
2. *Andy Gibb*—17.0 percent.
3. *Billy Joel*—9.0 percent.
4. *James Taylor*—5.0 percent.
5. *Peter Frampton*—5.0 percent.

6. *John Denver*—4.0 percent.
7. *Rod Stewart*—3.0 percent.
8. *Shaun Cassidy*—2.3 percent.
9. *Paul McCartney*—2.2 percent.
10. *Jackson Browne*—1.9 percent.
10. *Elton John*—1.9 percent.
10. *Stevie Wonder*—1.9 percent.

Whose favorite female singer was:

1. *Linda Ronstadt*—20.1 percent.
2. *Barbra Streisand*—19.8 percent.
3. *Olivia Newton-John*—10.3 percent.
4. *Debby Boone*—8.2 percent.
5. *Natalie Cole*—5.9 percent.
6. *Carole King*—4.6 percent.
7. *Carly Simon*—3.6 percent.
8. *Diana Ross*—2.2 percent.
9. *Stevie Nicks*—1.9 percent.
9. *Helen Reddy*—1.9 percent.

Whose favorite singing group was:

1. *Bee Gees*—27.2 percent.
2. *Fleetwood Mac*—8.7 percent.
3. *Styx*—4.2 percent.
4. *Kansas*—3.9 percent.
5. *Chicago*—3.8 percent.
6. *Beatles* (still!)—3 percent.
7. *Eagles*—2.9 percent.
8. *Earth, Wind and Fire*—2.6 percent.
9. *Boston*—2.3 percent.
10. *Beach Boys*—2.1 percent.

•**PEOPLE'S CHOICE.** A 1979 *People* magazine poll turned up the following favorites in various musical categories:

1. *Favorite male singer*—Billy Joel.
2. *Favorite female singer*—Linda Ronstadt.
3. *Favorite groups*—Bee Gees.
4. *Favorite singer among older-than-55ers*—Tony Bennett.
5. *Second most popular male singer*—Neil Diamond.
6. *Second most popular female singer*—Olivia Newton-John.
7. *Most popular group among American males*—Chicago.

• SATURDAY NIGHT FEVER. Without any question, the most listened to music in the United States in 1978 was the disco sound, which became a multibillion-dollar industry in a period of less than two years. Some numbers.

1. *Proportion of disco songs on* Billboard's *list of 100 top songs of 1978*—20 percent.
2. *Number of all-disco stations in the United States*—200.
3. *Americans who go to discos*—19 percent of population 12 year of age and older.

SOURCES
Associated Councils of the Arts, *Americans and the Arts.*
Newsweek, "Disco Takes Over," April 2, 1979.
People, "People Readers Poll," March 5, 1979.
Seventeen.

IN SPECTATOR SPORTS

American tastes in spectator sports have remained pretty much the same throughout the 1970s, with football solidly number one, baseball second, and basketball a fading third in appeal. Here is a closer look, based on a 1978 Gallup poll for *TV Guide.*

• THE BASIC NUMBERS. Here is how the top spectator sports in the United States fare against one another when ranked according to the proportion of Americans who watch them on TV:

1. *Pro football*—60 percent.
2. *College football*—55 percent.
3. *Baseball*—49 percent.
4. *College basketball*—43 percent.
5. *Pro basketball*—41 percent.
6. *Pro tennis*—15 percent.
7. *Boxing*—11 percent.
8. *Golf*—10 percent.
9. *Auto racing*—6 percent.
10. *Soccer*—6 percent.

• THE DEMOGRAPHICS OF SPECTATORDOM. A 1973 Harris survey, designed to find out which spectator sports were the favorites of Americans, turned up some definite demographic patterns:

1. Football is number one among southerners and westerners but is number two, behind baseball, among easterners and midwesterners.
2. Baseball's constituency is made up chiefly of older, small-town Americans and is more popular with grammar-school graduates than with college graduates.
3. Blacks like football as much as whites do but show less interest in baseball. Blacks are four times as likely as whites to give the nod to boxing.
4. Jews are less likely to choose baseball or football as their favorite sports than are white Protestants or Catholics but show proportionately greater fondness for basketball, golf, tennis, and bowling than do Protestants or Catholics.

•INSTANT REPLAYS. The *TV Guide* survey determined that most television viewers are satisfied with the amount of sports carried on the tube, but there are signs of dissatisfaction in certain areas, chiefly golf and pro wrestling.

Proportion of viewers who would like to see:

1. *More golf*—2 percent.
2. *Less golf*—16 percent.
3. *More professional wrestling*—4 percent.
4. *Less professional wrestling*—12 percent.
5. *More baseball*—16 percent.
6. *Less baseball*—10 percent.

•NOT SO DAMN YANKEES. According to an R. H. Bruskin survey taken in 1978, one out of every four American baseball fans was rooting for the New York Yankees during their 1978-stretch drive with the Boston Red Sox. Nearly 23 percent were pulling for the Bostonians. Figure a dead heat. No other American League team drew nearly as much support throughout 1978, with the Seattle Mariners and the Toronto Blue Jays coming in at the tail end of the popularity spectrum. The year's most popular National League team was the Cincinnati Reds (favored by 25 percent). The Dodgers (with 13 percent) were a distant second and the Giants (11 percent) third.

•THE FIGHTING IRISH. Myths die hard. Rockne is gone and the Gipper almost forgotten, but Notre Dame is still the most popular college football team in America. Nearly one out of five Americans in 1978, according to the R. H. Bruskin report, considered Notre Dame his favorite college team. Alabama (10 percent) was number two and Texas (9 percent) third.

• TEEN CHOICES. The most popular male and female sports figures among teenage girls, based on the results of a 1978 *Seventeen* teen trends survey, are as follows.
Most popular women in sports:

    1. *Chris Evert*—27.0 percent.
    2. *Nadia Comaneci*—19.0 percent.
    3. *Dorothy Hamill*—16.5 percent.
    4. *Tracy Austin*—13.0 percent.
    5. *Billie Jean King*—3.0 percent.
    6. *Olga Korbut*—3.0 percent.

Most popular men in sports:

    1. *Bruce Jenner*—38.0 percent.
    2. *Jimmy Connors*—5.0 percent.
    3. *Bjorn Borg*—4.0 percent.
    4. *O. J. Simpson*—4.0 percent.
    5. *Steve Cauthen*—2.5 percent.
    6. *Pete Rose*—2.5 percent.
    7. *Roger Staubach*—1.5 percent.
    8. *Johnny Bench*—1.0 percent.
    9. *Julius Erving*—1.0 percent.
   10. *Mark Fidrych*—1.0 percent.
   11. *Steve Garvey*—1.0 percent.
   12. *Joe Namath*—1.0 percent.

• OH, HOWARD. When *TV Guide* asked respondents to name their most favorite and least favorite sports announcer, here is how the numbers came out.
Best liked:

    1. *Howard Cosell*—20 percent.
    2. *Frank Gifford*—13 percent.
    3. *Don Meredith*—10 percent.

Least liked:

    1. *Howard Cosell*—39 percent.
    2. *Curt Gowdy*—2 percent.

3. *Joe Garagiola*—2 percent.
4. *Don Meredith*—2 percent.

SOURCES
R. H. Bruskin and Associates.
Harris Survey.
Don Kowett, "TV Sports, America Speaks Out," *TV Guide*, August 19, 1978.
Seventeen.

IN HOW WE LOOK

The few surveys that have looked into the matter show clearly that (*a*) most Americans are very much concerned about how they look, and (*b*) American women are only slightly more appearance conscious than American men.

• **THE BASIC NUMBERS.** From a 1975 Needham, Harper and Steers survey, these numbers on the men and women who indicated that dressing well was an important part of their lives:

1. *Women*—81 percent.
2. *Men*—72 percent.
3. *Women younger than 25*—84 percent.
4. *Men 25 to 34 (the largest group in sampling)*—73 percent.

• **MEN'S DEPARTMENT.** From Luciano Franzioni, a designer with Hart, Schaffner & Marx, this view of where American men in 1979 stand in the way of basic fashion tastes.
Men who prefer the:

1. *Natural-shoulder look*—4 percent.
2. *"Safe," middle-of-the-road styles*—56 percent.
3. *"British" look*—15 percent.
4. *"Western" look (jeans, etc.)*—6 percent.
5. *"California" or "resort" look*—3 percent.

• **SIZING UP.** If the findings of a 1977 Roper poll are an accurate reflection of American tastes in the opposite sex, men are more figure conscious than women, but women, on the other hand, are more likely to be impressed by clothing. The numbers, based on the "one or two things about physical appearance" that a man or woman tends to notice first when meeting a person of the opposite sex.

What men first notice about women:

1. *Figure or build*—44 percent.
2. *Face*—33 percent.
3. *Clothing*—26 percent.
4. *Eyes*—18 percent.
5. *Smile*—18 percent.
6. *Hair*—18 percent.
7. *Legs*—8 percent.

What women notice about men:

1. *Clothing*—33 percent.
2. *Face*—31 percent.
3. *Eyes*—29 percent.
4. *Smile*—23 percent.
5. *Figure or build*—20 percent.
6. *Hair*—17 percent.
7. *Teeth*—10 percent.
8. *Height*—10 percent.

•**FASHION PLATES.** Keeping up with the changing fashions in clothing is something that just about half the American people find enjoyable, with women more favorably disposed to the idea than men. From a 1977 Roper poll, these numbers on the percentage of Americans who either like or dislike the idea of fashion in clothing changing from year to year.

Americans who like the idea:

1. *Total*—49 percent.
2. *Women*—54 percent.
3. *Men*—43 percent.
4. *Self-described liberals*—60 percent.
5. *Self-described conservatives*—45 percent.

Who do not like the idea:

1. *Total*—13 percent.
2. *Women*—14 percent.
3. *Men*—13 percent.

Who do not pay much attention to changing fashions:

1. *Total*—37 percent.
2. *Women*—31 percent.
3. *Men*—43 percent.

·**Ms. Conceptions.** From *Women's Wear Daily*, a survey of how American women describe themselves with respect to their fashion tastes.

Women who:

1. *Like to be among the first with a new look*—4 percent.
2. *Like to assemble own different look*—27 percent.
3. *Are conservative (like to adopt established fashion)*— 31.5 percent.
4. *Are not concerned about fashion*—31 percent.

·**Women on Men.** When Hart, Schaffner and Marx surveyed a sampling of 500 women to find out how women feel about various aspects of male dress and male behavior, here is what they learned.

Proportion of women who like men:

1. *With dark hair*—79 percent.
2. *In a vested business suit*—57 percent.
3. *With well-proportioned pants (rather than pants that are too tight or too loose)*—88 percent.
4. *In a classic dress shirt*—70 percent.
5. *In classic briefs rather than mini-underwear or boxer shorts*—57 percent.
6. *In a fitted turtleneck*—56 percent.
7. *In boxer swim trunks rather than bikini trunks or mid-rise trunks*—43 percent.
8. *In the nude when they (men) sleep rather than in pajamas, short pajamas, or a night shirt*—50 percent.

·**Office Dressing.** More American workers than ever before are wearing what they *like* to wear to work and not what they *have* to wear. The numbers, according to a 1977 Roper poll.

Men who:

1. *Wear jeans to work*—36 percent.
2. *Wear a business suit to work*—14 percent.
3. *Are executives or professionals and wear a business suit to the office*—38 percent.
4. *Are executives or professionals and wear denims*—11 percent.
5. *Are younger than 30 and wear jeans*—30 percent.

Women who:

1. *Wear skirt or slacks with a blouse or sweater*—31 percent.
2. *Wear a pantsuit*—27 percent.
3. *Wear a regular-length dress or a suit with skirt*—15 percent.
4. *Wear jeans*—13 percent.

• **M E N O N M E N .** *The Playboy Report on American Men* found significant differences among various segments of the male population on the question of what forms of masculine adornment evoke approval and what forms do not. Some sample numbers.

Proportion of men who approve either "strongly" or "somewhat" of:

1. *Hairpieces*—66 percent.
2. *Designer clothes*—62 percent.
3. *Jewelry*—54 percent.
4. *Shoulder bags*—38 percent.
5. *Cosmetics*—7 percent.
6. *Hairstyling*—78 percent.

In all the categories above, acceptance was greater among the Innovators (younger, more progressive-thinking men) than among Traditionalists and Conventionals.

SOURCES
Hart, Schaffner and Marx.
Needham, Harper and Steers.
The Playboy Report on American Men.
The Roper Organization.
Women's Wear Daily.

IN JEWELRY

Nearly 40 percent of Americans 18 and older buy at least one piece of jewelry according to a survey by *Jewelers' Circular Keystone*, a trade magazine. Here is a sampling of our tastes in jewelry, based on buying patterns in 1977.

• **P O L L I N G   S T O N E S .** The most frequently purchased colored stones (and, presumably, the most popular) in 1977, based on proportion of overall market, were:

1. *Turquoise*—20.0 percent.
2. *Opal*—14.0 percent.
3. *Jade*—9.0 percent.
4. *Ruby*—9.0 percent.
5. *Pearl*—8.5 percent.
6. *Emerald*—5.0 percent.
7. *Garnet*—3.0 percent.
8. *Birthstone*—2.0 percent.

Some demographic notes: Men are more likely to buy opals and turquoise, but women's tastes run to rubies, emeralds, and pearls. Midwesterners favor opal more than any other stone, with pearls second; and opal is strongest among purchasers 25 to 44 years of age.

• **T I M E   S T U D Y .** Only about half the watches now being sold in the United States are the traditional mechanical kind, and the other groups—digital, quartz, analog—keep gaining ground. Here are the 1977 industry figures:

1. *Mechanical*—45.5 percent.
2. *Self-winding mechanical*—13.0 percent.
3. *Digital LED*—20.5 percent.
4. *Battery*—10.5 percent.
5. *Digital LCD*—6.0 percent.
6. *Quartz analog*—3.5 percent.

For men only:

1. *Mechanical*—35 percent.
2. *Self-winding mechanical*—16 percent.
3. *Digital LED*—22 percent.
4. *Battery*—12 percent.
5. *Digital LCD*—10 percent.
6. *Quartz analog*—5 percent.

Demographics: younger people show a stronger preference for digitals, and mechanicals are favored by westerners and people 55 years old and older.

• **H O N O R E D   M E T A L S .** When it comes to choosing the metals for their stones to be set in, Americans overwhelmingly choose gold. The numbers:

1. *Gold or white gold*—62.0 percent.
2. *Silver*—29.0 percent.
3. *Platinum*—1.5 percent.

• HARD NUMBERS. When Americans buy diamonds—and 9.5 million bought them in 1977—here is how they buy them:

1. *Rings*—60 percent.
2. *Necklaces and pendants*—22 percent.
3. *Earrings*—12 percent.
4. *Pins*—2 percent.
5. *Bracelets*—1.5 percent.

SOURCE
Jewelers' Circular Keystone, February 1978.

IN DOGS

The most reliable indicator of American preferences in dog breeds is provided by the Aemrican Kennel Club, which keeps a record of all pedigree registrations. Here is how registrations have gone over the past ten years.

• THE GENERAL PICTURE. The poodle remains the single most popular breed of dog in the United States, but its numerical edge over the rest of the pack is dwindling—mainly because more people are choosing some of the more exotic breeds. Once you get past the poodle, the list of most popular breeds in the United States, based on 1977 American Kennel Club figures, looks like this:

2. *Doberman pinschers*—79,250.
3. *German shepherds*—67,000.
4. *Cocker spaniels*—53,000.
5. *Irish setters*—43,500.
6. *Labrador retrievers*—42,000.
7. *Beagles*—41,000.
8. *Dachshunds*—35,000.
9. *Miniature schnauzers*—35,000.
10. *Golden retrievers*—31,000.
11. *Shetland sheepdogs*—24,500.
12. *Collies*—24,000.

13. *Lhasa apsos*—22,500.
14. *Yorkshire terriers*—21,500.
15. *Siberian huskies*—20,000.

• **CHANGING TIDES**. The annual number of pedigree registrations in the United States has remained fairly constant over the past ten years, but certain breeds have gained in popularity while others have lost favor. The breeds losing favor are:

1. *Poodles.*
2. *Saint Bernards.*
3. *German shepherds.*
4. *Beagles.*
5. *Pomeranians.*
6. *Yorkshire terriers.*

The breeds gaining favor are:

1. *Lhasa apsos*—up from 30th in 1971 to 13th in 1977.
2. *Doberman pinschers*—up from 13th in 1971 to 2nd in 1977.
3. *Siberian huskies*—up from 26th in 1971 to 15th in 1977.
4. *Cocker spaniels*—up from 13th in 1971 to 4th in 1977.

SOURCE
American Kennel Club, Inc.

IN HEROES AND HEROINES

When it comes to putting celebrities on a pedestal—and then dumping them—Americans are probably the most fickle people in the world. Still, some celebrities have managed to stay in the public favor much longer than others. Here is a sampling of America's taste in heroes, based on several of the more recent magazine polls.

• **TEN ANGELS**. From a 1978 *Seventeen* teen trends survey, the favorite female entertainment stars:

1. *Barbra Streisand*—17.0 percent.
2. *Kate Jackson*—8.0 percent.
3. *Carol Burnett*—6.5 percent.
4. *Cheryl Ladd*—5.0 percent.
5. *Sally Field*—4.8 percent.

6. *Kristy McNichol*—4.8 percent.
7. *Jacyln Smith*—4.0 percent.
8. *Suzanne Somers*—3.8 percent.
9. *Diane Keaton*—3.0 percent.
10. *Jane Fonda*—2.0 percent.

•**LADIES' CHOICE.** From the Most Famous Persons *Ladies' Home Journal* 1978 Poll:

1. *Funniest man*—Bob Hope.
2. *Funniest woman*—Carol Burnett.
3. *Most intelligent man*—Albert Einstein.
4. *Most intelligent woman*—Madame Curie.
5. *Most famous sports figure*—Bruce Jenner.
6. *Sexiest man*—Burt Reynolds.
7. *Sexiest woman*—Farrah Fawcett-Majors.
8. *Man who has done most good for world*—Abraham Lincoln.
9. *Woman who has done most good for world*—Eleanor Roosevelt.
10. *Man who has done most damage to the world*—Adolf Hitler.
11. *Woman who has done most damage to the world*—Anita Bryant.

Favorite male entertainment stars:

1. *John Travolta*—9.5 percent.
2. *Robert Redford*—9.3 percent.
3. *Burt Reynolds*—7.5 percent.
4. *Richard Dreyfuss*—6.5 percent.
5. *Kris Kristofferson*—4.0 percent.
6. *Alan Alda*—3.5 percent.
7. *Parker Stevenson*—3.5 percent.
8. *John Ritter*—3.3 percent.
9. *Sylvester Stallone*—3.0 percent.

Favorite female political figures:

1. *Muriel Humphrey*—8.5 percent.
2. *Barbara Jordan*—8.0 percent.
3. *Rosalynn Carter*—7.0 percent.
4. *Shirley Temple Black*—6.0 percent.
5. *Betty Ford*—4.5 percent.
6. *Bella Abzug*—3.0 percent.
7. *Golda Meir*—3.0 percent.

8. *Ella Grasso*—2.5 percent.
9. *Shirley Chisholm*—2.5 percent.
10. *Lillian Carter*—1.0 percent.

Favorite male political figures:

1. *Jimmy Carter*—14.0 percent.
2. *Gerald Ford*—11.0 percent.
3. *Edmund G. "Jerry" Brown, Jr.*—7.0 percent.
4. *Ronald Reagan*—5.0 percent.
5. *Edward Kennedy*—4.0 percent.
6. *Henry Kissinger*—2.5 percent.
7. *Walter Mondale*—2.0 percent.
8. *Anwar el-Sadat*—1.2 percent.
9. *Menachem Begin*—1.0 percent.
10. *Richard Nixon*—1.0 percent.

• **G A L L U P C H O I C E S .** The top-ten lists of the most admired men and women in 1978, as determined by the Gallup poll, are as follows.

Men:

1. *Jimmy Carter.*
2. *Pope John Paul II.*
3. *Billy Graham.*
4. *Anwar el-Sadat.*
5. *Gerald Ford.*
6. *Ronald Reagan.*
7. *Edward Kennedy.*
8. *Richard Nixon.*
9. *Menachem Begin.*
10. *Henry Kissinger.*

Women:

1. *Betty Ford.*
2. *Rosalynn Carter.*
3. *Golda Meir.*
4. *Pat Nixon.*
5. *Barbara Walters.*
6. *Jacqueline Kennedy Onassis.*
7. *Anita Bryant.*
8. *Barbara Jordan.*
9. *Queen Elizabeth II.*
10. *Shirley Chisholm.*

• **THE PEOPLE POLL.** From a survey of subscribers to *People* magazine, two-thirds of whom are younger than 35 and 44 percent of whom attended college:

1. *Best-looking man*—Robert Redford.
2. *Prettiest woman*—Jaclyn Smith.
3. *Favorite TV actor*—Robin Williams.
4. *Favorite TV actress*—Jean Stapleton.
5. *Most boring male TV personality*—Howard Cosell.
6. *Most boring female TV personality*—Farrah Fawcett-Majors.
7. *Most trusted political figure*—Jimmy Carter.
8. *Least trusted political figure*—Richard Nixon.
9. *Most effective woman leader*—Coretta Scott King.
10. *Favorite actor*—Paul Newman.
11. *Favorite actress*—Faye Dunaway.

SOURCES
Gallup Poll.
Ladies' Home Journal, July 1978.
People, March 5, 1978.
Seventeen.

IN HOUSING

The two factors that appear to have the most bearing on the preferences and tastes Americans have in housing are the area in which the house is located and the conveniences in the house. So suggests a 1978 study by *Better Homes and Gardens*. A closer look.

• **CONTEMPORARY VIEWS.** Given the choice, most Americans (55 percent according to the *Better Homes and Gardens* survey) would choose a new house that has never been occupied over one that was built several years ago and occupied by a previous owner.

• **OUTWARD BOUND.** More American home owners now say they prefer to live in the suburbs (43 percent) rather than in an urban area (11 percent), but the first choice of 37 percent of the home-owning population is rural areas. For the record, about 18 percent of middle- to higher-income home owners live in urban areas, and nearly 49 percent live in the suburbs.

• **D R E A M   H O U S E .** It looks as if the most salable kind of house in the United States today is a three-bedroom affair with two bathrooms. Beyond this, these are some of the features Americans would prefer and the proportion who prefer them:

1. *More bedrooms*—15 percent.
2. *Another bathroom*—25 percent.
3. *A larger kitchen*—27 percent.
4. *More convenience features in the kitchen*—8 percent.
5. *A formal dining room*—77 percent.
6. *More closet space*—33 percent.

• **S I T T I N G   P R E T T Y .** Some representative American attitudes on bathrooms, based on a *Better Homes and Gardens* consumer study.

1. *Homeowners who consider the number of bathrooms "very important" in a home-buying decision*—62 percent.
2. *Who consider bathrooms unimportant*—3 percent.
3. *Who consider the average-size bathroom (five feet by eight feet) too small*—54 percent.
4. *Who'd be willing to pay extra for concealed fluorescent lighting*—56 percent.

The same survey also found that if the average American could design his or her own dream bathroom, chances are it would have *two* sinks, a heat lamp, an exhaust fan, a full-length mirror, and a large window.

SOURCE
Better Homes and Gardens, Building and Remodeling, 1978.

IN CARS

Whether or not our tastes in cars have changed since 1970, our buying patterns are somewhat different, although big cars still dominate American highways.

• **T H E   B A S I C   N U M B E R S .** The proportion of the auto-buying market commanded by each category of car in 1978:

1. *Subcompact*—10.0 percent.
2. *.Compact*—22.0 percent.
3. *Intermediate size*—24.5 percent.
4. *Standard*—19.5 percent.
5. *Luxury*—7.5 percent.
6. *Imports*—16.0 percent.

• TOP TEN. The ten best-selling American-made cars in 1978, by nameplate:

1. *Chevrolet*—621,000.
2. *Cutlass Supreme*—407,000.
3. *Fairmont*—406,000.
4. *Malibu*—374,000.
5. *Monte Carlo*—355,000.
6. *Ford*—333,000.
7. *Thunderbird*—304,500.
8. *Olds 88*—274,000.
9. *Camaro*—260,000.
10. *Cadillac*—249,000.

SOURCE
Motor Vehicle Manufacturers Association of the United States.

IN MOVIES

A movie can take off for any number of reasons: the stars, the story, the promotion; so it is a dicey business trying to figure out just what it is that Americans like in movies. Complicating the problem even more is the fact that the composition of American movie audiences has changed drastically over the past thirty years, with only a small proportion of Americans 40 and older going to more than a few movies a year. Still and all, when you look down the list of movies that have flexed the most box-office muscle through the years, certain patterns emerge. Here are some of them.

• READY WHEN YOU ARE, C.B. About one out of every four movies on the *Variety* list of the forty "rental champ" movies of all time has been of either the "spectacle" or the "disaster" type, on the order of *Star Wars* (the biggest grosser of them all), *Gone with the Wind, The Ten Commandments,* and *Earthquake.*

• **HANDKERCHIEF CITY.** Somebody you like dies in approximately half the films on *Variety*'s top-forty list. A few of the tearier examples are *Love Story, Gone with the Wind,* and *One Flew Over the Cuckoo's Nest.* Only about 40 percent of the movies on the list have endings that can be described as genuinely happy. The rest are either sad or borderline.

• **STAR GAZING.** "Name value" appears to have been a factor in the success of only about half the top films on the current *Variety* list, but certain stars' names crop up more frequently than others.

1. *Charlton Heston*—5 mentions.
2. *Richard Dreyfuss*—4 mentions.
3. *Robert Redford*—3 mentions.
4. *Burt Reynolds*—2 mentions.
5. *Dustin Hoffman*—2 mentions.
6. *Paul Newman*—2 mentions.
7. *John Travolta*—2 mentions.
8. *Mel Brooks*—2 mentions.

• **VARIETY'S TOP FORTY.** The following is a list of the forty movies that have returned the highest rental revenues to distributors, as of January 1, 1979. The list may be deceptive, however, since the higher admission prices of movies today puts older films at a disadvantage.

1. *Star Wars.*
2. *Jaws.*
3. *The Godfather.*
4. *Grease.*
5. *The Exorcist.*
6. *The Sound of Music.*
7. *The Sting.*
8. *Close Encounters of the Third Kind.*
9. *Gone with the Wind.*
10. *Saturday Night Fever.*
11. *One Flew Over the Cuckoo's Nest.*
12. *Smoky and the Bandit.*
13. *American Graffiti.*
14. *Rocky.*

15. *Animal House.*
16. *Towering Inferno.*
17. *Jaws II.*
18. *The Graduate.*
19. *Dr. Zhivago.*
20. *Butch Cassidy and the Sundance Kid.*
21. *Airport.*
22. *The Ten Commandments.*
23. *Heaven Can Wait.*
24. *The Poseidon Adventure.*
25. *Mary Poppins.*
26. *The Goodbye Girl.*
27. *Blazing Saddles.*
28. *A Star Is Born.*
29. *King Kong.*
30. *M.A.S.H.*
31. *Ben Hur.*
32. *Earthquake.*
33. *Hooper.*
34. *Oh, God.*
35. *Young Frankenstein.*
36. *Fiddler on the Roof.*
37. *Billy Jack.*
38. *All the President's Men.*
39. *The Godfather II.*
40. *Thunderball.*

• **N E W G O L D .** If we consider only those films released in 1978, the *Variety* top-ten list, with rental revenues, looks like this:

1. *Grease*—$83,091,000.
2. *Close Encounters of the Third Kind*—$54,000,000.
3. *Animal House*—$52,368,000.
4. *Jaws II*—$49,299,000.
5. *Heaven Can Wait*—$42,517,000.
6. *The Goodbye Girl*—$41,000,000.
7. *Star Wars (reissue)*—$38,375,000.
8. *Hooper*—$31,500,000.
9. *Foul Play*—$25,065,000.
10. *Revenge of the Pink Panther*—$25,000,000.

Analysis, in the words of *New York Times* movie critic Vincent Canby: a "mass American movie audience that is predominantly teen-aged, more fond of romance than violence, and inclined to giggle its appreciation for a movie's desire to please as often as for a truly comic result."

• **X - C ESS**. The proportion of American moviegoers who go to X-rated movies is on the decline, although there is no way of knowing whether it is a matter of personal preference or availability. The numbers:

1. *Americans who saw an X-rated movie in 1978*—15 percent.
2. *In 1975*—19 percent.
3. *In 1972*—25 percent.

• **THE PEOPLE'S CHOICE**. The best-loved American movie of all time, according to a 1978 poll taken by R. H. Bruskin, is *Gone with the Wind; Star Wars* is a distant second. Nearly one out of five Americans in the Bruskin sampling chose *Gone with the Wind* as the best movie of all time, with females (34 percent) showing nearly twice the affection for the film as males (18 percent). Surprisingly, *Gone with the Wind* outdistanced *Star Wars* among 18- to 24-year-old Americans (14 percent to 11 percent respectively). All told, *Star Wars* drew a 4.5 percent response rating, followed by *Roots* (3.5 percent), *The Sound of Music* (2.9 percent), and *The Ten Commandments* (2.5 percent).

SOURCES
R. H. Bruskin.
Vincent Canby, "The Bottom Line on Hit Films is Generally Pretty Gross," *New York Times*, May 28, 1979.
Variety.

VI OUR EVERYDAY HABITS

EATING

Nearly everything about American eating habits—what we eat, how much we eat, where we eat, even with whom we eat—has been changing over the past twenty years, although nobody seems to know if these changes are for the better or the worse.

• **INSIDE STORY.** First of all, we are eating less. In 1910 the average daily food consumption level per capita in the United States was just under 4.5 pounds. Today it is 4 pounds. We are also eating different amounts of certain foods. Here are some representative annual consumption levels for various foods and how those levels in the late 1970s differ from those of 1970:

1. *Beef*—126.0 pounds (up 11 percent).
2. *Pork*—61.0 pounds (down 15 percent).
3. *Fish*—13.0 pounds (up 10 percent).
4. *Chicken*—44.0 pounds (up 10 percent).
5. *Turkey*—9 pounds (up 12 percent).
6. *Butter*—4.5 pounds (down 20 percent).
7. *Fresh fruit*—85.5 pounds (up 5 percent).
8. *Fresh vegetables*—101.0 pounds (up 3 percent).
9. *Refined sugar*—95.5 pounds (down 6 percent).
10. *Corn syrup and sugar in processed foods*—39.5 pounds (up 100 percent).

• **ROUGH FIGURES.** The number of strict vegetarians in the United States is still on the small side, but not so the number who are cutting down on meat and moving to a more vegetable-oriented diet. Some numbers from a 1978 Roper poll:

1. *"Strict" vegetarians in the United States*—825,000 (just under .5 percent of adult population).
2. *"Mainly" vegetarians*—about 2.6 percent.
3. *People who say they are careful about how much meat they eat*—17 percent.
4. *Who no longer eat meat often or regularly*—75 percent.

The Roper survey also showed that most people who follow a vegetarian diet do it for health reasons (56 percent), while 16 percent do it for humanitarian reasons and 25 percent do it for reasons of economy.

•**PANTRY PRIDE.** A look inside the cupboards, refrigerators, and pantries of American households gives the following picture of the American diet, based on a W. R. Simmons survey.

Proportion of households using the following foods in the month prior to the survey:

1. *White bread*—85.0 percent.
2. *Coffee*—83.5 percent.
3. *Margarine*—83.0 percent.
4. *Cold cereal*—81.0 percent.
5. *Catsup*—81.0 percent.
6. *Bananas*—74.5 percent.
7. *Canned soup*—74.5 percent.
8. *Peanut butter*—73.0 percent.
9. *Canned tuna*—68.0 percent.
10. *Bacon*—68.0 percent.
11. *Frankfurters*—67.0 percent.

•**DAY BY DAY.** *The Perrier Study of Fitness in America* offers the following day-to-day picture of American eating habits.

Average number of days per week that each of these commonly eaten foods and beverages are part of our menus:

1. *Water*—7.
2. *Milk or cheese*—6.
3. *Mineral or bottled water*—6 (among people who drink it).
4. *Fresh fruit*—4.5.
5. *Colas and other soft drinks*—4.
6. *Diet soft drinks*—4.
7. *Candies, cookies, or cake*—4.
8. *Breakfast cereals*—4.
9. *Beef or lamb*—3.5.
10. *Wine*—3.5.
11. *Beer*—3.
12. *Hard liquor*—2.5.
13. *Poultry*—2.

•**JUNKIES.** Now that children make up an increasingly smaller chunk of the population, the per-capita consumption of junk foods—candy, for instance—is down, but the numbers are deceptive. The key fact: Americans are eating far more caloric sweeteners—mostly sugar and corn syrup—than ever before. Here are some of the chief sugar sources.

Proportion of households housing the following foods on a typical day:

1. *Cookies*—45.0 percent.
2. *Ice cream*—62.0 percent.
3. *Frozen desserts or cakes*—16.0 percent.
4. *Instant puddings*—21.0 percent.
5. *Potato chips*—63.5 percent.
6. *Powdered drinks*—31.0 percent.
7. *Whipped-cream topping*—34.0 percent.
8. *Cake mixes*—32.0 percent.

Some related numbers:

1. *Per-capita consumption of candy*—15.5 pounds in 1977 (down by about 25 percent since the 1950s).
2. *Americans who eat cookies*—26 percent (holding steady).
3. *Americans who eat ice cream or some related dessert*—90 percent.
4. *Who eat it several times a week*—25 percent.
5. *Who eat it every day*—10 percent.

• **B u r g e r   B l i t z .** If all the hamburgers Americans eat each year were stretched out side by side, the resultant line of ground beef would stretch around the world four times. Some other burger numbers:

1. *Number eaten yearly in the United States*—34 billion.
2. *Average per week*—3 for *total* population.
3. *Average eaten per year at a McDonald's alone*—11 per person.

• **T a b l e   M a t t e r s .** So much for *what* we eat. Here is a look at how we do it at home—and with whom, based on a Newspaper Advertising Bureau survey:

1. *Meals eaten at home (all situations)*—about 85 percent.
2. *Weekday breakfasts eaten at home*—92 percent.
3. *Weekday lunches*—62 percent.
4. *Weekday dinners*—82 percent.
5. *Weekend dinners*—68 percent.
6. *Dinner meals eaten at kitchen table*—52 percent.

7. *At a dining table in a dining room*—28 percent.
8. *On a tray in a living room or family room*—8 percent.

And from a 1978 *Advertising Age* survey, a closer look at our mealtime habits:

1. *How long the average dinner meal lasts*—20 minutes or less.
2. *How often the entire family sits down to dinner together*—about three times a week.
3. *American families who eat breakfast together*—75 percent.
4. *Households in which the television set is on during the evening meal*—32 percent.

From the Newspaper Advertising Bureau, these numbers for the proportion of meals eaten out:

1. *Weekday lunches*—37 percent.
2. *Weekday dinners*—17 percent.
3. *Weekend breakfasts*—15 percent.
4. *Weekend lunches*—28 percent.
5. *Weekend dinners*—32 percent.

And these numbers for Americans who eat specific meals out:

1. *Men who eat lunch away from home during the week*—40 percent.
2. *Who eat dinner away from home during the week*—16 percent.
3. *Women who eat lunch out*—30 percent.
4. *Dinner out*—16 percent.
5. *Families in the $8,000-to-$15,000 income bracket who eat dinner out in a typical week*—12 percent.
6. *Families in the $20,000-and-over income bracket*—24 percent.

•**SKIPPING OUT.** Breakfast is the meal Americans are most likely to skip. National Restaurant Association figures suggest that one out of four adult Americans skips breakfast on a regular basis. The largest proportion of breakfast skippers (34 percent) is in the 18–34 age-group, and the smallest proportion (8 percent) is in the older-than-60 age-group. Curiously, breakfast-skipping patterns are pretty much the same in all income groups. Among breakfast skippers in the United States, the most common reason for missing the meal is that they "don't like to eat in the morning."

•**LEAVING HOME**. Two things have combined to make eating in restaurants an almost universal American experience: the increased number of working mothers and the advent of the fast-food restaurant. Here are some numbers that show how we do it. Where we go when we eat out (based on a National Restaurant Association survey):

1. *Hamburger place*—41 percent.
2. *Full-menu restaurant*—12 percent.
3. *Pizza place*—12 percent.
4. *Ice-cream parlor*—11 percent.
5. *Cafeteria*—9 percent.
6. *Chicken place*—8 percent.
7. *Budget steak house*—7 percent.

The fast-food chains we go to, based on findings of a Newspaper Advertising Bureau survey of Americans 12 years old and older who visited the following places at least once in the month prior to the survey:

1. *McDonald's*—54 percent.
2. *Burger King*—25 percent.
3. *Dairy Queen*—24 percent.
4. *Kentucky Fried Chicken*—23 percent.
5. *Pizza Hut*—15 percent.

And from a 1978 Gallup poll, what is costs us per head:

1. *At a fast-food restaurant*—$2.
2. *At a family-style restaurant*—$3.
3. *At a specialty restaurant*—$10 (not counting booze or wine).
4. *Median price for dinner eaten at a restaurant in 1978*—$3.75; but higher in the West, at $4.95, and lower in the South, at $3.00.

•**BULGE BATTLE**. You cannot really talk about eating in the United States unless you also talk about dieting.

From the *Woman's Day* nutrition study:

1. *Americans currently on a diet*—20 percent.
2. *Who use artificial sweeteners*—20 percent.

3. *Who fast during an average week*—7 percent.
4. *Who admit they overeat*—23 percent.

From a *Glamour* magazine diet survey:

1. *American women who say they are on a diet "most of the time"*—49 percent.
2. *Who take weight off and then put it on again*—76 percent.
3. *Who eat more when they are by themselves than when they are around others*—77 percent.
4. *Who feel guilty about overeating*—50 percent.
5. *Who think they are "naturally" overweight*—78 percent.
6. *Who get hungry when they watch other people eat*—73 percent.

• **VITAMIN BUFFS.** Although the official word from the government is that we do not need them as long as we eat a balanced diet, Americans are nonetheless spending about $1.2 billion a year on vitamin pills, with the market growing at a rate of 10 percent annually.

1. *Americans who take vitamin pills*—about 30 percent.
2. *College students (Survey of College Market) who take them*—48 percent.
3. *College women who take pills once a day or more often*—25 percent.
4. *College men who take vitamin pills once a day or more often*—18 percent.
5. *Proportion of vitamin market shared by "natural" vitamins*—about 50 percent.

SOURCES
Gallup Poll.
Glamour.
National Restaurant Association.
Newspaper Advertising Bureau.
Perrier Study of Fitness in America.
The Roper Organization.
W. R. Simmons.
Leo J. Shapiro, and Dwight Bohmbach, "Eating Habits Force Changes in Marketing," *Advertising Age,* October 30, 1978.

Statistical Abstract of the United States: 1978.
Survey of the College Market.
Woman's Day, Family Food Study.

DRINKING (SOFT)

Less coffee and milk, more carbonated drinks: That is the general picture of American beverage consumption over the past twenty-five years. Here is a closer look.

• **PERKING DOWN**. Americans now drink an average of 9.2 pounds of coffee per person per year, which breaks down to about 560 cups. High as these figures may seem, they represent only half the coffee we were drinking in 1946, when the average yearly coffee consumption rate per capita was in excess of 1,000 cups. Coffee gets brewed in about 84 percent of American homes, and 30 percent of the population now drink a decaffeinated brand. Most Americans (72 percent) say they drink coffee for the "taste of it," but nearly half the women in one California study admitted that coffee helped to "wake them up" and about 42 percent admitted they drank coffee to "get them going in the morning."

• **IN THE BAG**. Roughly half the American population drink tea, but the total amount of tea Americans drink is still only one-tenth of the amount of coffee that gets drunk each year. On the other hand, tea consumption has been increasing at a steady level ever since 1960.

• **COLA NUTS**. Americans are now guzzling down carbonated drinks at the rate of 359 cans per person per year, which helps to explain why national sales for soft drinks at the wholesale level are rapidly approaching the $12-billion mark. Two out of every three carbonated drinks sold in the United States are cola drinks, and diet-cola drinks make up about 15 percent of the soft-drink market. Lemon-lime drinks (7 Up, etc.) are the second most widely drunk carbonated soft drink after colas (around 20 percent of the population drink them). Recent surveys show that most soft drinks (about 60 percent) are drunk at home and about 30 percent of these drinks are taken with a meal.

SOURCES
Pepsico.
Statistical Abstract of the United States: 1978.

DRINKING (HARD)

Americans are drinking more alcohol today than at any other time in our history, but there have been some recent—and striking—changes in the *kind* of drinking we do. What has been happening, in short, is that whiskey consumption—particularly of bourbon—is on the decline, and wine and spirits consumption is on the upswing.

• THE BASIC NUMBERS. A "drinker," in the eyes of the U.S. Department of Health, Education, and Welfare, is anybody who drinks at least one alcoholic beverage a month, but the department also classifies drinkers into three categories: "light," "moderate," and "heavy." The barometer on which this categorization is based is the amount of absolute alcohol a person absorbs on an average day, with the dividing line between "moderate" and "heavy" being one ounce a day. (To absorb an ounce of absolute alcohol, you have to drink any of the following: two shots of straight whisky; two 4-ounce glasses of wine; or two beers.) Here are the current U.S. estimates, based on a 1974 Harris survey and a 1977 Gallup poll.

1. *Abstainers and infrequent drinkers*—about 29 percent of the population 12 years old and older.
2. *Light drinkers (less than 0.2 ounce a day)*—36 percent.
3. *Moderate drinkers (between 0.2 ounce and 1 ounce a day)*—23 percent.
4. *Heavy drinkers (1 ounce or more a day)*—12 percent.

Men:

1. *Abstainers and infrequent*—23 percent.
2. *Light*—33 percent.
3. *Moderate*—26 percent.
4. *Heavy*—16 percent.

Women:

1. *Abstainers and infrequent*—44 percent.
2. *Light*—36 percent.

3. *Moderate*—14 percent.
4. *Heavy*—6 percent.

•**THE DEMOGRAPHICS.** Several demographic factors color our alcohol-consumption statistics. Heavy drinkers, for instance, are more likely to be found in the 21–24 age-group than in any other age bracket and less likely to be found in the 65-and-older group (one macabre analysis of this fact is that most *really* heavy drinkers never make it to 65!). Surveys have shown, too, that abstainers outnumber heavy drinkers among persons with less than an eighth-grade education, but the reverse is true among college graduates. Religion? Jews show a smaller proportion of abstainers than Catholics or Protestants but also have the lowest proportion of heavy drinkers. The highest proportion of heavy drinkers is found among Catholics, and the highest proportion of abstainers is found among Protestants. As far as ethnic factors go, at least one survey, done in 1967, shows that when compared with other Americans of similar socioeconomic backgrounds, Irish Americans tend to have a greater proportion of problem drinkers.

•**TIPPLING TRENDS.** A survey by the marketing department of *Time* magazine turned up the following patterns of liquor and wine consumption in the United States between 1967 and 1977:

1. *Table wine*—consumption up 254 percent since 1967.
2. *Bottled cocktails*—up 203 percent.
3. *Rum*—up 156 percent.
4. *Vodka*—up 122 percent.
5. *Cordials and liqueurs*—up 115 percent.
6. *Canadian whiskey*—up 111 percent.
7. *Brandy and cognac*—up 51 percent.
8. *Scotch*—up 50 percent.
9. *Gin*—up 26 percent.
10. *Bourbon*—down 23 percent.
11. *Blended whiskeys*—down 37 percent.

•**BY THE GALLON.** Given the different levels of drinking that characterize American imbibing habits, per-capita-consumption numbers are of questionable value. But here they are anyway, courtesy of the U.S. Department of Health, Education, and Welfare. The averages pertain to Americans 15 years old and older and do *not* include abstainers.

1. *Hard liquor*—about 250 shots a year (no major change since 1971).
2. *Beer*—72 cans a year (up about 13 percent since 1971).
3. *Wine*—40 bottles a year (up 41 percent since 1971).

• **HEAD COUNT.** Some of the numbers relating to beer drinking in the United States:

1. *Men who drink beer*—60 percent.
2. *Women who drink beer*—30 percent.
3. *College students who drink beer*—68 percent.
4. *College males who drink beer either "once a day or more often," or "a few times a week"*—51 percent (according to the Survey of College Market).
5. *College females who drink with the same frequency*—20 percent.
6. *Light beer*—about 10 percent of the market.
7. *Imported beer*—about 2 percent of the market.

• **WHO DRINKS WHAT?** One of the things *The Perrier Study of Fitness in America* tried to determine was whether eating patterns differed between Americans who are active exercisers and Americans who are nonactive. The findings.

"High active" exercisers drink:

1. *Less beer than nonactive and obese Americans.*
2. *Less liquor than nonactives.*
3. *Less mineral or bottled water than nonactives.*

People of normal weight drink:

1. *About the same amount of hard liquor as obese people.*
2. *Less beer than obese people.*
3. *Less mineral water than obese people.*

• **GRAPE EXPECTATIONS.** By 1982, according to some projections, roughly three-fourths of the wine drunk in the United States will be table wine. This represents a virtual turnaround from 1967, when 50 percent of all the wine Americans drank were dessert wines and only 30 percent were table wines. Some other wine numbers:

1. *American adults who drink wine at least once a month*—16 percent.
2. *Who drink three glasses a week or more*—6 percent.
3. *Who drink seven or more glasses a week*—2 percent.

4. *American households in which wine is drunk regularly* —6 percent.
5. *Households in $15,000-and-over income bracket in which wine is drunk regularly*—20 percent.

Other patterns: The largest proportion of American wine drinkers (20 percent) live in the West, and southerners drinks less wine than anybody.

• TIPPLING TEENS. The teen-age drinking problem is bad, and it seems to be getting worse. Some sample numbers. From a 1974 Harris Survey:

1. *High school students who get drunk four times a year or more*—23 percent.
2. *Who are considered "problem drinkers"*—5 percent.
3. *Eighth-graders who were drunk at least once during 1973*—33 percent.
4. *Who were drunk four times or more in 1973*—33 percent.

From a 1978 National Institute on Alcohol Abuse and Alcoholism study:

1. *Average age at which American children in 1975 took their first drink*—12.9 (down from 13.6 in 1965).
2. *Children who've tasted alcohol by the age of ten*—40 percent.
3. *Teenage boys who drink alcohol*—79 percent.
4. *Teenage girls who drink alcohol*—70 percent.
5. *Teens who drink once a week*—40 percent.
6. *Who drink alone*—35 percent.

• AMERICA VERSUS THE WORLD. Here is a closer—and approximate—look at the countries that drink the most (based on per-capita consumption) of the various types of alcoholic beverages as determined by the *Journal of Studies on Alcohol, Inc.*, of Rutgers University.

Spirits, in liters (there are 7.78 liters in a gallon):

1. *Peru*—12.5.
2. *Soviet Union*—12.5.
3. *U.S.A.*—10.0
4. *Canada*—9.5.
5. *West Germany*—9.1.

Wine, in liters:

1. *Portugal*—166.5
2. *Italy*—143.5.
3. *France*—142.0.
4. *Switzerland*—58.5.
5. *Austria*—45.0.

(U.S. Consumption—8.5 liters.)
Beer, in liters:

1. *West Germany*—191.5.
2. *Czechoslovakia*—188.5.
3. *Belgium*—185.5.
4. *Australia*—182.0.
5. *New Zealand*—177.5.

(U.S. consumption—109.0 liters.)
Pure absolute alcohol, in liters:

1. *Portugal*—23.5.
2. *France*—22.5.
3. *West Germany*—15.0.
4. *Belgium*—14.4.
5. *Austria*—14.0.

(U.S. consumption—10.5 liters.)

SOURCES
Anheuser-Busch Breweries.
Gallup Poll.
Harris Survey.
Journal of Studies on Alcohol.
Perrier Study of Fitness in America.
Statistics on Consumption of Alcohol and on Alcoholism, 1976.
Survey of the College Market, 1977.
U.S. Department of Health, Education, and Welfare, *Alcohol and Health,* 1974.
U.S. National Institute on Alcohol Abuse and Alcoholism.

SLEEPING

The average American spends in an average lifetime about 20 years asleep. Yet, it has only been over the past few years that sleep researchers have gained any sort of understanding of why and how we sleep. Here is a little of what we know.

• **THE BASIC NUMBERS**. Most Americans get—and need —about 7.5 hours of sleep a night, but it is generally accepted that most of us get more sleep than we actually need. A lot depends on age, occupation, and life-style. Pregnant women need two hours more sleep, on average, than women who are not pregnant. People in mentally active jobs need more sleep than people whose jobs require purely physical energy. And older people need less sleep than younger people.

• **EARLY TO BED**. One out of three American adults goes to bed each night between 10:30 P.M. and 11 P.M. By midnight four out of five Americans are asleep. Rural Americans tend to go to bed earlier than urbanites and suburbanites.

• **NIGHT MOVES**. There are four basic sleeping positions (and numerous variations thereof). The average numbers of people who sleep in these positions, according to sleep expert Dr. Samuel Dunkell, are:

1. *Semifetal* (side position)—60 percent.
2. *Prone* (face down, arms and legs apart)—25 percent.
3. *Full fetal* (knees to chest)—7.5 percent.
4. *Royal* (on back)—7.5 percent.

Dr. Dunkell suggests that sleeping positions mirror personality traits. People who sleep in the semifetal position, he says, are well balanced. Prone sleepers tend to be fussy and domineering. Royal sleepers are self-reliant and assured. Full-fetal sleepers tend to be inhibited and insecure.

• **PAJAMA GAMES**. Data on what we wear to bed are sketchy, but here are some estimates based on the handful of surveys that have been done:

1. *Women who wear nightgowns*—more than 90 percent.
2. *Men who wear pajamas*—55 percent.
3. *Men who sleep in underwear*—35 percent.
4. *Men who sleep in the nude*—10 percent.
5. *College men who sleep in the nude*—20 percent.
6. *Women who sleep in the nude*—2 percent.

• **R E D   E Y E   S P E C I A L S .** Estimates on the number of Americans who have difficulty falling asleep range from 21 million (14 percent of adult population) to 48 million (32 percent). Some sleep specialists estimate that as many as one out of every two Americans has trouble sleeping on occasion and that in one out of seven cases the problem is serious. Here are some of the numbers from a 1972 HEW survey among young people with sleeping problems:

1. *Teenagers who report insomnia problems from time to time*—44 percent.
2. *Who have nightmares or bad dreams "quite frequently"* —3 percent.
3. *Teenage girls who have bad dreams from "time to time"*—47 percent.
4. *Teenage boys*—39 percent.
5. *Teenagers who sleepwalk*—5 percent (boys slightly more likely than girls).

Patterns? Neither nationality, race nor income seems to have any relationship to insomnia, but age and sex apparently do. Older people complain more about sleeping difficulties than younger people, and women more than men. The segment of the population voicing insomnia complaints the most are older, married females.

• **M I D N I G H T   E X P R E S S .** Something like 8.5 million Americans took sleeping pills at least once during 1977, and nearly two million Americans, according to the National Institute on Drug Abuse, took the pills every night for two consecutive months or longer. Some related numbers.

1. *Americans who take sleeping pills at least once during the year*—about 5 percent.
2. *Who take them on a regular basis*—about 1 percent.
3. *Proportion of drug related deaths in 1976 that involved either a tranquilizer or a sleeping pill*—35 percent.

Trends? There was a 73 percent decline between 1971 and 1976 in the number of prescriptions for barbiturate sleeping pills— the direct result of a federal law passed in 1970 that put barbiturates into a more restrictive drug category. The use of non-barbiturate sleeping pills, however, has jumped during the same period.

• **DREAMLAND.** Nearly everybody dreams, and probably the most extensive study ever done on the subject was carried out in the mid-1960s by Calvin S. Hall and R. L. Van de Castle. It involved the analysis of home dreams of more than 1,000 college students. Here's what emerged.

1. *People who report having aggressive dreams—*47 percent.
2. *Friendly dreams—*38 percent.
3. *Dreams in which the dreamer is going somewhere—*32 percent.
4. *In which the dreamer is involved in a specific activity—*25 percent.
5. *Dreams about misfortune or failure—*16 percent.
6. *Sex-related dreams—*less than 10 percent.
7. *Sex-related dreams in which there is actual intercourse going on—*less than 3 percent.

Most dreams (80 percent) take place in a setting that is familiar to the dreamer, and only rarely (4 percent of the time) does a dream take place in a bizarre or surrealistic setting. Other people are generally present in our dreams, but usually we know who they are. Guest appearances ("Here's Johnny!") from movie stars, athletes, politicians, and other celebrity types are rare.

SOURCES

Calvin S. Hall and R. L. Van de Castle, *The Content Analysis of Dreams,* 1966.
Pajama Wearers and Attitudes, 1957.
Dr. Samuel Dunkell.
U.S. Department of Health, Education, and Welfare, *Behavioral Patterns of Youths 12–17.*
Wilse B. Webb, *Sleep, the Gentle Tyrant,* 1975.

TALKING

Working on the premise that conversation is the "glue that binds our society together," the Newspaper Advertising Bureau (NAB) ran a survey in March 1977 among 3,000 American adults, the idea being to find out what subjects Americans talk about the most when they converse with friends, relatives and acquaintances. Here's what the survey said about what we talk about, as well as some other numbers on our talking habits.

• THE BASIC NUMBERS. From the NAB survey, proportion of adult Americans who talk frequently:

1. *About current events*—47 percent.
2. *About the economic situation*—20 percent.
3. *About politics*—20 percent.
4. *About either sports, education, amusement, or the arts* —25 percent.

These findings are consistent with the results of NORC General Social surveys, which show that more than twice as many Americans (about 40 percent) say they talk "very often" about their "present financial situation" than say they talk "very often" about current issues such as women's rights, abortion laws, and the country's scientific community.

• THE DEMOGRAPHICS. A demographic analysis of the NAB survey findings shows that men and women have about the same degree of conversational interest in news and current events; but women tend to talk more about family matters and acquaintances, whereas men are more likely to talk about work, politics, sports, and entertainment. Younger people (18- to 24-year-olds) converse more about entertainment, sports, jobs, and school than do older people, but older Americans talk more about politics and current events. The survey also showed that while Americans with higher education levels are more likely than lesser-educated Americans to talk about politics, the conversational frequency for other kinds of news events is pretty much the same among Americans in all educational and income-level groups.

• TOPIC LIST. Here is a list of the subjects Americans talk about the *most*, based on the choices made by the respondents in the NAB survey.

Proportion of Americans who say one of the subjects they talk about "most often" is:

1. *Economic situation*—20 percent.
2. *Job or career*—19 percent.
3. *Sports*—19 percent.
4. *Family matters apart from children*—17 percent.

5. *Children or grandchildren*—15 percent.
6. *Movies, TV, reading*—13 percent.
7. *Religion*—11 percent.
8. *School*—11 percent.

• **HUNG UP.** From the American Telephone and Telegraph Company, who ought to know, comes word that in 1977 the average American spoke on the phone about 6 times a day. The specific number is 5.75, which is up from 5.45 in 1973. We also spend an average of 8 minutes on the phone when we are talking long-distance.

SOURCES
NORC.
Newspaper Advertising Bureau.
American Telephone and Telegraph.

PERSONAL GROOMING

Americans spend more money—and probably more time—on personal grooming than the residents of any other nation, and the numbers get bigger every year. Here is how we do it.

• **THE BASIC NUMBERS.** Vanity is now a $9-billion industry in the United States. For instance:

1. *Average per-capita expenditure on personal-grooming items*—$40 a year.
2. *Total spent on hair products*—$2.5 billion.
3. *On face creams, makeup, and cosmetics*—$2.0 billion.
4. *On shaving products*—$1.4 billion.
5. *On razor blades alone*—$400 million.

• **TAKING IT OFF.** Current market surveys show that about 95 percent of American men shave on a regular basis (the remaining 5 percent presumably have beards). The particulars:

1. *Americans who use electric razors*—25 percent.
2. *Who use after-shave lotion*—50 percent, but higher among young people.
3. *Who use a heated shave-cream dispenser*—15 percent.

• **ARM'S LENGTH.** Now for the underarm-deodorant story:

1. *Men who use deodorant regularly*—75 percent.
2. *Women who use it regularly*—85 percent.
3. *College women who use it more than once a day*—33 percent.
4. *College men who use it twice a day*—20 percent.
5. *Deodorant users who favor aerosol type*—about 50 percent.
6. *Roll-on type*—30 percent.

• **HAIR TODAY.** Americans spend about $750 million a year (about $3.40 per person) on shampoos, with dandruff and medicated shampoos occupying a big piece of the market. The numbers:

1. *Men who shampoo at least once a month*—75 percent.
2. *Women who shampoo at least once a month*—85 percent.
3. *Those 18 and younger who wash their hair at least once a week*—85–90 percent.
4. *College men who wash their hair more than once a day*—54 percent.

• **WASHED UP.** It's pretty much taken for granted that Americans spend more time in the bath or shower than anybody else in the world. And the numbers from a 1977 Roper Poll more than drive home the point. Here are some of them:

1. *Americans who say they take some sort of bath in an average 24-hour period*—90 percent.
2. *Who average more than one shower or bath a day*—5 percent.
3. *Men who shower*—75 percent.
4. *Who take baths*—25 percent.
5. *Women who shower*—50 percent.
6. *Who take baths*—50 percent.

And from a 1977 *Beauty Fashion Magazine* survey:

1. *Teenage girls (16 to 19) who shower daily*—65 percent.
2. *Who take at least one bath a week*—55 percent.
3. *Women who use an additive in the bath every time they bathe*—50 percent.

Most surveys indicate that younger and richer people are more likely to shower than they are to bathe, and that showers are more popular than baths in big cities.

SOURCES

Drug Topics, Annual Survey June 20, 1978.
Newspaper Advertising Bureau.
Survey of the Collge Market.
Seventeen.

KEEPING HOUSE

Well, somebody has to do it. And the most recent surveys show that Americans today, especially working women, are spending less time than ever before on basic house or apartment cleaning activities.

• THE BASIC NUMBERS. The best estimate of the average time now being spent on housework in the average American household is between ten and 15 hours a week, although the cleaning time will, of course, vary according to the size of the household and how many children there are. From the American Soap and Detergent Association, these numbers, based on proportion of households in which the following chores are done at least once every two weeks:

1. *Sweeping and vacuuming*—98 percent.
2. *Dusting*—92 percent.
3. *Washing floors*—91 percent.
4. *Waxing and polishing*—43 percent.
5. *Removing stains*—32 percent.
6. *Cleaning windows*—4 percent.

Of all the rooms in the typical American house, the kitchen gets the most housekeeping attention. The dining room gets the least attention.

• LOADING UP. Also from the American Soap and Detergent Association, these numbers on American laundry habits:

1. *Average number of weekly washloads in typical American family household*—6.
2. *In households of five or more*—10.
3. *Households in which the laundry is still done by hand* —13 percent.
4. *Americans who do their washing on Monday* (still)— 22 percent.

5. *On Saturday*—15 percent.
6. *Who go to laundromats*—4 percent.

• **Up Against the Vacuum Cleaner.** From sociologist Anne Oakley's book-length study on the sociology of housework:

1. *The least liked housecleaning chore among American housewives*—ironing.
2. *The best liked chore*—cooking.
3. *American women who are either dissatisfied or very dissatisfied with housework*—70 percent.

When Angus Campbell and his colleagues questioned American women on their housecleaning attitudes, they found that women in higher-income homes express more dissatisfaction with housework than do lower-income women, even though higher-income women spend *less* time actually doing housework. (An estimated one out of eight women in the United States has somebody come in now and then to help out with the housework.) City women, generally, complain more about housework than suburban women. Educated women complain more than women who haven't graduated from high school. And women who are satisfied with the home or apartment they live in complain less than women who feel their home or apartment isn't adequate for their needs.

SOURCES
The National Cleaning and Laundry Census, American Soap and Detergent Association.
Angus Campbell, *The Quality of American Life*.
Anne Oakley, *The Sociology of Housework*, 1974.

DRIVING

Few activities apart from the more common biologically related habits—eating, sleeping, etc.—are as central to the American experience as is going some place in a car. Indeed, according to one study by the Motor Vehicle Manufacturers Association, a car, a truck, or a taxi is involved in nearly 90 percent of all the activities Americans take part in outside the home.

• **T** HE **B** ASIC **N** UMBERS . First a look at *who* drives:

1. *American adults who know how to drive a car*—75 percent.
2. *Men drivers*—54 percent of driving population.
3. *Drivers younger than 25*—20 percent of driving population.

Now a look at where we go when we drive:

1. *Car trips that are business-related*—36 percent (but they account for 42 percent of the yearly national mileage, which—get your calculator—is about 1.7 trillion miles).
2. *Errands*—15 percent (only 7.5 percent of the yearly national mileage total).
3. *Social purposes*—10 percent.
4. *Vacations*—1 percent.

• **S** HORT **T** AKES . The average American car ride lasts about 10 miles if it is for business (one way), 12 miles if it is a social visit to friends, 4.5 miles if it is a shopping trip. For vacations, the average is 160 miles—one way.

• **T** OLL **T** AKERS . Here are the most recent numbers on who does—and who does not—car-pool.

1. *Americans who drive themselves to work*—70 percent (higher in smaller cities).
2. *Who car-pool*—17 percent.
3. *Who use mass transit*—6 percent.

• **B** UCKLING **U** NDER . The latest National Highway Safety Administration figures show that 19.5 percent of American drivers, or less than one out of five, use seat belts. Here is a more specific breakdown:

1. *Drivers 24 to 49 years old*—19 percent.
2. *Drivers older than 50*—15 percent.
3. *Drivers younger than 24*—19 percent.
4. *Midwesterners*—17 percent.
5. *Westerners*—27 percent.
6. *Women*—21 percent.
7. *Men*—17 percent.

• S w e d i s h A n g e l s . Recent surveys suggest a relationship between the kind of car a person drives and the likelihood the driver will use seat belts. Owners of smaller imported cars, for example, use seat belts much more frequently than owners of larger, American-built cars. The seat-belt-usage rate among Volvo owners (45 percent) is four times the usage rate of owners of Chrysler Cordobas; and owners of Dodge Colts, Toyotas, Volkswagens, and Capris show a frequency use rate that is nearly three times that of owners of Lincoln Continentals, Mercury Cougars, and Cadillacs.

• F a i l S a f e . Some older cars—particularly those built in 1974—have certain interlock features designed to "force" drivers to fasten seat belts, but the research shows that even among owners of these cars, the seat-belt-usage rate is only 25 percent.

• F e n d e r B e n d e r s . The United States has been averaging between 16 and 17 million motor vehicle accidents a year since 1970, which breaks down to a rate of about one accident for every ten cars. If you consider drivers only, as well as the fact that it usually takes two drivers to make an accident, the average annual *driver* accident rate is now one accident for every four drivers.

• O v e r t h e L i m i t . A U.S. Federal Highway Administration study in 1975 showed that 83 percent of Americans driving on main rural highways exceeded the 55-miles-per-hour speed limit during off-peak hours, with 28 percent traveling, on average, faster than 60 miles per hour. On the other hand, the proportion of drivers who average better than 70 miles per hour has dropped from 14 percent in the early 1970s to around 1 percent since the imposition of the 55-miles-per-hour speed limit.

• T h e T i c k e t , P l e a s e . NORC General Social Surveys since 1972 indicate that about 41 percent of American drivers have received at least one ticket for a traffic violation other than illegal parking.

SOURCES
Motor Vehicle Manufacturers Association.
NORC.

National Safety Council.
Statistical Abstract of the United States: 1978.

READING

Everybody (well, almost everybody) in America reads *something*, but how much we read—and what we read—is a question that not even book publishers feel qualified to answer. Recent survey data suggest that (*a*) television has not eaten into our reading habits as much as a lot of people think and (*b*) though television may be the most time-consuming leisure activity in the United States, reading provides the most satisfaction.

·**NEWS HOUNDS.** There is no shortage of data on our newspaper-reading habits, thanks to an ongoing research program conducted by the Newspaper Advertising Bureau as part of the Newspaper Readership Project. Here are some highlights from recent surveys.

Proportion of Americans who read a newspaper:

1. *At least once a day*—69 percent (no difference between men and women).
2. *At home*—80 percent.
3. *After the evening meal*—40 percent.
4. *At or before breakfast*—16 percent.
5. *By going through the entire paper and reading whatever is interesting*—about 62 percent.
6. *Who also watch TV news*—70 percent.
7. *Who open the paper to a general news page*—88 percent (women more so than men).
8. *Who read the business and finance page*—75 percent.
9. *The sports page*—75 percent (men more so than women).
10. *The obituary page*—87 percent.
11. *The comics*—84 percent.
12. *The columnists*—86 percent (women more so than men).

·**READERS' CHOICE.** A 1978 study by Ottoway Newspapers, Inc., a newspaper chain that operates in a number of medium-sized American cities, garnered the following data regarding the most "widely read" sections of the paper. Remember, these finding reflect the newspaper-reading habits of Americans in small and medium-sized towns.

1. *Editorial page*—89 percent.
2. *Classified section*—80 percent.
3. *Family section*—73 percent.
4. *Comics*—62 percent.
5. *Business*—58 percent.
6. *Sports*—37 percent.

• K I D S ' C O L U M N . A look at the newspaper-reading habits of children, from a Newspaper Research Bureau survey:

1. *Six- to eight-year-olds who have ever read a newspaper—* 33 percent.
2. *Fifteen- to 17-year-olds who have ever read a newspaper —81 percent.*
3. *Nine- to 11-year-olds who read the Sunday comics—64 percent.*
4. *Twelve- to 14-year-olds who use the newspaper for their social studies projects—41 percent.*
5. *Who like the idea of using the newspaper for schoolwork—65 percent.*
6. *Boys 15 to 17 who read the sports page "most of the time"—62 percent.*
7. *Boys 12 to 14 who read the sports page "most of the time"—67 percent.*
8. *Teenage girls who read personal-advice columns—40 percent.*
9. *Teenage boys who read personal-advice columns— 12 percent.*

• C O M I C R E L I E F . From the same survey, this short list of the three most widely read comic strips:

1. *Blondie*—65 percent.
2. *Peanuts*—64 percent.
3. *Andy Capp*—60 percent.

• B O O K W O R M S . A 1978 study, commissioned by the Book Industry Study Group and conducted by Yankelovich, S elly and White, Inc., showed that around 94 percent of Amer ans read something, but only 55 percent of the population can be described as book readers. Some of the numbers:

1. *Average number of books read each year by the reading population*—16.
2. *Proportion of Americans who read at least twenty books a year*—25 percent.
3. *Who read less than one book a month*—53 percent (according to a 1975 Harris survey).
4. *Who buy more than one hardback book a year*—15 percent (according to W. R. Simmons).
5. *Average amount Americans spend on books each year*—$35.
6. *Americans who do not read books at all*—45 percent.
7. *Who belong to a book club*—20 percent.
8. *Who say they read for pure pleasure*—36 percent.
9. *Who read for general knowledge*—25 percent.
10. *Number of hours the average reader spends reading in a week*—14 hours.

And this from the Library Association: Twenty percent of Americans own a library card.

• READING DEMOGRAPHICS. Most readers (58 percent) are women, with the heaviest readership concentrated in the 30–39 age-group. Some other figures from the Harris survey and *The Playboy Report on American Men:*

1. *Women readers who work full-time*—42 percent.
2. *Who do not work*—21 percent.
3. *Who are in households where the family income is $25,000 or more*—33 percent.
4. *Who draw creative satisfaction from reading*—42 percent.
5. *Men readers who say they draw creative satisfaction from reading*—32 percent.
6. *Men (18 to 49) who read more than twenty books a year*—22 percent.
7. *Who read eleven to twenty books a year*—12 percent.
8. *Who are single and read more than twenty books a year*—29 percent.
9. *Who are married and read more than twenty books a year*—18 percent.
10. *Who do not read any books at all or read only one or two a year*—31 percent.
11. *Who read less than one book a month*—64 percent.

• No-Shows. Here is a closer look at the 45 percent of Americans who do not read books at all, according to the Book Industry Study.

Nonreaders who:

1. *Are black*—22 percent of non-readers.
2. *Earn less than $10,000 a year*—43 percent.
3. *Did not go beyond the eighth grade*—33 percent.
4. *Say they do not read because they do not have the time*—23 percent.
5. *Because they have bad eyes*—14 percent.
6. *Because they lack reading competence*—13 percent.

• Lettered Children. Here is what a 1972 U.S. government study of 12- and 17-year-olds turned up on the reading habits of American teens:

1. *American 12- and 17-year-olds who spend at least "some" time during the day reading books*—80 percent (but no distinction here between reading for school and reading for pleasure).
2. *Who spend more than an hour a day reading*—50 percent.
3. *Median reading time for girls*—one hour and twenty minutes.
4. *For boys*—less than an hour.

• Roving Eyes. The average American reads at a rate of between 200 and 250 words a minute, which is also the reading speed of the average eighth-grader. There are, of course, exceptions.

1. *Reading speed of college students with A or B averages*—325–350 words a minute.
2. *Of avid readers*—300 words a minute.
3. *Of speed-reading-school graduates*—500 words a minute.

• The Top Twenty. The most widely read magazines in the United States, based on circulation figures for the last half of 1978, are (rounded off to the nearest thousandth):

1. *TV Guide*—19,881,000.
2. *Reader's Digest*—18,301,000.
3. *National Geographic*—9,960,000.
4. *Family Circle*—8,277,000.

5. *Better Homes and Gardens*—8,277,000.
6. *Woman's Day*—8,003,000.
7. *McCall's*—6,503,000.
8. *Ladies' Home Journal*—6,002,000.
9. *National Enquirer*—5,720,000.
10. *Good Housekeeping*—5,198,000.
11. *Playboy*—4,825,000.
12. *Penthouse*—4,510,000.
13. *Redbook*—4,431,000.
14. *Time*—3,311,000.
15. *The Star*—3,009,000.
16. *Newsweek*—2,959,000.
17. *Cosmopolitan*—2,659,000.
18. *American Legion*—2,598,000.
19. *Sports Illustrated*—2,337,000.
20. *People*—2,319,000.

• **BLACK MARKET**. Not surprisingly, the magazines most widely read by black Americans are those written specifically for the black market. Some illustrative numbers, based on a 1977 poll by Lee Slurzberg Research.

Magazines most widely read by black women:

1. *Ebony*—48 percent.
2. *Jet*—40 percent.
3. *Essence*—27 percent.
4. *Good Housekeeping*—18 percent.
5. *Better Homes and Gardens*—18 percent.
6. *Black Stars*—12 percent.
7. *Ladies' Home Journal*—12 percent.
8. *Family Circle*—10 percent.
9. *Woman's Day*—9 percent.
10. *American Home*—8 percent.
11. *Vogue*—7 percent.

By black men:

1. *Ebony*—39 percent.
2. *Jet*—38 percent.
3. *Sports Illustrated*—21 percent.
4. *Black Sports*—14 percent.
5. *Black Stars*—10 percent.
6. *Essence*—9 percent.
7. *Black Enterprise*—8 percent.

8. *Black Business Digest*—5 percent.
9. *Encore*—3 percent.

SOURCES
Associated Councils on the Arts, *Americans and the Arts*.
Newspaper Advertising Bureau.
Playboy Report on American Men.
Publishers Weekly, November 6, 1978.
Magazines Publishers Association.
Lee Slurzberg.
U.S. Department of Health, Education, and Welfare, *Behavioral Patterns in School of Youths 12–17*.

LISTENING TO THE RADIO

The radio listening habits of Americans haven't been studied as much by social scientists as have our television viewing habits, which has obscured the degree to which radio is part of our everyday lives.

• **THE BASIC NUMBER.** From the Radio Advertising Bureau, this glimpse of radio ownership.

1. *American households containing at least one radio*—99 percent.
2. *Containing six or more sets*—41 percent.
3. *Containing at least one clock radio*—60 percent.
4. *Automobiles with a radio*—95 percent.
5. *Amount of money Americans spend yearly on new radios*—$3,500,000.

• **LISTENING IN.** From a 1978 NORC survey, a look at how much we listen to radio each day.

1. *Proportion of Americans who listen to the radio at least one hour a day*—38 percent.
2. *Two hours a day*—21 percent.
3. *Three hours a day*—8 percent.
4. *Four hours a day*—7 percent.
5. *More than four hours a day*—20 percent.
6. *Less than one hour a day*—less than 1 percent.

• **THE DEMOGRAPHICS**. From the Radio Advertising Bureau's research department, a look at who listens and how much:

1. *Teens average listening time daily*—3 hours.
2. *Adults*—about 3½ hours.
3. *Men 18 to 24*—4 hours.
4. *Men 50 and older*—2 hours and 54 minutes.
5. *Women 18 to 24*—3 hours and 46 minutes.
6. *Women 50 and older*—3 hours and 12 minutes.

Patterns? None that stand out, except for age. Income seems to have no bearing on the amount of time an American spends listening to the radio. And even age is important only among persons under 18 and older than 50, where the average is lower than among other age groups.

• **TUNED IN**. Some reasons people listen to the radio and the proportion of Americans who fall into each category:

1. *To keep up with the news*—92 percent.
2. *To find out what's going on in local community*—77 percent.
3. *For pleasure and relaxation*—88 percent.
4. *To keep from getting lonely*—59 percent.
5. *To keep from getting bored*—55 percent.
6. *To stay cheerful and happy*—61 percent.

SOURCE
Radio Advertising Bureau.

GAMBLING

Depending on whose estimate you believe, Americans gamble anywhere from $20 billion to $500 billion a year. Money apart, gambling itself is nearly as widespread a habit as drinking alcoholic beverages. To date the most detailed study of gambling in America was done for the U.S. government by the Institute for Social Research (ISR) at the University of Michigan. Here is some of what it turned up.

• **THE BASIC NUMBERS**. The majority of American adults (61 percent according to the study) gamble, whether at the track, at a casino, with a bookie, at a friendly card game, or at a Friday night bingo session in a church. The ISR (not to be confused with the IRS, which would dearly love a piece of American gambling action) estimates that we gamble around $22.5 billion a year, which averages out to about $390 for every adult American who gambles. An estimated one out of ten Americans bets *illegally*—that is, plays the numbers or bets with a bookie; and less than 30 percent of American adults have *never* placed a bet in their lives.

• **THE DEMOGRAPHICS.** The ISR did some detailed demographic analyses of gambling patterns. Here are some of them, based on the proportion of people who fall into each category:

1. *Women who gamble*—55 percent.
2. *Men who gamble*—68 percent.
3. *Women who gamble illegally*—5 percent.
4. *Men who gamble illegally*—17 percent.
5. *Catholics who gamble*—80 percent.
6. *Protestants who gamble*—54 percent.
7. *Jews who gamble*—77 percent.
8. *Atheists who gamble*—40 percent.
9. *Jews who gamble illegally*—19 percent.
10. *Catholics who gamble illegally*—16 percent.
11. *Protestants who gamble illegally*—9 percent.
12. *College graduates who gamble*—79 percent.
13. *High-school graduates who gamble*—66 percent.
14. *Whites who gamble*—62 percent.
15. *Nonwhites who gamble*—52 percent.
16. *Whites who gamble illegally*—10 percent.
17. *Nonwhites who gamble illegally*—17 percent.
18. *Whites who are heavy illegal bettors*—2 percent.
19. *Nonwhites who are heavy illegal bettors*—5 percent.
20. *Americans 65 and older who gamble*—23 percent.
21. *Americans 18 to 24 years old who gamble*—73 percent.
22. *Americans earning more than $15,000 who gamble*—74 percent.
23. *Americans earning under $10,000 who gamble*—less than 50 percent.
24. *Northeasterners who gamble*—80 percent.
25. *Southerners who gamble*—25 percent.

•GAMES GAMBLERS PLAY. Here is a breakdown of the kinds of gambling that Americans do, based on the proportion of gamblers who bet in each activity:

1. *State lotteries*—48.0 percent.
2. *Bingo*—19.0 percent.
3. *Horse racing at the track*—14.0 percent.
4. *Off-track betting parlors*—13.5 percent.
5. *Casino games*—9.4 percent.
6. *Illegal sports cards*—3.0 percent.
7. *Numbers*—3.0 percent.
8. *Horses with a bookie*—2.4 percent.
9. *Sports with a bookie*—1.9 percent.

But in terms of average dollars wagered per year by each gambler, the list looks like this:

1. *Off-track betting parlors*—$1,118.
2. *Sports with a bookie*—$623.
3. *Horse racing at the track*—$448.
4. *Casino games*—$448.
5. *Horses with a bookie*—$416.
6. *Numbers*—$273.
7. *Bingo*—$74.
8. *Illegal sports cards*—$44.
9. *State lotteries*—$25.

•EXPENSIVE THRILLS. ISR researchers asked their respondents to rate various gambling activities on the basis of an excitement scale ranging from one to eight. Here is how the various games fared.

The total sample:

1. *Horses at the track*—3.98 rating.
2. *Cards with friends*—3.74.
3. *Gambling casinos*—3.41.
4. *Slot machines*—3.39.
5. *Bingo*—3.19.
6. *Sports with friends*—3.11.
7. *Lottery*—2.80.
8. *Dog tracks*—2.77.
9. *Dice*—2.54.
10. *Horses off-track*—2.06.
11. *Sports cards*—1.96.

12. *Sports with a bookie*—1.90.
13. *Numbers*—1.74.

Bettors who gamble on specific games:

1. *Horses at the track*—6.59.
2. *Gambling casinos*—5.80.
3. *Dog tracks*—5.50.
4. *Sports cards*—5.44.
5. *Slot machines*—5.26.
6. *Bingo*—5.08.
7. *Sports with friends*—5.01.
8. *Horses off-track*—4.35.
9. *Lottery*—4.11.
10. *Sports with a bookie*—3.87.
11. *Numbers*—3.52.

SOURCE
Institute for Social Research, *Gambling in the United States*, 1974.

SMOKING

Men are doing it less. Women are doing it more. And even though the country's smoking rate, on the whole, is down, people who smoked heavily in the early 1970s are smoking even more heavily than ever today.

• T H E   B A S I C   N U M B E R S . Nearly one out of three American adults (about 54 million) now smokes cigarettes, and an additional 6 million smoke either a pipe or cigars. There are about 3 million more Americans smoking today than in 1960, but the proportion of cigarette smokers is down by about 4 percent. The proportion of men who smoke is well down from the 1970 total, but the rate of women smokers is rising, with about 6 million more women smoking cigarettes today than in 1970.

• P A C K I N G   I t   I N . Men are more likely to be heavy smokers than are females. Here are the statistics that prove it.
Proportion of:

1. *Men who smoke more than 35 cigarettes a day*—17 percent.

2. *Women who smoke more than 35 cigarettes a day*—10 percent.

3. *Men who smoke fewer than 15 cigarettes a day*—28 percent.

4. *Women who smoke fewer than 15 cigarettes a day*—40 percent.

• **T A R R E D O U T .** About 30 percent of all cigarette sales in the United States today involve low-tar brands (that is, those having 15 milligrams of tar or less).

• **A T H L E T I C S M O K E .** Most people assume that Americans involved in athletics are generally nonsmokers, but *The Perrier Study of Fitness in America* found little difference among active and nonactive athletic groups in either the proportion of smokers or the amount of cigarettes smoked per day. Some representative figures:

1. *Bowlers who smoke*—51 percent.
2. *Swimmers who smoke*—45 percent.
3. *Calisthenics people who smoke*—41 percent.
4. *Tennis players and players of other racquet sports who smoke*—25 percent.

• **K I C K I N G I T .** Roughly one out of five smokers, according to a study by Dr. William Mariencheck of the University of Tennessee Hospital, fails when he or she tries to kick the habit. The success rate jumps, however, to 33 percent among people who quit because of lung cancer or bronchial problems. Troubled women 20 to 35 years old have the toughest time quitting, and on-the-move executives have the second toughest time of all.

• **F A T C H A N C E S .** The generally accepted belief that people who stop smoking automatically put on weight is disputed by American Cancer Society studies, which show that only one out of three persons who stops smoking gains weight while one out of three persons actually loses weight. The remaining third holds the same weight.

SOURCES

American Cancer Society.
The Perrier Study of Fitness in America.
U.S. National Center for Health Statistics.

USING DRUGS

It is a safe assumption, based on the most recent data, that at least one out of four Americans has had some experience with what the federal government chooses to call a "controlled substance." Tougher to establish is exactly how many Americans use drugs on a regular basis and how the patterns have changed throughout the 1970s. About the only things that can be said for certain are that (a) young Americans are more involved with drugs than older Americans and (b) the proportion of Americans who have tried marijuana at least once has doubled since the late 1960s..

• JOINT ACCOUNTING. A survey conducted in 1977 for the National Institute on Drug Abuse (NIDA) produced the following numbers on marijuana usage in the United States:

1. *Americans who have ever tried marijuana*—about 25.0 percent of population 12 years old and older.
2. *Who describe themselves as current users*—about 14.5 percent.
3. *Seventeen years old and younger who have tried marijuana*—28.0 percent.
4. *Who describe themselves as current users*—16.0 percent.
5. *Sixteen and 17 years old who have ever tried it*—47.0 percent.
6. *Who describe themselves as current users*—29.0 percent.
7. *Young adults (18 to 25) who have ever tried it*—60.0 percent.
8. *Who describe themselves as current users*—12.0 percent.
9. *Americans 35 and older who have ever tried it*—7.0 percent.
10. *Who describe themselves as current users*—1.0 percent.

A 1977 Gallup poll showed that marijuana smoking was twice as prevalent among college-educated Americans than among high-school-educated Americans, and three times as prevalent among blacks than among whites. But the NIDA demographic breakdowns show that among younger smokers, whites hold a proportional edge. The Gallup survey also showed that, on the whole, men are twice as likely to be marijuana smokers than are women, but NIDA survey findings suggest that among younger smokers, the gap between the two sexes is somewhat narrower. The regional findings of both surveys are similar, with NIDA figures showing that marijuana smoking is three times as prevalent in the Northeast and West as it is in the South.

• S n o w   B l i n d . The most recent surveys (1978) suggest that roughly 10 million Americans (5.5 percent of the population 12 years old and older) have tried cocaine at least once, but only a fraction of that number are regular users. From surveys by the Addiction Research Foundation of Ontario on cocaine usage in the United States:

1. *Americans who take cocaine daily*—about 450,000 (less than 0.25 percent of population).
2. *Who use it an average of two days a month*—about 1 million.
3. *Eighteen- to 25-year-olds who have tried cocaine*—19.0 percent (according to the NIDA survey).
4. *Who describe themselves as current users*—3.5 percent.

• T r i p p e r s . All signs point to a sharp drop in the number of Americans, particularly young Americans, using LSD and other hallucinogens. From the 1977 NIDA survey:

1. *Americans who have used LSD or other hallucinogens* —6 percent of population 12 and older.
2. *Who describe themselves as current users*—about 900,-000.
3. *Twenty-six-year-olds and older who have used LSD*— 2.5 percent.
4. *Eighteen- to 25-year-olds who have used it*—20.0 percent.
5. *Who describe themselves as current users*—2 percent.

• U p s   a n d   D o w n s . The number of Americans using stimulants, sedatives, and tranquilizers has been rising steadily throughout the 1970s, but nobody has yet figured out a way to determine how many people are taking pills for legitimate medical reasons and how many are popping for the sake of popping. Some of the more recent numbers.

From Susan Edminston's report on the tranquilizer valium, published in *Today's Health:*

1. *Americans who use valium*—17 percent.
2. *Women who use it*—20 percent.
3. *People who use it for anxiety or insomnia*—30 percent.
4. *For muscle spasms*—18 percent.
5. *For epilepsy and cerebral palsy*—3 percent.
6. *For anxiety related to organic diseases*—45 percent.

From the NIDA survey, these percentages for young adults aged 18 to 25:

1. *Who have ever used stimulants*—21.0 percent.
2. *Who use them now*—2.5 percent.
3. *Who have ever used sedatives*—18.5 percent.
4. *Who use sedatives now*—3.0 percent.
5. *Who have ever used tranquilizers*—13.5 percent.
6. *Who use them now*—2.5 percent.

Other NIDA survey findings show that despite the fact that the use of stimulants, sedatives and tranquilizers by teenagers is rising, the percentage of current users (about 1 percent) is minuscule compared with the percentage of teenagers who drink (31 percent) or smoke marijuana (16 percent). Similarly, the proportion of those 26 years old and older who take these pills, though rising, is still under 0.5 percent of that population group.

• **C o m i n g D o w n** . Most of the recent surveys among high-schoolers seem to indicate that the 1980s will see a marked decline in the use of most drugs. The University of Michigan's Institute for Social Research did a survey in the late 1970s that showed that 90 percent of high-school seniors disapproved of the use of heroin, cocaine, LSD, and barbiturates, and more than 80 percent were against the idea of trying any of these substances even once.

SOURCES

Susan Edminston, "The Medicine Everybody Loves," *Today's Health,* January, 1978.

Gallup Poll.

Institute for Social Research.

National Institute for Drug Abuse.

WATCHING TELEVISION

With at least one television set a fixture in 98 percent of U.S. households, it is no surprise that watching television is now the most time-consuming leisure activity in our history. Here is the picture.

• **THE BASIC NUMBERS.** About 95 percent of Americans watch at least one television show on an average day, according to the latest NORC surveys. Nearly one-third of the population watch at least two hours a day, and close to half (47 percent) of the adult population watch an average of three hours of television or more daily. The average amount of time a television set stays on in American homes is now about six hours and ten minutes. The median time is about three hours. In both instances, the figures are slightly down from 1977 figures, but the networks do not appear to be panicking.

• **THE DEMOGRAPHICS.** Television-viewing habits throughout the United States vary considerably, as you might expect, according to demographic factors. Here is how A. C. Nielsen estimates the weekly viewing activity of various population segments:

1. *Children aged 2 to 5*—27.5 hours.
2. *Children aged 6 to 11*—24.5 hours.
3. *Female teens*—21.5 hours.
4. *Male teens*—22.5 hours.
5. *Women aged 25 to 54*—30 hours.
6. *Men aged 25 to 54*—24.5 hours.
7. *Women older than 55*—35 hours.
8. *Men older than 55*—32 hours.
9. *Households of one or two people*—36.5 hours.
10. *Households of five or more people*—61 hours.

A final demographic note: The median television-viewing time among college-educated Americans is two hours and twenty-four minutes, about a third less than the national median.

• **ATTENTION GRABBERS.** Only about 38 percent of children who watch television (according to a Newspaper Advertising Bureau study) devote their full attention to what is going on on the screen. Some of the other things kids do when they watch television in the morning:

1. *Eating or drinking*—42 percent.
2. *Talking*—11 percent.
3. *Playing games*—8 percent.
4. *Dressing or undressing*—14 percent.
5. *Household chores*—1 percent.
6. *Reading or writing*—2 percent.

The same general patterns hold true for afternoon and evening viewing except that kids do less eating and drinking and more talking at those times.

• P R I M E   T I M E . Roughly one-third of the total time Americans spend in front of their televisions is spent during the so-called prime-time hours: Monday through Saturday from 8 P.M. to 11 P.M. and Sunday from 7 P.M. to 11 P.M. The second most watched period is weekdays from 10 A.M. to 4:30 P.M., with Saturday and Sunday from 7 A.M. to 1 P.M. a close third. The demographics here are predictable. Young children make up the smallest proportion of prime-time audiences but are big watchers in the morning. Women are much more likely than men to watch television from 10 A.M. to 4 P.M., which is when the soaps dominate; and men are more likely than women to watch television on weekend afternoons, which is when sports dominate.

SOURCES
NORC.
Newspaper Advertising Bureau.
A. C. Nielsen Company.

STAYING IN SHAPE

Clearly, Americans were more fitness-minded in the 1970s than at any other time in our history, but even so, it is tough to separate out the proportion who work out and play games for fun and relaxation and those who do it specifically to stay in shape. In any event, the most recent surveys suggest that although the proportion of Americans who exercise enough to be fit keeps rising, the number who do it enough to actually *be* fit is relatively small.

• **T H E   B A S I C   N U M B E R S .** According to *The Perrier Study of Fitness in America* about 60 percent of Americans now say they exercise on a regular basis, compared with 24 percent who made the claim in the early 1960s. A closer look at the numbers, though, shows that only a small proportion of this number is exercising with any real degree of regularity.

Proportion of Americans who get:

1. *At least five hours a week of vigorous physical activity*—15 percent.
2. *Three-and-a-half to five hours*—16 percent.
3. *Two-and-a-half to three-and-a-half hours*—28 percent.
4. *No exercise at all*—41 percent.

• **H o w   W e   D o   I t .** Again from the Perrier study, a look at the fitness activities with the largest constituencies:

1. *Walking*—22 percent of adults 18 and older.
2. *Swimming*—17 percent.
3. *Calisthenics*—14 percent.
4. *Bicycling*—13 percent.
5. *Running or jogging*—11 percent.
6. *Tennis*—9 percent.
7. *Basketball*—7 percent.
8. *Hiking*—7 percent.
9. *Softball*—7 percent.
10. *Baseball*—6 percent.

The fastest-growing fitness activities in the United States are running, calisthenics, and racquet sports—all up a good 50 percent or better since 1970. Activities on the decline are swimming, hiking, and bicycling.

• **F i t   R e w a r d s .** Americans who exercise at least five hours a week—the "high actives," in the words of the Perrier study—report a better sense of well-being than those who do not exercise at all. The "benefit gap" between the two groups (as measured in percentage-point differences between actives as a group and nonactives reporting the described feelings) are:

1. *Feelings of optimism*—24 points higher among high actives.
2. *Being influential*—19 points.

3. *Feeling energetic*—33 points.
4. *Feeling relaxed*—13 points.
5. *Feeling outgoing*—13 points.

• **FITNESS FALLOUT.** One aim of the Perrier study was to differentiate the life-styles and health patterns of active exercisers from those of nonactives, but the differences turned out to be slight. Some of the findings:

1. *Active exercisers who smoke*—38 percent.
2. *Nonactives who smoke*—35 percent.
3. *Actives who were not sick at all in 1977*—39 percent.
4. *Nonactives who were not sick at all in 1977*—41 percent.
5. *Actives who were sick about three or four days in 1977* —21 percent.
6. *Nonactives who were sick the same amount of time*— 11 percent.
7. *Actives who spent nine days or more in bed in 1977*— 10 percent.
8. *Nonactives who spent the same amount of time in bed*—23 percent.

Additionally the Perrier study uncovered no major differences in sleeping habits or eating habits except that high-active exercisers tend to be a little more nutrition-minded than once-a-week exercisers. Some related numbers:

1. *High-active exercisers who say that their activity affects the way they eat*—42 percent.
2. *Low-active exercisers who say the same thing*—24 percent.
3. *Runners who say the same thing*—60 percent.
4. *Active exercisers who say their athletic habits increase their appetite*—46 percent.
5. *Decrease their appetite*—9 percent.

• **ON THE RUN.** When a "runners only" segment of the Perrier study was asked to talk about motivation for running, here is what the most active runners gave as their chief motives:

1. *Staying in shape*—21 percent.
2. *Building good stamina*—17 percent.
3. *Toning legs and other muscles*—15 percent.
4. *Good, solid exercise*—13 percent.

Here is what they said *was not* a factor in their running:

1. *Fun of it*—17 percent.
2. *Relaxation*—12 percent.
3. *Losing weight*—12 percent.
4. *Chance to compete with self*—14 percent.

And what the perceived benefits were:

1. *Greater sense of well-being*—80 percent.
2. *Less tension*—62 percent.
3. *Better appearance*—48 percent.
4. *More self-confidence*—33 percent.
5. *Better sex life*—28 percent.

SOURCES
The Perrier Study of Fitness in America.

VII OUR RELATIONSHIPS

LOVE AND COURTSHIP

No subject in America is written about, sung about and talked about more, yet, studied less than love. But maybe not for long. Over the past few years a handful of sociologists and social psychologists have moved into a territory once considered the exclusive domain of poets. Here is a glimpse of what they've come up with in the way of numbers.

• **A T F I R S T S I G H T .** In 1970, a team of researchers headed by Eugene J. Kanin probed more than 700 younger lovers in order to find out *when* in the relationship they knew they were in love. The results, alas, pretty much demolish the idea of love at first sight.

1. *Men who said that love came prior to the fourth date—* 20 percent.
2. *Women who said the same thing—* 15 percent.
3. *Men who weren't sure by the twentieth date if they were in love—* 30 percent.
4. *Women who felt the same way—* 43 percent.

• **T H E R E A L T H I N G .** From sociologists Elaine and G. William Walster, these numbers on how often it comes along, and how long it lasts.

1. *Americans who were in love at least once by their late teens—* 97 percent.
2. *How often "true" love comes to the average American in a lifetime—* 1.2 times for men, and 1.3 times for women, according to a study by W. M. Kephart, cited by the Walsters.
3. *How much less passionately the average married couple feels about each other after 10 to 17 years of marriage as compared to after three years of marriage—* 14 percent less, according to a study by psychologist Zick Rubin.
4. *Casualty rate of college love affairs—* about 50 percent.
5. *College love affairs that break up because of a "mutual" decision—* 15 percent.

• **S H E ' S F U N N Y T H A T W A Y .** According to a *Redbook* survey on male sexuality, the quality in women that men treasure the most is the love that the woman has for the man. The numbers, based on the percentage of men who consider the following traits important in the ideal partner:

1. *"Her love for me"*—85 percent.
2. *Intelligence*—80 percent.
3. *Shapely legs*—70 percent.
4. *Sense of humor*—65 percent.
5. *Self-confidence*—47 percent.
6. *Slim hips and rear*—38 percent.
7. *Large hips and rear*—30 percent.
8. *Large breasts*—30 percent.
9. *Small breasts*—30 percent.
10. *Pretty face*—28 percent.

And what women consider important in men, based on a 1971 *Psychology Today* poll:

1. *The ability to love*—96 percent.
2. *Willingness to stand up for beliefs*—92 percent.
3. *Warmth*—89 percent.
4. *Self-confidence*—86 percent.
5. *Gentleness*—86 percent.

And *least* important:

1. *Past sexual conquests*—only 4 percent consider this trait very important or essential in a man.
2. *Height*—11 percent.
3. *Physical strength*—21 percent.
4. *Physical attractiveness*—29 percent.

• Y O U N G   L O V E . From a 1977 Gallup Youth Survey, some numbers on the romantic escapades of teenagers:

1. *American teens who, by age 16, had already had their first date*—61 percent.
2. *Teen boys 16 to 18 years old who say they kiss on the first date*—50 percent.
3. *Teen girls 16 to 18 years old who report the same thing*—37 percent.

And from a *Seventeen* survey, these dating attitudes and practices among teenage girls:

1. *Teen girls who like the boy to take the lead in making out*—71 percent.

2. *Who don't mind shyness in a boy*—50 percent.
3. *Who like the macho image*—15.5 percent.
4. *Who would date a boy over parents' objections*—71 percent.
5. *Who would date a younger boy*—50 percent.
6. *Who expect the boy to pay all expenses*—50 percent.
7. *Who are turned off by heavy drinkers*—89 percent.
8. *Who appreciate intellectuality*—50 percent.
9. *Who are turned on by a boy who is a good dancer*—50 percent.
10. *Who believe strongly that the girl should take the lead in making out*—5 percent.

• **MUTUAL ATTRACTION.** A study in the late 1960s involving students from three U.S. colleges and one Canadian college revealed the following value scale of qualities college students look for in dating partners. Each student was given a list of eighteen traits to rank according to importance. Here is how the lists came out for men and women.

Men:

1. *Dependable character.*
2. *Mutual attraction.*
3. *Emotional stability.*
4. *Pleasing disposition.*
5. *Desire for home and children.*
6. *Good cook.*
7. *Refinement.*
8. *Ambition.*
9. *Good health.*
10. *Education and intelligence.*
11. *Good looks.*
12. *Sociability.*
13. *Similar educational background.*
14. *Similar religious background.*
15. *Chastity.*
16. *Favorable social status.*
17. *Similar political background.*
18. *Good financial prospects.*

Women:

1. *Emotional Stability.*
2. *Dependable character.*
3. *Mutual Attraction.*

4. *Pleasing disposition.*
5. *Desire for home and children.*
6. *Ambition.*
7. *Education and intelligence.*
8. *Refinement.*
9. *Similar educational background.*
10. *Good health.*
11. *Similar religious background.*
12. *Good financial prospects.*
13. *Sociability.*
14. *Favorable social status.*
15. *Chastity.*
16. *Good cook.*
17. *Good looks.*
18. *Similar political background.*

SOURCES

Gallup Poll.

Judy Gaylin, "What Do Girls Look for in Boys," *Seventeen*, March 1979.

Eugene J. Kanin et al., "A Research Note on Male-Female Differentials in the Experience of Heterosexual Love," 1970.

W. M. Kephart, "Some Correlates of Romantic Love," 1967.

Carol Tavris, "*Redbook* Report on Male Sexuality," February 1979.

Elaine and G. William Walster, *A New Look at Love*, 1977.

MARRIAGE

Marriage has been taking its lumps as of late, but it is in no danger of expiring, as the statistics well show.

• **THE BASIC NUMBERS.** As mentioned earlier (see Part I, "Americans at a Glance") more than 90 percent of Americans marry at least once in their lifetimes. At present 70 percent of all American men older than 18 are married, and 65 percent of all American adult women are married. Some other number facts about American marriages:

1. *Proportion of currently married people who have been divorced at least once*—20.0 percent.
2. *Marriages in which husband and wife are the same age*—12.0 percent.
3. *In which husband is one or two years older than wife* —26 percent.
4. *Husband is three or four years older than wife*—20.0 percent.
5. *Five to nine years older than wife*—16.5 percent.
6. *Ten or more years older than wife*—7.0 percent.
7. *Marriages in which wife is older than husband*—14.5 percent.
8. *Marriages in which husband and wife have different religious backgrounds*—10.0 percent (and rising).
9. *Interracial marriages*—1.0 percent.

• OLD-FASHIONED IDEAS. In putting together their book *Husbands and Wives,* Dr. Anthony Pietropinto and Jacqueline Simenauer asked nearly 4,000 married men and women what influences led them to marriage. Here are some of the replies:

1. *Love*—56 percent of women; 39 percent of men.
2. *Desire to set up a home*—26 percent.
3. *Companionship*—25 percent.
4. *Pressure to get married*—5 percent of women.

• GETTING ALONG. One of the most detailed views of marital life in America emerged from the Institute for Social Research study, *The Quality of American Life.* Here is a synopsis of some of the findings:

1. *Married couples who "never" fight about money*—22 percent.
2. *"Rarely"*—35 percent.
3. *"Sometimes"*—32 percent.
4. *"Often"*—8 percent.
5. *"Very often"*—4 percent.
6. *Couples who do things together "all the time"*—38 percent.
7. *"Very often"*—31 percent.
8. *"Often"*—16 percent.
9. *"Sometimes"*—12 percent.
10. *"Hardly ever"*—4 percent.

11. *Wives who say their husbands understand them "very well"*—42 percent.
12. *"Fairly well"*—48 percent.
13. *"Not very well"*—7 percent.
14. *"Not very well at all"*—3 percent.
15. *Husbands who say their wives understand them "very well"*—50 percent.
16. *"Fairly well"*—44 percent.
17. *"Not very well"*—5 percent.
18. *"Not very well at all"*—1 percent.

• **S A T I S F A C T I O N** . Most surveys, including the Institute for Social Research survey, show that a very high proportion of married people in the United States describe their marriages as either "very happy" or "pretty happy." A 1978 NORC survey showed a 97-percent satisfaction rate (based on people who described their marriages as "very happy" or "pretty happy"), and nearly 90 percent of the couples surveyed by the Institute for Social Research expressed very high marital-satisfaction levels. And whenever married couples in the United States are asked if they have ever wished they had married anybody else, the proportion of men and women who answer "never" is generally upwards of 70 percent, with less than 10 percent saying they have second thoughts often.

• **B E D D Y   B Y E** . Of the one hundred married couples interviewed for a study published in *Family Circle*, 80 percent described their marriages as either "very happy" or "happy," but 90 percent said they had a "less than perfect sexual relationship."

• **C A L I F O R N I A   S U I T E S** . California has one of the highest divorce rates in the United States. But the findings of a 1979 *Los Angeles Times* poll suggest that marriage may not be as battered an institution in California as most people think. Some of the highlights.

Californians who say they are "completely satisfied" with their present marital situation:

1. *Total adult population*—60 percent.
2. *Married*—70 percent.
3. *Single*—35 percent.
4. *Divorced*—35 percent.

"Fairly well satisfied":

1. *Total*—23 percent.
2. *Married*—24 percent.
3. *Single*—23 percent.
4. *Divorced*—18 percent.

"Not too satisfied":

1. *Total*—5 percent.
2. *Married*—3 percent.
3. *Single*—7 percent.
4. *Divorced*—9 percent.

"Not at all satisfied":

1. *Total*—5 percent.
2. *Married*—2 percent.
3. *Single*—7 percent.
4. *Divorced*—10 percent.

Other findings:

1. *Married people who consider a divorce very likely*—8 percent.
2. *Who think their marriage will survive*—70 percent.

Although women were slightly more likely to express dissatisfaction with their current marital status than men, the overall differences between male and female responses were relatively small.

• **WHO RULES THE ROOST.** A 1971 study by Richard Center, Bertram Raven, and Aroldo Rodrigues presented this picture of the balance of power in American marriages:

1. *Marriages in which the husband and wife have separate, but reasonably equal, areas of responsibility*—70 percent.
2. *Marriages in which the huband and wife share in making all big decisions*—20 percent.
3. *Marriages in which the husband makes all the decisions*—10 percent.
4. *Marriages in which the wife makes all the decisions*—5 percent.

• **THE SECOND TIME AROUND.** It could well be better. The latest Census Bureau statistics show that less than 10 percent of remarried divorced people get divorced a second time. Divorced men, incidentally, are three times more likely to remarry than divorced women.

• **B YE   B YE ,   B IRDIE** . Conventional wisdom has always held that when the last child leaves the household, the woman of the house is supposed to feel a sense of loss and go into what is known as the "empty nest" syndrome. But a 1978 study by Elizabeth Bates Harkins suggests that the effects of the syndrome are generally mild (if they happen at all) and usually disappear within two years. Indeed, the study points out that the majority of American women are better off psychologically once the kids have flown the coop—just so long as the departure does not come as a surprise and is not the result of something tragic.

SOURCES

Hugh Carter and Paul C. Glick, *Marriage and Divorce: A Social and Economic Study*, 1970.

Richard Center, Bertram H. Raven and Aroldo Rodrigues, "Conjugal Power Structure; A Re-examination," 1971.

Ellen Frank and Carol Anderson, "How Important Is Sex to a Happy Marriage?" *Family Circle*, March 13, 1979.

Elizabeth Bates Harkins, "Effect of Empty Nest Transition on Married Women," 1978.

Eleanor B. Luckey, "Number of Years Married as Related to Personality Perception and Marital Satisfaction," 1966.

Anthony Pietropinto and Jacqueline Simenauer, *Husbands and Wives: A Nationwide Survey of Marriage*, 1979.

B. C. Rollins and H. Feldman, "Marital Satisfaction over the Family Life," 1970.

Benjamin Schlesinger, "Remarriage as Family Reorganization for Divorced Persons: A Canadian Study," 1970.

U.S. Bureau of the Census, Statistical Abstract of the United States: 1978.

U.S. Bureau of the Census, *Divorce, Child Custody and Child Support*, 1979.

DIVORCE

Although in the late 1970s there were some signs that the divorce rate in the United States was leveling off, the ten years between 1970 and 1979 registered the highest number of divorces in this country's history. The numbers speak for themselves.

• **T HE B A S I C N U M B E R S .** An average of about two million Americans have been getting divorced each year since 1975, which is about two-and-a-half times the number of people who were divorced in the early 1960s and 25 percent more than the 1970 total—this during a period in which the number of marriages was actually declining. The actual divorce rate, which was 2.5 per 1,000 population in 1965, has more than doubled and is now 5.1 per 1,000. Based on the numbers alone, the average married person who is 30 years old now stands a one in three chance of being divorced within the next ten years and an estimated 40 percent of current marriages will fail if the present trend persists. That is the bad news. The good news is that the number of children involved in divorce cases is down somewhat. Some of the statistical fallout of the divorce rate:

1. *Proportion of American women who are either divorced or separated*—14.0 percent (up from 5.0 percent in 1970).
2. *White women 25 to 34 who are divorced or separated* —14.5 percent in 1977.
3. *Black women in the same age-group who are either divorced or separated*—36.0 percent in 1977.
4. *Proportion of American men 45 to 54 who are divorced or separated*—8.0 percent in 1977.
5. *American women 45 to 54 who are divorced or separated*—12.0 percent in 1977.
6. *Median age at divorce after first marriage*—30.5 for men; 28.0 for women (no change since 1975).
7. *Median duration of marriage*—6.5 years (up from the 1950 median but the same throughout 1970).
8. *Children per divorce*—1.03 (down from 1.22 in 1970).

• **P A Y I N G F O R I T .** A Census Bureau study gathered in 1976 and published in 1979 produced some surprising numbers relating to the economic aspects of divorce. Here are some of them:

1. *Divorced mothers receiving child support*—about 40 percent.
2. *Unmarried mothers receiving child support*—4 percent.
3. *Average child support being paid by fathers in 1975*—$2,430.
4. *Divorced or separated women for whom child support was less than 10 percent of total income*—50 percent.
5. *Was more than 50 percent of total income*—5 percent.

• GROUNDS. George Livinger's study of 600 divorced couples in the late 1960s turned up the following reasons for the split.

Cited by women:

1. *Mental cruelty*—40 percent.
2. *Financial problems*—39 percent.
3. *Physical abuse*—36 percent.
4. *Drinking*—27 percent.
5. *Infidelity*—24 percent.

Cited by men:

1. *Mental cruelty*—30 percent.
2. *Infidelity*—20 percent.
3. *Financial problems*—9 percent.
4. *Drinking*—5 percent.
5. *Physical abuse*—3 percent.

• MALE ADVANTAGE. Several recent studies on the trauma of divorce suggest that, everything else being equal, women have a tougher time dealing with it than men.

From a study by David Chiriboga and Loraine Cutler:

1. *Women who said their health suffered greatly during the divorce ordeal*—53 percent.
2. *Men who said the same thing*—43 percent.
3. *Women who had trouble sleeping*—35 percent.
4. *Men who had trouble sleeping*—12 percent.
5. *Women who were severely depressed*—44 percent.
6. *Men who were severely depressed*—21 percent.
7. *Women who gained weight*—30 percent.
8. *Men who gained weight*—33 percent.

9. *Women who drank more*—34 percent.
10. *Men who drank more*—32 percent.

• **B R E A K I N G L O O S E .** Divorce itself may be a miserable experience, but, if nothing else, the sex life of the average divorced woman is better than it was during the marriage—at least that was so in the 1960s, according to a study by Paul H. Gebhard.

Of the 632 divorced women whom Gebhard studied, the proportion who had sexual intercourse:

1. *At least once since the divorce and found it satisfying* —82 percent.
2. *With more than one partner*—70 percent.

Gebhard found that most divorced women get back on "the sex trail" within a year after the end of their marriage.

SOURCES
Angus Campbell, *Quality of American Life.*
David Chiriboga and Loraine Cutler, "Stress Responses Among Divorced Men and Women," 1979.
Paul Gebhard, "Postmarital Coitus Among Widows and Divorcees," 1970.
George Livinger, "Sources of Marital Dissatisfaction among Applicants to Divorce," 1966.
U.S. National Center for Health Statistics, Vital Statistics of the U.S.

MOTHERHOOD

Having a baby is something that happens in the lives of three out of four American women before they reach the age of 35. But the major trend over the past twenty years is that women are simply not having as many babies as they once did, and are finished up with childbearing at an earlier age.

• **T H E B A S I C N U M B E R S .** The number of women who have babies each year in the United States has been averaging about 3,150,000 since 1973. This translates to a birthrate of about 14.8 per 1,000. The birthrate is down by about 38 percent since 1960 and by 22 percent since 1970. It is also down in all age brackets except for the 10–14 age-group where the rate is only 1.2 per 1,000, anyway. The 1976 rates in other age-groups are as follows:

1. *Fifteen- to 19-year-olds*—53.5 per 1,000 (down from 89.1 in 1960).
2. *Twenty- to 24-year-olds*—112.1 (down from 258.1 in 1960).
3. *Twenty-five- to 29-year-olds*—108.8 (down from 197.4 in 1960).
4. *Thirty-five- to 39-year-olds*—19.0 (down from 56.2 in 1960).
5. *Forty- to 45-year-olds*—4.3 (down from 15.5 in 1960).
6. *Forty-five- to 49-year-olds*—0.2 (down from 0.9 in 1960).

• **EXPECTATION RATE.** More married Americans than ever before are now saying that they do not want *any* children, and fewer are saying that they want more than four children. The "expectation" rates for white women and black women are fairly similar. In 1976 the Census Bureau asked married American women between the ages of 18 and 24 how many children they expected to have before they dropped out of the baby-making business. Here is how the percentages came out.

For white women:

1. *None*—5.5 percent.
2. *One*—12.5 percent.
3. *Two*—56.5 percent.
4. *Three*—18.5 percent.
5. *Four or more*—7.5 percent.

For black women:

1. *None*—5.0 percent.
2. *One*—16.5 percent.
3. *Two*—50.0 percent.
4. *Three*—22.5 percent.
5. *Four or more*—5.5 percent.

For both black and white women, the trend in expectation rates is the same: more women saying they expect to have none, one, or two; fewer women saying they expect to have three, four, or more.

• **E ARLY A RRIVALS** . The proportion of American women who have their first babies either before, or within seven months of, marriage has remained fairly stable throughout the 1970s, but it is still on the high side—about 22 percent for all women and better than 50 percent for black women. Black women, too, are twice as likely to have their first child by the age of 18 than are white women. And generally speaking, women from lower-income families and lower educational levels start having babies earlier (and also get married earlier) than women in higher socioeconomic groups.

• **W HERE'S P OPPA** ? Nearly one out of seven babies (about 15 percent) in the United States today is born out of wedlock. But even though this proportion is up from 10.7 percent in 1970, the actual *number* of out-of-wedlock babies is on the decline. The reason for this apparent paradox is that the overall birthrate among married women has dropped, which has produced a rise in the *proportion* of unmarried mothers. The numbers:

1. *Births to unmarried women in 1976—468,000.*
2. *To girls younger than 15—10,000.*
3. *To girls 15 to 19—225,000.*
4. *To girls younger than 19—50 percent.*
5. *To black women—58 percent.*

• **F INISHING U P** . The average American mother today has her first baby at the age of 22—about two years after she gets married. Most women are usually finished with childbearing by the age of 26. Sixty years ago the average married woman did not have her last child until the age of 32.

• **R ELUCTANT M OTHERS** . A 1976 study by the National Survey of Family Growth suggests that more than one of every ten babies born in the United States each year is either "not wanted" or "probably not wanted" at the time of conception. The percentage of unwanted births among various demographic groups looks like this:

1. *All married and unmarried mothers—12.0 percent.*
2. *Married mothers—10.0 percent.*
3. *Married white mothers—8.0 percent.*
4. *Married black mothers—21.0 percent.*

5. *Married and unmarried mothers with less than a high-school education—17.5 percent.*
6. *Married and unmarried mothers who are college graduates—4.5 percent.*

• A B O R T I O N   S T O R Y . For every ten babies born in the United States in 1976, there were three legal—and no one knows how many illegal—abortions. And some people are predicting that by the time 1980 rolls around, there will be almost as many abortions in the United States as there are live births. Even the Hyde Amendment, which limited the circumstances under which a woman could have a government-funded abortion, has seemingly failed to make much of a dent in the abortion rate. Some of the numbers:

1. *Legal abortions in 1976—1,179,300.*
2. *Proportion of abortions performed on married women —22 percent.*
3. *On women younger than 20—32 percent.*
4. *On black and Hispanic women—25 percent.*
5. *On women who had at least one living child—35–40 percent.*

SOURCE
U.S. Bureau of the Census, *Statistical Abstract of the United States: 1978.*

RAISING KIDS

The child-rearing practices and attitudes of American parents are clearly more permissive today than they were, say, twenty-five years ago, but the trend toward permissiveness seems to have leveled off, and, if anything, the drift is toward more traditional views. Here are some glimpses of child-rearing patterns gleaned from several of the more recent studies.

• S P A R I N G   T H E   R O D . *The General Mills American Family Report 1976–77* divided American parents into three groups, based on attitudes toward discipline:

1. *Permissive—26 percent.*
2. *Middle-of-the-roaders—51 percent.*
3. *Strict—23 percent.*

Mothers, in general, tend to be more permissive in their parenting views than fathers; and younger parents, as a rule, are more permissive than older parents. It appears, too, that the larger the family is, the more permissive in their attitudes the parents tend to be.

• D I S H I N G   I T   O U T . The two most common forms of punishment in American homes today are yelling and scolding, and spanking. Here is a list of the major disciplinary measures taken in American family homes (based on findings reported in *The General Mills American Family Report*), and the proportion of parents who take them:

1. *Yelling or scolding*—52 percent.
2. *Spanking*—50 percent.
3. *Sending the kids to their rooms*—38 percent.
4. *Not allowing the kids to go out to play*—32 percent.
5. *Not letting the kids watch television*—25 percent.
6. *Sending the kids to bed*—23 percent.
7. *Threatening the kids*—15 percent.
8. *Assigning extra chores*—12 percent.
9. *Holding back allowance*—9 percent.

• R E W A R D S . Most American parents reward their kids with a kiss or a hug. When it comes to more *tangible* rewards, the list looks like this:

1. *Taking the kids someplace special*—48 percent.
2. *Buying them something special*—40 percent.
3. *Giving them something special to eat*—26 percent.
4. *Giving them money*—20 percent.
5. *Allowing them extra television viewing*—20 percent.

Patterns? Younger parents generally tend to be more demonstrative than older parents, and strict parents are more likely than permissive parents to buy the children something specific rather than hand out a straight cash payment.

• O N L Y   H U M A N . Most American parents, regardless of how they view discipline, admit to being "frequently or occasionally inconsistent in disciplining their children," and about one-third of parents concede they have "often" or "sometimes" lost control and punished children more than they deserved. Strict parents are more likely to admit to inconsistencies in the parenting approach than permissive parents; and single parents show the highest degree of self-doubt, with 71 percent saying they are occasionally or frequently inconsistent.

• **H E L P W A N T E D .** Most American parents are reluctant to seek outside advice when their children have behavioral problems, but a high proportion of them recognize that they need help in certain parenting areas. The areas singled out the most are:

1. *Drug problems*—49 percent.
2. *New teaching methods in school*—42 percent.
3. *Convincing the children not to smoke*—37 percent.
4. *Disciplinary problems*—36 percent.
5. *General problem of being a parent*—34 percent.
6. *Medical problems*—34 percent.
7. *Nutrition*—34 percent.
8. *Teaching children about religion*—32 percent.
9. *Teaching children about sex*—31 percent.

On the other hand, only 18 percent of American parents say they would seek outside help if their child was "very unhappy" and only 44 percent say they would seek advice if their child got into trouble with the police.

• **T O U C H Y S U B J E C T S .** Some of the problems parents find difficult to discuss with their children, and the proportion of parents who have these difficulties:

1. *Homosexuality*—45 percent.
2. *Death*—42 percent.
3. *Sex*—42 percent.
4. *Family problems*—25 percent.
5. *Own shortcomings*—24 percent.
6. *Money*—22 percent.
7. *Own feelings*—21 percent.
8. *Smoking*—15 percent.
9. *Illegal drugs*—13 percent.
10. *Drinking*—12 percent.

• **B I G D E A L S .** The biggest hassles faced by parents of children younger than 12, and the proportion of parents who complain about these hassles, concern the following:

1. *Children snacking between meals*—32 percent.
2. *Whining or crying*—30 percent (mainly among parents whose children are 6 or younger).

3. *Children not eating what they should*—27 percent.
4. *Children asking for things they see advertised*—26 percent.
5. *Irresponsibility (children not doing chores)*—26 percent (mostly parents of children older than 6).
6. *Disrespect from children*—26 percent.
7. *Children's temper tantrums*—35 percent (mostly parents of children younger than 6).
8. *Children watching too much television*—23 percent.
9. *Children not going to bed on time*—23 percent.
10. *Children not telling the truth*—16 percent.

•**O**n **the T**ake. About half the teenagers in the United States receive an allowance (according to a 1972 U.S. Department of Health, Education, and Welfare survey), but the terms vary among different situations. Some examples:

1. *Families in which kids have to perform chores or duties to earn allowance*—70 percent.
2. *In which allowance is sometimes withheld as a means of punishment*—25 percent.
3. *In which both parents decide on the amount of allowance*—50 percent.
4. *In which the mother decides the allowance figure*—27 percent.
5. *In which the father decides*—19 percent.

Girls, in general, are more likely to receive an allowance than boys—probably because a higher percentage of teenage boys have jobs by the time they are 16 or 17.

•**R**ating **G**ame. Parents may not be the best judges of how their children behave, but who else is in a better position to make those judgments. Here is a listing of some of the feelings parents expressed about their children in a 1972 HEW survey.
Proportion of parents who:

1. *Consider their children fussy eaters*—10 percent.
2. *Are concerned about their children's weight*—20 percent.
3. *Are pleased with their children's ability to make and keep friends*—82 percent.
4. *Are well acquainted with the majority of their children's friends*—75 percent.

5. *Are satisfied with how their kids are doing in school*— 95 percent.
6. *Describe their children as being "very nervous"*—4 percent.
7. *Describe their children as being "not nervous at all"*— 50 percent.
8. *Say they have "no trouble at all" raising their children*—60 percent.
9. *Describe their children as being in "excellent health"*—96 percent.

•FREEDOM NOW. The degree of autonomy enjoyed by the average American teenager varies according to the age of the child and to the specific activity. Here is a look at what kids can—and cannot—do on their own, and the percentage of kids who fit into each category:

1. *Can spend their allowance money as they see fit*—52 percent.
2. *Can choose the friends they want to pal around with*—54 percent for boys; 39 percent for girls.
3. *Can choose the clothes they want*—33 percent.
4. *Can stay out as late as they want*—20 percent for 17-year-old boys; less than 10 percent for 17-year-old girls.

•TELEVISION MONITORS. A Gallup poll in 1977 showed that nearly half the parents in the United States restrict the *types* of programs their children watch, and more than a third limit the number of hours their children watch television. The numbers:

1. *Parents who restrict the types of programs their children watch*—49 percent.
2. *Parents of children aged 4 to 7 who do so*—63 percent.
3. *Parents of children aged 8 to 12 who do so*—60 percent.
4. *Parents who restrict the number of hours their children watch TV*—36 percent.
5. *Parents of children aged 13 to 17 who do so*—30 percent.
6. *Parents of children aged 8 to 12 who do so*—43 percent.

•RUNAWAYS. Approximately one out of every ten American teenagers has run away from home at least once, but only

3 percent of the American teenage population have run away more than once. No major differences separate the runaway patterns of boys and girls, although the proportion of runaways is much higher among older teens than among younger teens.

SOURCES

Gallup Poll.

The General Mills American Family Report 1976–77.

U.S. Department of Health, Education, and Welfare, *Behavioral Patterns of Youth 12–17*, 1972.

FRIENDSHIP

Americans are probably as gregarious as anybody in the world (with the exception, perhaps, of Australians who, according to Gallup surveys, are *the* most gregarious people on earth), and, as the proportion of single people in the population continues to rise, the value we place on friendship appears to be increasing.

• THE BASIC NUMBERS. A survey by the Gallup International Research Institute looked into the number of close friends the people in various countries had. Here's how Americans fared:

1. *Americans with only one or two close friends*—10 percent.
2. *With between three and five close friends*—22 percent.
3. *With between six and nine*—16 percent.
4. *With ten or more*—47 percent.
5. *With none*—3 percent.

In general, Americans are slightly more friendship-oriented than Europeans and considerably more friendship-oriented than Asians or Africans. Nearly 52 percent of the sampling of the population from India, for instance, had *no* close friends outside the family.

• FRIENDS INDEED. From Frank Andrews and Stephen Withey, a glimpse of how much satisfaction Americans derive from their friendships.

1. *Americans who are delighted with their friends*—12 percent.

2. *Pleased*—45 percent.
3. *Mostly satisfied*—37 percent.
4. *Mixed*—1 percent.
5. *Mostly dissatisfied*—1 percent.
6. *Americans who are delighted with the things they do and the times they have with their friends*—15 percent.
7. *Pleased*—43 percent.
8. *Mostly satisfied*—31 percent.
9. *Mixed*—8 percent.
10. *Mostly dissatisfied*—2 percent.

• ROOM AT THE TOP. The desire to make new friends and develop new social relationships tends to vary among Americans according to a number of factors, chief among them age.

From the *Playboy Report on American Men:*

1. *Students 18 to 22 who list developing new relationships as one of the two or three things most important to them*—30 percent.
2. *Non-students 18 to 22*—21 percent.
3. *Twenty-three to 29-year-olds*—14 percent.
4. *Thirty to 40-year-olds*—13 percent.
5. *Forty to 50-year-olds*—10 percent.

And Angus Campbell found that the more friends a person has, the more that person is likely to want to make *new* friends. Only 25 percent of the respondents in *The Quality of Life* study who had fewer friends than average, for instance, expressed any real interest in making new friends.

SOURCES

Frank M. Andrews and Stephen B. Withey, *Social Indicators of Well-Being.*

Angus Campbell et al., *The Quality of American Life.*

The Playboy Report on American Men.

VIII SEX

WHAT TURNS US ON

Since humans are the only animals for whom biology does not dictate the arousal preliminaries, a good deal of sex research has focused on what is, and what is not, sexually arousing to various types of people. Here is what we know about Americans.

• THE GENERAL PICTURE. The sexual revolution appears to have narrowed the gulf that separates men and women in terms of what things are arousing to each sex, but there are still some significant differences. Probably the biggest single difference is that women are not as aroused by purely *visual* stimuli as men are. On the other hand, men do not seem to have as many erogenous zones.

• EROTICA. The proliferation of pornography in the form of movies, photographs, books, has seemingly reduced the arousal properties of erotica in general, but the patterns of female and male responses are probably no different today from what they were when Kinsey looked into the matter in 1953. Here is a glimpse of what he found out then:

1. *Men who get stimulated by erotic photographs*—77 percent.
2. *Women who get stimulated by erotic photographs*—32 percent.
3. *Men who get stimulated by sexy literature*—59 percent.
4. *Women who get stimulated by sexy literature*—60 percent.
5. *Men who get stimulated by hearing dirty stories*—47 percent.
6. *Women who get stimulated by hearing dirty stories*—14 percent.

• DIFFERENT STROKES. The most recent studies on sexual arousal have turned up some definite correlations between a person's age, personality, and sexual experience and the arousal properties of erotica. Some examples:
Erotic films appear to have *more* arousal power:

1. *Among younger people than among older people.*
2. *Among women who are sexually experienced than among women who are not sexually experienced.*

3. *In settings where there are only a few people than in settings where there are a lot of people.*

4. *In settings where the atmosphere is casual than in settings that are stiff (no pun intended) and formal.*

Two other notes of interest: (*a*) there seems to be no relationship between what is usually referred to as "moral character" and the degree to which you get aroused by erotic materials; and (*b*) the guiltier you are about sex, the less likely you are to be aroused by erotica.

• PROJECTION FIGURES. One of the things researchers for *The Report of the Commission on Obscenity and Pornography* did was to gather small groups of people together, show them different variations of explicit sex in films, and poll them afterward to learn which scenes they found most arousing. The general findings:

1. *Straight heterosexual sex*—more sexually arousing for men and women combined than any other type of explicit sex scene.

2. *Group sex*—a bigger turn-on for men (bigger, in fact, than straight heterosexual sex), but less so for women.

3. *Homosexual scenes*—greater arousal level for men watching two women making love than for women watching two men making love; but women are less turned off by scenes depicting female homosexuality than are men by scenes of male homosexuality.

4. *Heterosexual oral sex*—arousing to both sexes, but more so to women than men.

5. *Sadomasochistic sex*—low arousal levels for both sexes.

6. *Masturbation*—greater arousal level for men watching women masturbate than for women watching men do it; but women are less "disgusted" by the sight of a woman masturbating than men are at the sight of a man masturbating.

• MEN'S DEPARTMENT. From the "*Redbook* Survey of Male Sexuality" comes the following list of what most men find sexually exciting.

Proportion of men who "strongly" or "moderately" agree that these turn-ons are "exciting":

1. *A woman taking the initiative*—80 percent.
2. *Perfume and other fragrances*—77 percent.

3. *Lacy lingerie*—75 percent.
4. *A woman using sexually explicit language*—45 percent.
5. *Vaginal odor*—40 percent.

The big turn-offs, according to the men surveyed in the poll are:

1. *Heavy makeup*—80 percent.
2. *Leg or underarm hair*—70 percent.
3. *A pregnant woman*—50 percent.
4. *A menstruating woman*—42 percent.

SOURCES

Alfred C. Kinsey et al., *Sexual Behavior in the Human Female*, 1953.

U.S. Government, *The Report of the Commission on Obscenity and Pornography*, 1970.

Carol Tavris, "*Redbook* Report on Male Sexuality," *Redbook*, February 1978.

WHAT BIRTH-CONTROL METHODS WE USE

The Pill is still number one, but sterilization is coming up fast on the outside.

• **THE BASIC NUMBERS.** About three out of four American couples practice birth control of one kind or another. Here is a rough breakdown, based on several recent surveys:

1. *The Pill*—22 percent.
2. *Vasectomy*—10 percent.
3. *IUD*—7 percent.
4. *Condoms*—7 percent.
5. *Diaphragm*—3 percent.
6. *Contraceptive foam*—3 percent.
7. *Withdrawal or rhythm*—5 percent.
8. *Tubal ligation for the purpose of birth control*—2 percent.
9. *Female sterilization for reasons other than birth control*—10 percent.

• **THE DEMOGRAPHICS.** Surveys relating to contraceptive practices in the United States have turned up some definite demographic patterns. Younger women, for instance, are much more likely to use the Pill than older women, and the same pattern holds true (albeit to a lesser degree) for the IUD, the diaphragm, and foam. More striking differences turn up when the contraceptive practices of blacks and whites are compared. White women and black women show similar patterns, but white men are three time more likely than blacks to use a condom, and ten times more likely to have had a vasectomy.

• DOCTOR'S CHOICE. A 1978 *Redbook* magazine poll showed that 46 percent of American gynecologists "usually" recommended the Pill to their patients. Among woman gynecologists, however, the most frequently recommended contraceptive aid was the diaphragm.

SOURCES
Redbook, August 1978.
U.S. Bureau of the Census, *Statistical Abstract of the United States: 1978.*

HOW IT WAS THE FIRST TIME FOR US

Two things have been happening to virginity in the United States: The relative proportion of virgins is decreasing; and the average age at which the deflowering occurs is getting lower for both men and women.

• THE BASIC NUMBERS. Given the fact that more than 90 percent of Americans eventually get married, the proportion of American men and women who remain virgins throughout their lifetime is very small—probably less than 2 percent. Here are some figures on the proportion of virgins among various age and gender segments of the population, based on the most recent surveys:

1. *Male virgins 18 to 34 years old*—13 percent (according to Morton Hunt's survey for *Playboy*).
2. *Female virgins 18 to 34*—23 percent.
3. *Male virgins 17 or younger*—25–35 percent.
4. *Female virgins 17 or younger*—66–75 percent.
5. *Proportion of middle-class white American women who were virgins on their wedding night*—10 percent since 1973.

• **D e m o g r a p h i c s .** Kinsey's findings in the 1950s showed some vast differences in the proportion of college males who had premarital intercourse and the proportion of noncollege males with premarital experience of intercourse. More recent surveys indicate a sharp reduction in the gap. This is what the demographic analyses show in general:

1. Although premarital intercourse is more frequent among lower-educated, lower-income groups than in higher socioeconomic groups, the difference is rapidly becoming insignificant.
2. Urban young men and young women are more likely to be sexually active before marriage than rural men and women.
3. Black males show a higher rate of premarital sexual activity than white males, but the difference in the sexual activity of black and white females is smaller.

• **W i l l Y o u L o v e M e T o m o r r o w ?** In a 1973 study Donald Carns looked into the conditions surrounding "first time" sexual experiences. This is what he learned:

1. *Women who were "in love" with the first man they slept with*—50 percent.
2. *Men who were "in love" with the first woman they slept with*—10 percent.
3. *Men who were "happy" after their first taste of sexual intercourse*—90 percent.
4. *Women who were "happy" after the first time*—66 percent. (NOTE: A good percentage of the women who were not happy explained later that they were "worried about getting pregnant," but later on, when these fears were eased, they had a more positive attitude about the experience.)
5. *Women who did not tell anybody else about their first sexual experience*—25 percent.
6. *Men who did not tell anybody else about it*—18 percent.
7. *Women who told more than five people*—22 percent.
8. *Men who told more than five people*—63 percent.

• **S t r i k i n g O u t .** Even in this era of casual sex, not every male-female liaison culminates in the sack. So a handful of studies over the past 10 years have examined the question of why people exercise restraint in the face of sexual opportunity. From a 1971 survey of college students by Richard Driscoll and Keith Davis.

Reasons men gave for *not* having intercourse:

1. *Worried about pregnancy*—22 percent.
2. *Unable to talk girl into it*—21 percent.
3. *The decision wasn't theirs*—14.5 percent.
4. *Didn't love the girl*—14 percent.
5. *Was worried about worsening relationship*—11 percent.

Reasons women gave for *not* having intercourse:

1. *Didn't love the boy*—37 percent.
2. *Thought it was morally wrong*—16 percent.
3. *Worried about pregnancy*—16 percent.
4. *Worried about feeling ashamed afterward*—15 percent.
5. *Worried about worsening relationship*—11 percent.

SOURCES

Donald Carns, "Talking About Sex: Notes on First Coitus and the Double Sexual Standard," 1973.

Morton Hunt, *Sexual Behavior in the 1970s*, 1974.

Richard H. Driscoll and Keith E. Davis, "Sexual Restraints: A Comparison of Perceived and Self-Reported Reasons for College Students," 1971.

HOW OFTEN WE HAVE IT

Sexologists keep telling us that there is no such thing as an "average" sexual frequency rate, and that you invite trouble when you start comparing numbers with other couples. On the other hand, pollsters keep asking married couples how often they do it. And keep getting answers.

• **THE BASIC NUMBERS.** A composite picture of all the various surveys that have been conducted over the past ten years to determine how often married couples have intercourse offers a frequency profile that looks something like this:

1. *Couples 18 to 24 years old*—about twelve times a month.

2. *Twenty-five to 34*—eight to eleven times a month.
3. *Thirty-five and older*—eight times a month or less.
4. *Forty-five and older*—about four times a month.

The results from a recent *Family Circle* survey among 100 couples of all ages paint the following overall picture:

1. *Never*—2 percent.
2. *Less than once a month*—8 percent.
3. *Two to four times a month*—47 percent.
4. *Two or three times a week*—31 percent.
5. *Four or five times a week*—12 percent.

• **H o w M u c h I s E n o u g h ?** The majority of American couples who get asked this question say they are satisfied with the frequency of their marital sexual activities, but one survey, *The Redbook Report on Female Sexuality*, showed that around 38 percent of American married women say they don't get enough sex. Dissatisfaction with sexual frequency is more prevalent among older women and better-educated women. As far as men are concerned, the majority of those men surveyed by Anthony Pietropinto and Jacqueline Simenauer said three to four times a week was the ideal frequency rate, with married men more likely to cite a lower ideal frequency rate than single men. Curiously, the older the average man gets, the less frequently he *has* intercourse, but the more frequently he thinks he *should* be having it.

SOURCES
Ellen Frank and Carol Anderson, "How Important Is Sex to a Happy Marriage?"
Shere Hite, *The Hite Report*, 1976.
Morton Hunt, *Sexual Behavior in the 1970s*.
Anthony Pietropinto and Jacqueline Simenauer, *Beyond the Male Myth*, 1977.
Carol Tavris and Susan Sadd, *Redbook Report on Female Sexuality*, 1974.

THE TECHNIQUES WE USE

If nothing else, the sexual revolution has injected an unprecedented degree of variety into the sexual scenarios of the average

American marriage. Virtually all the surveys show that American men and women are more open with one another in their sexual encounters and are experiencing sex in a variety of different ways.

• **P o s i t i o n P a p e r**. Although the "missionary" position remains the single most widely practiced sexual position in the United States today, more couples than ever have become restless enough to experiment with other positions. From Morton Hunt's book-length *Playboy* survey comes the following two statistics:

1. *Married couples who use the "female superior" (female on top) position at least occasionally*—75 percent.
2. *Married women who almost never use the missionary position*—11 percent.

• **O r a l R e p o r t**. Let us start with the way it *was*. In the Kinsey era oral sex was conspicuously absent from the marriages of more than half the American married population and was a regular item in the sex diet of only a small proportion of married couples. But the surveys taken throughout the 1970s show a tremendous upsurge in both fellatio and cunnilingus. The proof:

1. *Proportion of marriages in which oral sex is practiced* —60 percent.
2. *Married couples younger than 35 who practice oral sex* —80 percent.
3. *Married persons younger than 25 who have experienced either fellatio or cunnilingus*—90 percent.
4. *Men who perform cunnilingus*—75 percent (according to the Pietropinto and Simenauer study).
5. *Married women who perform fellatio on their husbands*—43 percent (according to *The Redbook Report on Female Sexuality*).

• **E d u c a t e d T a s t e s**. Historically, oral sex has been more prevalent among college-educated men and women than among non-college-educated persons, but recent surveys suggest that the demographic differences are narrowing. Even so, single men (who are generally younger) are more oral-sex oriented than married men, and white men, in general, are more likely to engage in oral sex than blacks.

• **P R O O F   O F   T H E   P U D D I N G .** Most surveys show pretty clearly that a large percentage of both men and women enjoy *receiving* oral sex, but women seem to derive less pleasure from *giving* it than men do. About 42 percent of the women interviewed for *The Hite Report* said they achieved orgasm during cunnilingus, but fellatio ranked fairly low on the list of sexual activities that brought these women the "greatest pleasure." The *Redbook* report turned up the following two numbers:

1. *Proportion of women who perform fellatio on their husbands and find it "very enjoyable"*—34 percent.
2. *Who perform fellatio on their husbands and do not enjoy it*—33 percent.

• **B U T T I N G   O U T .** Anal sex appears to be an idea whose time has come—and gone. Here is how the figures look:

1. *American couples who have tried anal sex*—25 percent (higher among younger couples than among older couples).
2. *Proportion of married women who say they do it "often"*—2 percent (according to the *Redbook* report).
3. *Proportion of married women who say they enjoy it*— less than 10 percent.
4. *Proportion of married men younger than 35 who say they enjoy anal sex*—9 percent.
5. *Proportion of American college students who say anal sex is something they would "enjoy doing more"*—4 percent (according to Pietropinto and Simenauer).

SOURCES
Shere Hite, *The Hite Report.*
Morton Hunt, *Sexual Behavior in the 1970s.*
Anthony Pietropinto and Jacqueline Simenauer, *Beyond the Male Myth.*
Alfred Kinsey, *Sexual Behavior in the Human Female.*
Alfred Kinsey, *Sexual Behavior in the Human Male.*

HOW GOOD WE ARE AT IT

Performance is a delicate subject among sex therapists, with most people in the field insisting that there is too much emphasis on the purely technical side of sex today and not enough emphasis on the emotional aspect. Still, it does look as if Americans are technically more adept at sex today than in decades past even though the incidence of impotence among some segments of the male population is on the rise.

• **H A N G I N G I N T H E R E .** Kinsey's findings in the late 1940s indicated that the average American man ejaculated within two minutes of entry. Recent surveys suggest men are holding back a lot longer. Some sexologists understandably question the accuracy of surveys in which the men themselves are asked to estimate how long they can go without ejaculating; but the most current figures show that a plurality of American men are somewhere in the five-to-ten-minute category. And 25 percent of the men interviewed in the *Redbook* study on male sexuality said they could prolong intercourse longer than eleven minutes. *Said.*

• **W E T R Y H A R D E R .** Most men (80 percent according to the most recent surveys) now make a conscious attempt to delay orgasm, but some men try harder than others. In general, college-educated men, as well as men who earn $25,000 or more annually, are more concerned about delaying orgasm (according to Pietropinto and Simenauer) than non-high-school graduates and lower-income men, and blacks, on the whole, are less likely to delay orgasm than whites.

• **E M I S S I O N C O N T R O L .** As far as anybody has been able to tell, there is no relationship between penis size and ejaculatory control, and no demographic influence that makes a difference one way or the other. The majority of American men say they have experienced premature-ejaculation problems at one time or another, but of all the sex problems treated at the Masters and Johnson Institute, premature ejaculation has the highest success rate through therapy—98 percent.

• **W O M E N ' S W O R L D .** Based on all the surveys that have been done on the subject, it would appear that more than 80 percent of American women experience orgasm either some of the time or most of the time when they have intercourse with their lovers or husbands. The biggest factor in whether a woman achieves orgasm or not appears to be the degree to which her mate is sensitive to her needs, but, mate notwithstanding, a woman's capacity to achieve orgasm seems to be more tied into individual differences rather than any sociological influences. The only demographic area in which frequency of orgasm shows any variation is education, with highly educated women enjoying a slight edge in the orgasm department. And the fact that a woman is very religious in no way affects her orgasmic frequency or intensity. Praise the Lord!

SOURCES

Shere Hite, *The Hite Report.*
Alfred Kinsey, *Sexual Behavior in the Human Male.*
Anthony Pietropinto and Jacqueline Simenauer, *Beyond the Male Myth.*
Carol Tavris and Susan Sadd, *Redbook Report on Female Sexuality.*

HOW KINKY WE ARE

Contrary to what much of the latest sexual literature might lead us to believe, Americans, by and large, have remained fairly conventional in their sexual practices, the chief move across new frontiers being in the area of oral sex. Here is a brief look.

• **ANIMAL HOUSE.** Kinsey shocked a lot of people with his suggestion that nearly 8 percent of the American male population had had some sexual experience with an animal, and that nearly one out of five rural college males had had "some animal experience to the point of orgasm." Some sexologists have questioned the accuracy of these findings, but even Morton Hunt in his recent survey for *Playboy* (1973–74) suggests that around 5 percent of American males today, plus 2 percent of American females, have had at least some sexual contact with animals.

• **WHIPPING BOYS.** The proportion of Americans who find pleasure in sadomasochistic variations of sex is difficult to figure, given the subjectivity of the term, but the *Playboy* survey put the number at well below 10 percent of the population. A sampling of Hunt's figures:

1. *Married men who said they had performed a sado-masochistic act*—3 percent.
2. *Married women who said they had performed a sado-masochistic act*—1 percent.
3. *Single men who said they had been on the "giving" end of a sadomasochistic sex act*—10 percent.
4. *Single women who said they had been on the giving end of a sadomasochistic sex act*—10 percent.
5. *Single men who said they had been on the "receiving" end of a sadomasochistic sex act*—6 percent.
6. *Single women who said they had geen on the receiving end of a sadomasochistic sex act*—10 percent.

• G ANGING U P . The incidence of group sex is undoubtedly on the rise in the United States, but the proportion of Americans who make a steady diet of it is still very small. Again, from Hunt:

1. *Married men who had been involved in a group-sex scene*—10 percent.
2. *Married women who had taken part in group sex*—2 percent.
3. *Single men who had experienced group sex firsthand* —25 percent.
4. *Single women who had experienced group sex firsthand* 7 percent.

From all indications, most people who try group sex do *not* repeat the experience.

• S WINGERS . The most intelligent guesstimate of how many married men and women have played—or are playing— the mate-swapping game is that less than 2 percent of the total married population have done so, with the majority of those who try it once not going back for a second tasting. A 1974 study by Duane Denfield suggests that women have a tougher time with the swinging life than do men, and that in more than half the situations—54 percent—it is the woman alone who initiates the decision to stop swinging. The reasons offered most frequently by couples who drop out of swinging are:

1. *Jealousy*—33 percent.
2. *Guilt*—20 percent.
3. *Threat to marriage*—20 percent.

4. *Outside emotional attachments*—14 percent.
5. *Divorce or separation*—10 percent.

SOURCES
Duane Denfield, "Dropouts from Swinging," 1974.
Morton Hunt, *Sexual Behavior in the 1970s.*
Alfred Kinsey, *Sexual Behavior in the Human Male.*

HOW MUCH WE CHEAT, AND WHY

The adultery numbers in the United States are tricky to in-terpret—and for many reasons. For one thing, the divorce rate confuses the percentages. (A fairly high percentage of divorced persons committed adultery during their first marriages but not in their second marriages.) Secondly, many of the surveys do not differentiate between an adulterous act per se (one involv-ing a married person) and acts in which the woman (or man) involved in the experience was married at the time. Finally, the surveys rarely differentiate between one-night stands and genuine affairs. But even with these problems, it is safe to say that a higher proportion of married men and women—particu-larly younger men and women—are having affairs today than were doing so, say, twenty years ago, although the proportion of married people who believe in—and practice—sexual fidelity is still very high.

• THE BASIC NUMBERS. Averaging out all the various surveys on the current—and past—adultery rate in the United States produces the following estimates:

1. *Men who are currently married and have had at least one extramarital sex experience during their marriage* —50 percent.
2. *Married men who have had more than one extramari-tal sex experience during their current marriage*—25 percent.
3. *Men who say they make it a practice to cheat on their wives*—less than 6 percent.
4. *Women who say they have had an extramarital sex experience during their current marriage*—about 10 percent.
5. *Married women younger than 25 who have had extra-marital sex*—20–25 percent.

6. *Married women who say they make it a practice to cheat on their husbands*—less than 3 percent.

• **BEDROOM BEEFS.** The motivations that lead men to look outside the marriage for sex are different from those which lead women to do so. Women who cheat are more likely to be disappointed with their marriage as a whole and more likely to be romantically attracted to the extramarital sex partner than are men. Men are more likely to be motivated by a dissatisfaction with marital sex. Men are also more likely to stray for the fun and excitement of it. Respondents in the *"Redbook Report on Male Sexuality"* give the following set of reasons for having the affair (some men picked more than one reason):

1. *A spontaneous happening*—47 percent.
2. *Variety*—45 percent.
3. *Not getting along with wife*—17 percent.
4. *Fell in love*—16 percent.
5. *Wife not a good lover*—16 percent.
6. *Needed understanding*—5 percent.
7. *Retaliation for wife's affair*—4 percent.
8. *Attracted "to another man"*—4 percent.

• **LIMITED EDITIONS.** Most adulterers—men and women alike—tend to limit their extracurricular sex to a limited number of partners, but women are much more likely to keep the numbers down than men. Somewhere between 40 and 50 percent of American women who have cheated on their husbands have limited the adventure to only one partner, and only 10 percent, according to one survey, have been involved with five or more partners. By contrast, roughly half the men in the *Redbook* poll who admitted to having extramarital sex said they had had three or fewer partners.

• **LIKELY CANDIDATES.** The adultery rate in the United States is slightly higher in urban areas than it is in rural areas, and appears to be twice as high among black men as it is among white men, according to Pietropinto and Simenauer's findings. Education, on the other hand, does not seem to be a factor in male adultery, although the infidelity rate among college-educated women *is* slightly higher than it is among non-college-educated women.

• **L A D I E S ' D A Y .** Most of the relatively limited data on extramarital sexual behavior have focused on men, but with the adultery rate rising among women, Lynn Atwater, a behavioral scientist at Seton Hall University, figured it was time to look at the women's side of the story. Her study, which involved forty married women who had had, or were having, an extramarital sexual relationship, produced these findings:

Women in the study who:

1. *Had given no conscious thought to extramarital sex early in the marriage*—95 percent.
2. *Personally knew somebody who had had an extramarital affair*—50 percent.
3. *Had a conversation about extramarital sex before actually making the move*—55 percent.
4. *Gave a lot of thought to becoming involved before doing so*—75 percent.
5. *Were emotionally involved with the man they hooked up with*—50 percent.
6. *Were in love with the man*—25 percent.
7. *Repeated the experience more than once*—63 percent.
8. *Intended to repeat it*—84 percent of repeaters.
9. *Described their marriage as unhappy*—50 percent.

• **M U M ' S T H E W O R D .** Most men who fool around (80 percent according to a study by Lewis Yablonsky quoted in *Playboy*) do it secretly and insist that their extracurricular activities do not hurt their marriage. The men who play kiss-and-tell—about 20 percent—admit that candor destroys the main relationship. Approximately 9 percent of respondents in the *"Redbook* Report on Male Sexuality" who had committed adultery said their wife knew about it.

SOURCES

Lynn Atwater, "Getting Involved," 1979.

Morton Hunt, *Sexual Behavior in the 1970s.*

Carol Tavris, "Redbook Report on Male Sexuality."

Anthony Pietropinto and Jacqueline Simenauer, *Beyond the Male Myth.*

Playboy, "Playboy Advisor," March, 1979.

OUR MASTURBATION HABITS

One of the more surprising aspects of the sexual revolution is that we are not only enjoying sex with other people more but also appear to be doing it more by ourselves.

• THE BASIC NUMBERS. The masturbation rate among American males has always been very high—better than 95 percent—but it has been only recently that masturbation has become an accepted sex practice for women. Here are some of the figures:

1. *American women who were masturbating in the early 1950s*—63 percent.
2. *American women masturbating today*—about 80 percent.
3. *Married women who have masturbated at least once since their marriage*—74 percent (according to the *Redbook* female sexuality survey).
4. *Married men who masturbate*—more than 70 percent, but higher among younger married men.

• SELF-FREQUENCY. Not only are more Americans masturbating than ever before but the frequency rate has gone up as well. Studies prior to the 1960s showed an average masturbation rate among American women of about two to three times a month, and an average rate for males of about two or three times a week. More recent surveys show that while the rate for men is still pretty much the same, the rate among single women is up about 50 percent.

• HEAD START. The latest surveys indicate that six out of ten American boys are already masturbating by the age of 13. This compares with four out of ten 13-year-olds who were doing it in the early 1950s. Among 13-year-old girls, the current proportion of masturbators is thought to be one of every three. And here again there has been a noticeable change since the Kinsey era when the proportion of preteens doing it was one out of six.

• FANTASY ISLAND. Fantasies are an intrinsic part of masturbation, but subject matter varies from person to person, and also along certain demographic lines. A few numbers:

1. *Women who think about a man they know very well (usually their present lover) when they masturbate—* 90 percent.
2. *Men who think about their present mate—*65 percent.
3. *Women who have rape fantasies—*less than 2 percent.
4. *Men who have rape fantasies—*about 30 percent, but the rape is rarely "forceful" or "brutal" (according to the *Redbook* male survey).
5. *White men who do not fantasize at all when they masturbate—*9 percent.
6. *Black men who do not fantasize when they masturbate* —13 percent.

• CRITIC'S CHOICE. For *The Shanor Study,* Karen Shanor interviewed hundreds of young and sexually active men and came up with a list of the ten most popular masturbatory fantasies among men:

1. *A nude or seminude female body (no mention, though, of whether the body is a familiar one or not).*
2. *Sex with a woman with whom the fantasizer had previously been involved.*
3. *A replay of a satisfying sexual experience.*
4. *Sex with two or more women.*
5. *Being considered a stud.*
6. *Watching a woman perform sex in an enticing way.*
7. *Clandestine sex.*
8. *Watching wife or lover having sexual relations with somebody else.*
9. *Sex with a much younger woman.*
10. *Sex with somebody other than present lover.*

• HEAVY HITTERS. A recent survey of the masturbation habits of *Forum* magazine's readership (*Forum* is a publication that caters to sexually oriented people) gives us some added insight into masturbation practices in the United States, never mind the special nature of the sampling. Here are some highlights.

Proportion of men who:

1. *Masturbate in the bathroom*—66 percent.
2. *In the bedroom*—82 percent.
3. *At work*—14 percent.
4. *Feel relaxed after masturbation*—92 percent.
5. *Are happy afterward*—30 percent.
6. *Use erotic literature as an aid*—75 percent.
7. *Use a vibrator*—30 percent.
8. *Use bed clothes or pillows*—30 percent.
9. *Reach orgasm in two to four minutes*—55 percent.
10. *Six to ten minutes*—26 percent.
11. *Eleven to fifteen minutes*—5 percent.
12. *Less than a minute*—5 percent.

SOURCES

Forum, "Forum's Masturbation Survey," March 1979.
Alfred Kinsey, *Sexual Behavior in the Human Female.*
Alfred Kinsey, *Sexual Behavior in the Human Male.*
Carol Tavris and Susan Sadd, *Redbook Report on Female Sexuality.*
Anthony Pietropinto and Jacqueline Simenauer, *Beyond the Male Myth.*

THE GAY LIFE

Given the fact that no two people can agree on how, exactly, you have to conduct your life in order to be technically classified a homosexual, it is hardly surprising that estimates on the number of homosexuals in the United States today are all over the ballpark. By far, the most ambitious study of homosexuality ever published was that undertaken in the late 1970s by The Institute for Sex Research, whose founder was none other than Alfred Kinsey.

• THE GENERAL PICTURE. It was Kinsey himself who, in the late 1940s, opened up a can of worms by suggesting that at some stage of their lives nearly 37 percent of American men and 20 percent of American women had had some form of homosexual experience. The general feeling now is that Kinsey's figures were grossly misleading. Estimates from the Institute for Sex Research today are as follows:

1. *Single women who are actively homosexual*—3 to 5 percent.

2. *Single women who are not actively homosexual but have had a homosexual experience past the age of 19* —13 percent.

3. *Single men who are actively homosexual*—about 6 percent.

4. *Single men who are not actively homosexual but have had a homosexual experience past the age of 19*—5 percent.

5. *Married men and women who are actively homosexual* —less than 1 percent of all married persons.

• **VARIATIONS ON THE GAY THEME.** Here is a brief glimpse of sex practices among gays:

1. *Sexual frequency rate of average homosexual*—roughly 6 to 8 times a month.

2. *Proportion of gay men who say their employees or fellow workers know about their sexual preference*—30 percent.

3. *Frequency with which gay men have sex with a stranger*—about 80 percent of the time.

4. *Frequency with which lesbians have sex with a stranger*—about 6 percent of the time.

5. *Proportion of lesbians who have had sex with more than ten partners*—less than 50 percent.

6. *Gay men who say they have had sex with 1,000 (yes, 1,000!) different partners*—28 percent.

7. *Lesbians who were involved in a serious one-to-one relationship at the time of the Institute study*—70 percent.

8. *Gay men who had a steady relationship at the time of the study*—50 percent.

9. *Gay men who "cruise" in parks*—30 percent.

10. *Favorite activity among white male gays*—receiving oral sex.

11. *Favorite activity among black male gays*—performing anal intercourse.

12. *Favorite sexual activity among lesbians*—receiving oral sex.

SOURCES

Alan F. Bell and Martin S. Weinberg, *Homosexualities*, 1978.

Time, "How Gay Is Gay," April 23, 1979.

IX OUR LEISURE PASTIMES

HOW WE DIVIDE OUR FREE TIME

The amount of free time Americans have at their disposal has been increasing steadily since the early 1950s, and with the increase has come a new wave of sociological interest in how we spend this free time. One of the ongoing problems in this research is the fact that many people combine so-called free time with working time, so it is difficult to set specific guidelines.

• **THE BASIC NUMBERS**. Depending on how you ask the question and how the respondent interprets "free time," the average American will say that anywhere from 24 to 44 hours of free time are at his or her disposal each week. An Associated Councils of the Arts survey in 1975 indicated that more than half the American adult population had *less* than 25 hours a week of free time at their disposal. But a more detailed study by John P. Robinson of the Communication Research Center (Cleveland State University) resulted in the following numbers:

1. *Average total free time for all Americans*—38.5 hours a week.
2. *Employed men who are married*—36.1 hours a week.
3. *Employed men who are single*—45.0 hours a week.
4. *Employed women who are married*—31.7 hours a week.
5. *Employed women who are single*—36.4 hours a week.
6. *Housewives*—44.4 hours a week.

In every grouping, Robinson says, there has been an increase of about 10 percent in total free time since 1965.

• **THE DEMOGRAPHICS**. Demographic analyses of free-time availability have numerous built-in problems, the biggest being the fact that there is no way to discount factors like unemployment, or free time that is "voluntarily" spent on some sort of job. This qualification notwithstanding, college graduates appear to average around six hours *more* available leisure than noncollege graduates, and blacks, on average, have five hours a week more than whites. Younger people (18 to 25) have more free time on their hands than people in any other age-group except retirees. No single group in the population has *less* leisure time, on average, than working women. The amount of free time women in general have at their disposal varies according to the size of the family and the amount of money that comes into the house.

• **PASSING TIME**. The range of activities that Americans take part in in their leisure time, and the ways in which leisure activities can be categorized, are almost infinite. The best that can be done is to offer some generalizations based on some very broad patterns.

1. *Home entertainment*: Most Americans spend the bulk of their leisure hours *inside* their homes, nearly half of this time being spent either watching television, listening to the radio, or reading a newspaper or magazine. The latest surveys now show that 90 percent of Americans watch some television in their leisure time, and that 46 percent of all American adults (according to a 1974 Gallup poll) list television as their "favorite" leisure activity. Older people are more television oriented than younger people. Blacks and poorer people tend to depend on television more for leisure diversion than do whites and higher-income Americans. And college graduates, on average, watch 33 to 50 percent *less* television than high-school graduates.

2. *Mixing*: Most Americans spend the biggest chunk of their outside-the-home leisure time with other people, taking part in what are broadly referred to as "social activities." One study puts the average number of hours spent "socializing" per week in the United States at seven, with blacks (ten hours) showing a greater tendency toward social interaction than whites (eight hours). There also appears to be a direct correlation between income and socializing activities, with richer people tending to spend *less* time, relatively speaking, with their friends than do poorer people. Education as a factor unto itself seems to have no bearing on the figures. But age does: Younger people spend on average five hours more per week with friends than do middle-aged and older people. Predictably, single people (nine hours) average more time with friends per week than do married people.

3. *Groupers*: Group activities take up anywhere from three to nine hours a week in the life of most Americans, but here, again, classifications are vague. What does seem clear is that college graduates are much more likely to spend time in or-

ganizational activity (an average of nine hours a week according to some studies) and that Americans in the 18-to-25 age bracket spend about twice as much time in organizational activities as do people in other age-groups.

4. *Breaking a sweat:* The latest data on the amount of time the average American spends each week on sports and physical-fitness activities show that only around 15 percent of the adult population logs in five hours or more. Around three out of ten American adults spend two-and-a-half hours a week or less in some sports or fitness activity, and 16 percent are in the three-to three-and-a-half-hour category.

• T E E N S A T L E I S U R E . Here is a look at how teens spend their free time, based on a 1972 HEW survey:

1. *Watching television at least once a day*—95 percent.
2. *Listening to the radio*—85 percent do it once a day.
3. *Listening to the radio at least one hour*—61 percent.
4. *Spending some time reading a newspaper*—86 percent.
5. *Reading books*—80 percent.

• T O T S A T L E I S U R E . Nobody has more time than little kids, and here is what the Newspaper Advertising Bureau turned up on the leisure patterns of young children.

Proportion of boys and girls aged 6 to 8 who do the following activities "a lot":

1. *Watching television*—84 percent for boys; 86 percent for girls.
2. *Getting together with friends*—79 percent for boys; 77 percent for girls.
3. *Participating in sports*—63 percent for boys; 47 percent for girls.
4. *Talking on the telephone*—27 percent for boys; 45 percent for girls.
5. *Listening to records*—27 percent for boys; 37 percent for girls.
6. *Reading newspapers*—13 percent for boys; 8 percent for girls.
7. *Reading magazines*—26 percent for boys; 23 percent for girls.
8. *Doing arts and crafts*—37 percent for boys; 46 percent for girls.

9. *Reading books and stories that are not part of school-work*—30 percent for boys; 46 percent for girls.
10. *Going shopping or window-shopping*—29 percent for boys; 33 percent for girls.
11. *Reading comic books*—29 percent for boys; 16 percent for girls.
12. *Going to a club or team meeting*—12 percent for boys; 16 percent for girls.
13. *Going to movies at least once a week*—6 percent for boys; 13 percent for girls.

• MEN OF LEISURE. The American male at leisure, from *Playboy Report on American Men:*

1. *Proportion of single men who name "developing new relationships" as an "important" leisure goal*—30 percent.
2. *Married men who feel the same way*—8 percent.
3. *Men who think "helping other people" is an important leisure goal*—about 20 percent (but higher among working-class men).
4. *Single men who name "keeping in good physical shape" as an important leisure value*—41 percent.

Some of the activities that American men do on a regular basis, and the proportion who do them:

1. *Watching television*—66 percent.
2. *Listening to music at home*—63 percent.
3. *Listening to the radio*—61 percent.
4. *Fixing things around the house*—57 percent.
5. *Socializing (dining out, going to parties)*—56 percent.
6. *Reading*—56 percent.
7. *Participating in outdoor activities*—52 percent.
8. *Getting away for a change of scenery*—48 percent.

SOURCES

Associated Councils of the Arts, *Americans and the Arts.*
Gallup Poll.
Newspaper Advertising Bureau. *Children, Mothers and Newspapers.*
The Perrier Study of Fitness in America.
Playboy Report on American Men.
Robinson, John P. *Changes in America's Use of Time, 1965–1975,* 1976.

MAKING MUSIC

Ignoring for the moment how accomplished we are in our musical pursuits, it is clear that a surprisingly high proportion of Americans—about one out of five—know how to play at least one musical instrument. And our involvement with music seems to be intensifying. Here are some notes on our musical habits.

• **THE BASIC NUMBERS.** A 1978 Gallup poll, commissioned by the Illinois-based American Music Conference, showed that at least 35 million Americans—about one-fifth of the adult population—play a musical instrument at least six times a year, and a 1975 Harris survey showed that an additional 34 million Americans would like to play a musical instrument. Some figures from both surveys:

1. *Americans 16 and older who sing in a choir*—10 percent (sampling includes school choirs).
2. *Who play in an orchestra*—3 percent.
3. *Who play a musical instrument*—28 percent.
4. *Americans 65 and older who play a musical instrument* —10 percent.
5. *College graduates who are amateur musicians*—28 percent.
6. *High-school graduates who are amateur musicians*—15 percent.

• **INSTRUMENT LANDINGS.** The most widely played instrument in the United States, according to the 1978 Gallup poll, is the piano. About 18 million Americans, or 36 percent of all amateur musicians, play it, and most of these pianists (79 percent) are women. The second most widely played instrument in the United States is now the guitar, which claims nearly 15 million players (30 percent of all amateur musicians). Once you get past piano and guitar, the eight most popular instruments among amateur musicians in the United States are:

1. *Organ*—6.2 million.
2. *Clarinet*—2.9 million.
3. *Drums*—2.7 million.

4. *Flute*—2.5 million.
5. *Trumpet*—2.3 million.
6. *Violin*—1.8 million.
7. *Harmonica*—1.5 million.
8. *Saxophone*—1.5 million.

Women players outnumber men players of the clarinet, flute, and violin, with the largest male-female gap among flutists, of whom 83 percent are women and 17 percent men. And for the remaining instruments—trumpet, harmonica, drums, and saxophone—men players outnumber women, accounting for more than 80 percent of players in each category.

• S O U L   M U S I C . Around 4 percent of adult Americans (according to the Harris survey) say that playing a musical instrument is the leisure-time activity that gives them the most creative or artistic satisfaction. The highest proportion of these people (8 percent) are found among young people 16 to 20. And while men and women, and whites and blacks, tend to measure out about the same in this category, college graduates (7 percent) are more likely to get high artistic satisfaction from music than are high-school graduates.

SOURCES
American Music Conference.
Associated Councils of the Arts, *Americans and the Arts.*

WHAT WE DO FOR ENTERTAINMENT BESIDES WATCHING TELEVISION

Most Americans (about 80 percent) rely mainly on television to provide them with entertainment. Here is a look at what the other 20 percent do.

• M O V I E   B U F F S . Movie attendance in the United States has gone up significantly since the late 1960s, but less than 30 percent of the population 12 years old and older sees more than one movie a month, and the movie population on the whole is overwhelmingly young. Some figures on American moviegoing habits, based on the 1975 Harris survey on the arts, and figures from the Motion Picture Association.

Americans who:

1. *See a movie once a month*—48 percent of 12- to 17-year-olds.
2. *See a movie once a month*—35 percent of college graduates.
3. *Have an interest in going to see famous old films*—58 percent.
4. *Rely on movies for "light entertainment"*—71 percent.
5. *See movies as a form of artistic expression*—11 percent.
6. *Choose a movie on the basis of who is in it*—34 percent (based on people who say the cast members are a "very important" choice factor).
7. *On the basis of what type of film it is*—53 percent.
8. *On the basis of what the critics say*—10 percent.
9. *On the basis of who directed it*—7 percent.

Generally speaking, the "heavy" moviegoing public is made up of either very young kids or younger college graduates. Americans older than 50 are the mainstays of the nonmoviegoing population.

• T H E A T R E   B U F F S . Roughly one out of three Americans sees at least one live theatrical production a year, but this sampling includes high-school productions. The theatregoing public is primarily an up-scale segment of the population, with attendance patterns fairly similar in all age-groups except for the older-than-50 crowd, where it drops well below the national norm. Live theatre has the toughest time drawing in the South. It prospers the most in the East and in the Middle Atlantic States.

• I N   C O N C E R T . One out of ten Americans is a "frequent concertgoer." But this figure includes both rock and classical music concerts, which explains why the highest proportion of concertgoers in any one age-group—19 percent—is found among the 16- to 20-year-olds. The proportion of Americans who go to classical concerts on a regular basis is probably less than 4 percent, and college graduates outnumber high-school graduates in this category by a three-to-one margin.

• M U S E U M   P I E C E S . About one out of five American adults is a "frequent museumgoer," but the proportion drops to 12 percent when you consider only art museums, and it drops even more when you consider only those Americans who go to a museum four times a year. American museums are visited primarily by younger people, with the highest proportion of attendees (30 percent) in the 21-to-34 age-group. Attendance patterns of science and history museums are similar to those of art museums, the chief difference being that men are more likely to be nonattenders of art museums than of science museums.

• ON BROADWAY. A *Playbill* magazine subscriber survey offers the following picture of the Broadway theatregoing crowd:

1. *Males*—52 percent.
2. *Singles*—54 percent.
3. *Median age for men*—35.
4. *Median age for women*—32.
5. *Out-of-towners (i.e., from outside New York metropolitan area)*—25 percent.
6. *Average number of plays seen by New York–resident theatregoer*—9.

SOURCES
Associated Councils of the Arts, *Americans and The Arts*.
Motion Picture Association.
Playbill.

OUR HOBBIES

Americans are spending annually about $2 billion on hobbies, with social scientists now telling us that the satisfaction a person is able to draw from his or her hobbies is a reliable barometer of life satisfaction in general.

• THE BASIC NUMBERS. Precise figures are not available, but it is a safe guess that more than 60 percent of American adults have some sort of hobby (apart from watching television). Here are some rough numbers based on Harris and W. R. Simmons projections.

Proportion of American adults who:

1. *Cook for fun*—26.0 percent.
2. *Collect stamps, coins, antiques, and the like*—36.0 percent.
3. *Do outdoor gardening*—38.0 percent.
4. *Do indoor gardening*—34.0 percent.
5. *Collect stamps*—8.0 percent of population 5 years old and older.
6. *Do needlework*—16.0 percent.
7. *Ride motorcycles*—6.5 percent.
8. *Belong to a literary, art, or discussion group*—9.0 percent.
9. *Play chess regularly*—5.0 percent.
10. *Play bridge*—5.0 percent.
11. *Take photographs that are more than just snapshots*—2.0 percent.
12. *Do something in arts or crafts*—40.0 percent.

In virtually every category cited above, participation rates rise with income and education. Age, though, only begins to affect participation rates when you get into the older-than-65 category, where the proportion of gardeners goes up and the proportion of collectors goes down.

• P U T T E R I N G   U P . Probably the most popular hobby in the United States (if it can be called a hobby) is "puttering around the house"—gardening, painting, fixing things up, carpentry. More than 80 percent of Americans say they find enjoyment in such activities, and the enjoyment levels are fairly consistent in all demographic groups, although rural Americans tend to be a little more "do-it-yourself" minded than urbanites, and blue-collar workers are more likely to putter than executives. The only demographic category in which the proportion of Americans who do *not* enjoy basic household activities is more than 25 percent is the 16-to-20 age-group, where only seven out of ten say they like such activities. Some additional numbers, based on a 1975 Harris survey:

1. *Men who derive creative or artistic satisfaction from doing carpentry, fixing things, etc.*—23 percent.
2. *Women who feel the same way*—6 percent.
3. *Men who have no use for household activities as a way of spending leisure time*—20 percent.

4. *Women who feel the same way*—13 percent.
5. *Married men 18 to 49 who "fix things up around the house" on a regular basis*—68 percent (according to the *Playboy Report on American Men*).
6. *Single men in the same category*—38 percent.

• **GREEN THUMBS**. Thirty-five to 40 percent of Americans are involved in some phase of gardening, with only one age-group—the 16- to 20-year-olds—not actively involved. The numbers:

1. *Homeowners who plant a vegetable garden*—40 percent.
2. *Women who pick gardening as the leisure activity that gives them the most creative and artistic satisfaction*—30 percent.
3. *Men who do the same*—23 percent.
4. *Sixteen- to 20-year-olds who do the same*—4 percent.
5. *Sixty-five-year-olds and older who do the same*—47 percent.

• **GROUPIES**. Data from NORC surveys on the proportion of American adults who belong to various groups and organizations look something like this:

1. *Church groups*—40 percent.
2. *Sports groups*—19 percent.
3. *Labor unions*—16 percent.
4. *School and service groups*—14 percent.
5. *Professional and academic societies*—12 percent.
6. *Fraternal groups*—11 percent.
7. *Hobby and garden clubs*—9 percent.
8. *Literary, art, and discussion groups*—9 percent.
9. *Service clubs*—8 percent.
10. *Veterans' groups*—8 percent.
11. *Nationality groups*—4 percent.
12. *Fraternities or sororities*—4 percent.

• **OUTDOOR LIFERS**. More than half the American population 12 years old or older participates in some sort of outdoors-oriented leisure pastime apart from sports like tennis and golf, but the proportion who make a regular practice of it (participating at least five times a year) is probably closer to 30 percent. The numbers look like this:

1. *Men who backpack or hike*—5.5 percent.
2. *Women who backpack or hike*—4.0 percent.
3. *Men who go hunting*—14.0 percent, with the highest proportion coming from the South and with a lower participation rate among college graduates than among non-high-school graduates.
4. *Men who go fishing*—33.0 percent.
5. *Women who go fishing*—14.5 percent.
6. *Men who go on camping trips*—17.0 percent.
7. *Women who go on camping trips*—12.5 percent.
8. *Men (18 to 49) who say they participate in outdoor activities (hiking, fishing, hunting, boating) on a regular basis*—52.0 percent.
9. *Men who describe fishing, hunting, or camping as one of the leisure activities that give them the most creative satisfaction*—20.0 percent.
10. *Women who do the same*—4.0 percent.

• **THREADERS**. Sewing and needlework are leisure activities that cut across most demographic boundaries, although there are some fairly predictable differences in the number of people (chiefly women) who sew purely for pleasure and people who sew for the necessity of it. The numbers:

1. *Households in which there is a sewing machine*—58 percent.
2. *Women who say they enjoy sewing*—40 percent.
3. *Women who consider themselves "heavy sewers" (at least two garments a month)*—20 percent.
4. *Women who do needlework*—16 percent.
5. *Women who list handiwork or sewing as an activity that brings them creative satisfaction*—39 percent.
6. *Women younger than 20 who do so*—20 percent.
7. *Women 50 to 64 who do so*—42 percent.
8. *Women who do not sew at all*—37 percent.

• **CRAFTY PEOPLE**. About 40 percent of Americans are involved to some degree in the crafts, but only about half that number are involved with any degree of regularity. Crafts people in general tend to be younger, richer, and more educated than people who are not involved in the crafts, and women in most of the fields outnumber men by nearly two to one. The numbers:

1. *Men and women who draw, paint, or sketch for enjoyment*—9 percent.
2. *Women who weave*—3 percent.
3. *Men and women who work in pottery or ceramics*— 6 percent.
4. *Men involved in creative woodworking*—7 percent.
5. *Men and women who make jewelry*—3 percent.
6. *Women who say they draw a great deal of creative or artistic satisfaction from their crafts activity*—17 percent.
7. *Men who do so*—10 percent.
8. *Whites who do so*—14 percent.
9. *Blacks who do so*—8 percent.

• PLEASURE COOKERS. About one out of every four American adults says he or she "cooks for fun," and the surprising statistic is that a good third of these pleasure cookers are men. Cooking for the fun of it is a leisure activity that shows strength in virtually all demographic groups, as evidenced by the following numbers:

1. *Women who describe cooking as an activity that brings them creative satisfaction*—10 percent.
2. *White women in this category*—9 percent.
3. *Black women in this category*—14 percent.
4. *Women in $15,000-and-over households in this category*—6 percent.
5. *Men and women who say they cook gourmet or special meals "often"*—23 percent.
6. *Men who say they know how to cook gourmet meals*— 33 percent.

• TEEN HOBBIES. Roughly 88 percent of the teenage girls polled in a 1978 *Seventeen* survey said they had a hobby. Here is what those hobbies were:

1. *Sports*—18.0 percent.
2. *Sewing or needlecraft*—17.0 percent.
3. *Music*—12.0 percent.
4. *Collecting things*—8.0 percent (records included).
5. *Reading*—6.0 percent.
6. *Dancing*—5.5 percent.
7. *Horseback riding*—3.5 percent.

8. *Cooking*—2.5 percent.
9. *Writing*—2.5 percent.
10. *Photography*—2.0 percent.

SOURCES
Associated Councils on the Arts, *Americans and the Arts.*
NORC.
Playboy Report on American Men.
Seventeen.
W. R. Simmons.

WHAT WE DO FOR PHYSICAL RECREATION

Estimates on the number of Americans involved in various physical recreation activities have a tendency to be all over the ballpark, and this is because the spokespeople for these activities have a tendency to inflate the figures and do not always differentiate between the regular participants and the one- or two-timers. Even so, it is obvious that the fitness and physical recreation boom in the United States is far from over and should carry us panting well into the 1980s, and beyond. Here are some of the more recent surveys, none of which has any particular recreational ax to grind and each of which bases its participation figures on a minimum yearly participation rate.

•**THE PUBLIC SPEAKS.** A U.S. Heritage Conservation and Recreation Service survey, conducted in 1977, revealed the following participation figures, based on a sampling of more than 4,000 Americans 12 years old and older who had taken part in the activities listed at least five times between June 1976 and June 1977:

1. *Jogged or walked for exercise*—55.0 percent (96 million).
2. *Went swimming in pool*—47.0 percent.
3. *Went bicycling*—37.0 percent.
4. *Went bowling*—35.0 percent.
5. *Went fishing*—34.0 percent.
6. *Went swimming in a lake or in the ocean*—33.5 percent.

7. *Played tennis*—23.0 percent.
8. *Went motorboating*—19.5 percent.
9. *Rode motorcycles or minibikes for fun*—19.0 percent.
10. *Went hiking or backpacking*—16.0 percent.
11. *Went hunting*—14.0 percent.
12. *Went camping in a developed area*—12.0 percent.
13. *Went sledding*—11.5 percent.
14. *Played golf*—11.0 percent.
15. *Went ice-skating*—9.0 percent.
16. *Went camping in an undeveloped area*—8.5 percent.
17. *Went horseback riding*—7.5 percent.
18. *Went waterskiing*—7.0 percent.
19. *Went canoeing or kayaking*—6.0 percent.
20. *Went sailing*—4.0 percent.
21. *Went snowmobiling*—4.0 percent.
22. *Went downhill skiing*—4.0 percent.
23. *Went scuba diving*—less than 1.0 percent (or 200,000).
24. *Went skateboarding*—less than 1.0 percent (or 200,000).
25. *Went parachute jumping*—less than 1.0 percent (or 200,000).

• MEN'S DEPARTMENT. Here is what *The Playboy Report on American Men* turned up in the way of activities in which men 18 to 49 participate "regularly":

1. *Outdoors sports (fishing, hunting, camping, hiking, backpacking)*—45 percent (22.5 million).
2. *Swimming*—32 percent.
3. *Baseball or softball*—23 percent.
4. *Tennis*—20 percent.
5. *Bicycling*—17 percent.
6. *Football*—17 percent.
7. *Jogging*—14 percent.
8. *Golf*—13 percent.
9. *Weight lifting*—13 percent.
10. *Motorcycling*—12 percent.
11. *Motorboating*—12 percent.
12. *Skiing*—10 percent.
13. *Racquetball, handball, or paddleball*—8 percent.
14. *Distance running*—8 percent.
15. *Horseback riding*—7 percent.

• **C O E D   F I G U R E S .** From *The Perrier Study of Fitness in America* come these participation figures for men and women 18 and older:

1. *Walking*—22 percent (34 million).
2. *Swimming*—17 percent.
3. *Calisthenics*—14 percent.
4. *Bicycling*—13 percent.
5. *Bowling*—13 percent.
6. *Running or jogging*—11 percent.
7. *Tennis*—9 percent.
8. *Basketball*—7 percent.
9. *Softball*—7 percent.
10. *Hiking*—7 percent.
11. *Baseball*—6 percent.
12. *Golf*—5 percent.
13. *Volleyball*—5 percent.
14. *Football*—4 percent.
15. *Frisbee*—4 percent.
16. *Table tennis*—4 percent.
17. *Weight lifting*—3 percent.
18. *Downhill skiing*—3 percent.
19. *Waterskiing*—3 percent.

• **J O C K E T T E S .** From a 1978 *Seventeen* survey, a glimpse of the fifteen sports in which American teenage girls are most involved:

1. *Swimming*—89.0 percent.
2. *Bicycling*—87.5 percent.
3. *Tennis*—75.0 percent.
4. *Jogging*—71.0 percent.
5. *Bowling*—64.0 percent.
6. *Badminton*—56.0 percent.
7. *Table tennis*—53.0 percent.
8. *Ice-skating*—50.0 percent.
9. *Boating*—47.5 percent.
10. *Roller-skating*—46.0 percent.
11. *Sledding or tobogganing*—44.0 percent.
12. *Horseback riding*—40.0 percent.
13. *Gymnastics*—39.0 percent.
14. *Skiing*—35.0 percent.
15. *Track*—15.0 percent.

Their involvement in *team* sports:

1. *Volleyball*—57 percent.
2. *Baseball or softball*—47 percent.
3. *Basketball*—40 percent.
4. *Soccer*—40 percent.
5. *Field hockey*—16 percent.

Some odds and ends.

Proportion of teenage girls who:

1. *Play baseball or softball five times a week or more*—8.5 percent.
2. *Consider themselves good at basketball*—8.5 percent.
3. *Own a ten-speed bike*—62.0 percent.
4. *Lift weights at least three times a week*—500,000 girls.
5. *Have been involved in some form of sports competition*—50.0 percent.

SOURCES
Perrier Study of Fitness in America.
Playboy Report on American Men.
Seventeen.
U.S. Bureau of the Census, *Statistical Abstract of the United States: 1978.*

OUR TRAVEL PATTERNS

The trend in American travel habits over the past ten years has been toward more frequent but shorter trips, with foreign travel on the rise again after a four-year lull in the mid-1970s.

• T H E B A S I C N U M B E R S . Just about half of all American adults (53 percent according to W. R. Simmons figures for 1977–78) take at least one trip of 100 miles or more (one way) a year, but reasons vary:

1. *Business or a convention*—10.0 percent.
2. *Visits to friends or relatives*—36.0 percent.
3. *Recreation*—14.5 percent.
4. *Sightseeing or entertainment*—22.5 percent.
5. *Pleasure trips in general*—38.0 percent.

• **GETTING THERE**. Americans take most of their trips (80 percent) by car. Some related numbers:

1. *American adults who took at least one airplane trip in 1977*—13.5 percent.
2. *Who took more than three airplane trips in 1977*—2.5 percent.
3. *Who traveled by ship in 1977*—3.0 percent.

• **GOING ABROAD**. The number of Americans who have been traveling abroad since the mid-1970s has been averaging between 6.5 and 7.5 million a year, which is nearly five times the number who were traveling to foreign shores each year in the 1960s. Yet, because the length of time the average American traveler spends abroad on a typical trip has *dropped*, the average expenditure on a foreign trip today is actually *less* than it was in the 1950s. The numbers:

1. *Americans who took a foreign trip in 1977*—about 6.0 percent.
2. *Who have taken a foreign trip since 1972*—17.5 percent.
3. *Who have taken at least three foreign trips within the past five years*—4.5 percent.
4. *Who currently own a U.S. passport*—8.5 percent.
5. *Who have visited Canada since 1972*—6.5 percent.
6. *Mexico*—4.0 percent.
7. *The British Isles*—2.5 percent.
8. *France*—1.5 percent.
9. *Bermuda or the Caribbean*—3.6 percent.
10. *Who travel on government business*—23.0 percent.

• **PASSPORTERS**. A U.S. Passport Office analysis of passport holders shows the following demographic breakdown:

1. *Men*—45.0 percent.
2. *Women*—55.0 percent.
3. *Business people or professionals*—26.0 percent.
4. *Students*—17.0 percent.
5. *Housewives*—14.0 percent.
6. *Sales workers or technical persons*—12.0 percent.
7. *Retired people*—7.5 percent.
8. *Clerks or secretaries*—4.5 percent.
9. *Teachers*—4.0 percent.

•**HAVE SLEEPING BAG, WILL TRAVEL**. From the *Playboy* 1977 Survey of the College Market come the following numbers regarding American collegians who travel.

Proportion of college students who:

1. *Take at least one airplane trip a year*—85.5 percent.
2. *Had taken at least one trip outside the United States during the period 1974–77*—39.5
3. *Had a valid U.S. passport*—19.5 percent.
4. *Had taken ten or more trips inside the United States within a period of twelve months*—19.0 percent.

•**DREAM TRIPS**. When Needham, Harper and Steers asked a sampling of American men and women what their particular travel fantasy was, and gave them a number of choices, here is how various age and gender groups responded.

Proportion who would like to take a trip around the world:

1. *Women (all ages)*—67 percent.
2. *Men (all ages)*—67 percent.
3. *Women 25 to 34*—83 percent.
4. *Men 25 to 34*—73 percent.
5. *Women 55 and older*—51 percent.
6. *Men 55 and older*—53 percent.

Proportion who would like to spend a year in London or Paris:

1. *Women (all ages)*—34 percent.
2. *Men (all ages)*—34 percent.
3. *Women 25 to 34 (the age-group that likes the idea best)*—40 percent.
4. *Men 25 to 34*—39 percent.
5. *Women 34 to 44*—34 percent.
6. *Men 34 to 44*—40 percent.
7. *Women 55 and older*—25 percent.
8. *Men 55 and older*—23 percent.

•**TRAVEL WOES**. A *Newsweek* market study turned up some of things the Americans who travel abroad worry about most. They are:

1. *Having the right clothes*—54 percent.
2. *Weather*—52 percent.
3. *Having enough cash*—40 percent.

4. *Food*—36 percent.
5. *Accommodations*—31 percent.

SOURCES
Needham, Harper and Steers.
Newsweek.
W. R. Simmons.
U.S. Passport Office.
U.S. Travel Data Center.

X HOW WE SPEND OUR MONEY

WHERE OUR MONEY GOES

Everybody knows that prices in the United States have been climbing since the 1950s, with the U.S. dollar taking an enormous amount of punishment in the late 1970s. Yet, throughout this inflationary spiral the overall pattern of consumer expenditures has changed relatively little, and, truth be told, we still pay relatively less for the basics—food, fuel, housing—than do people in most countries.

• B A S I C L I V I N G . One of the ways the cost of living in the United States is measured is by something known as the consumer price index (CPI). The CPI is nothing but a scale by which prices of selected items before and after a specific year—it has been 1967 throughout the 1970s—can be compared. You start with a rating of 100 for 1967, which means that a CPI of 150 represents a 50-percent increase over 1967, and a CPI of 90 represents a 10-percent decline. Forget the declines. Here was the CPI as of March 1979:

1. *All items used in CPI scale*—207.1 (up 107.1 percent since 1967).
2. *Food and beverages*—222.5 (up 122.5 percent).
3. *Housing*—215.5 (up 115.5 percent).
4. *Transportation*—197.5 (up 97.5 percent).
5. *Medical*—232.5 (up 132.5 percent).
6. *Entertainment*—183.5 (up 83.5 percent).

• B I G G A I N E R S . A few of the specific items that have registered the biggest cost jump since 1967:

1. *Coffee*—420.0 (smile, it was 451.0 in 1977).
2. *A semiprivate room in a hospital*—326.0.
3. *Fuel oil*—more than 300.0 as of March 1979, and rising.
4. *Fish*—268.0.
5. *Medical services*—233.5.
6. *Household services*—230.5.
7. *Physicians' fees*—222.0.
8. *Auto insurance*—218.0.
9. *Fruits and vegetables*—209.0.
10. *Meat*—203.0.
11. *Gasoline*—195.0.
12. *Used cars*—186.0.

13. *Personal-care goods—182.5.*
14. *Clothing—160.0.*

• H O L D I N G S T E A D Y . The *smallest* price increases since 1967 have come about in the following areas:

1. *Television sets—101* (1 percent rise since 1967).
2. *Drugs and prescriptions—142.*
3. *Women's wear—149.*
4. *Eggs—152.*

• G E O G R A P H Y . The major cities in which the CPI rose the most, up until 1977, were:

1. *Houston—190.0.*
2. *Baltimore—186.0.*
3. *New York—185.5.*
4. *Boston—183.5.*
5. *Washington—183.5.*
6. *Minneapolis–Saint Paul—183.0.*

And the least:

1. *Honolulu—171.0.*
2. *Chicago—175.0.*
3. *St. Louis—176.5.*
4. *Seattle—177.5.*
5. *Milwaukee—178.0.*

• B U D G E T C R U N C H E S . The proportional makeup of budget expenditures in the average American home varies according to several factors (among them, size of family, area) but none more so than income. The U.S. Bureau of Labor Statistics groups American families into three broad income ranges: low, $10,000; intermediate, $17,000; and high, $25,000. Here is a comparative look at how the money gets spread around in each group.

Food:

1. *Low—30.5* percent of overall budget.
2. *Intermediate—24.0* percent.
3. *High—20.5* percent.

Housing:

1. *Low—20.0* percent.
2. *Intermediate—23.5* percent.
3. *High—24.0* percent.

Transportation:

1. *Low*—7.0 percent.
2. *Intermediate*—8.5 percent.
3. *High*—7.5 percent.

Clothing and personal care:

1. *Low*—10.5 percent.
2. *Intermediate*—9.0 percent.
3. *High*—9.0 percent.

Medical care:

1. *Low*—9.5 percent.
2. *Intermediate*—6.0 percent.
3. *High*—4.0 percent.

Social Security:

1. *Low*—6.0 percent.
2. *Intermediate*—5.5 percent.
3. *High*—4.0 percent.

Personal income taxes:

1. *Low*—7.0 percent.
2. *Intermediate*—13.5 percent.
3. *High*—20.0 percent.

Total (basics):

1. *Low*—82.5 percent.
2. *Intermediate*—76.0 percent.
3. *High*—71.0 percent.

•**DOLLARS AND CENTS.** Here, roughly, is what an average American family earning $17,000 a year is paying per month for various items in the budget:

1. *Food*—about $240, which includes $60 for food consumed outside the home.
2. *Housing*—$320 for rent or mortgage.
3. *Furnishings*—$100.
4. *Clothing*—$100 (assuming they are fussy about labels).
5. *Health care*—about $80.
6. *Transportation*—$250, which includes payments, gas, repairs, insurance.
7. *Utilities*—$175.

8. *Recreation*—$110.
9. *Reading materials*—$8.
10. *Education*—$65, if there is a child in college.
11. *Gifts and contributions*—$75.

• **TUITION BLUES.** Obviously it depends on the school, but yearly tuition, room, and board at the average American college in 1979 was around $2,000, not counting long-distance phone calls and bail money. Get up there in Ivy League territory and you are talking about $8,000 a year, including tuition, room, board, and books. The increase has been about 77 percent since 1968.

• **PUMPING CIRCUMSTANCES.** Some of the gas numbers, as they soared in the 1970s.

1. *Average price of a gallon of regular gas in 1970*—36 cents.
2. *In mid-1979*—85 cents.
3. *Average number of gallons used by each car in 1970*—722.
4. *In 1976*—680.
5. *Amount of gas (total gallons) we're using today, compared to 1970*—about 30 percent more.
6. *What they pay in France for a gallon of gas*—$2.00 (February, 1979).

• **TAX BITTEN.** The average American now gets stung by the IRS for about $2,100 a year. This represents an average of about 21 percent of gross income and does not include federal, state, local, and other taxes. All told, three out of the eight hours a typical American works each day go to pay that worker's tax burden for the year.

• **AMERICA VERSUS THE WORLD.** Here is a look at how the inflation rate in the United States shapes up against the inflation rate in other countries, based on the consumer price index as of 1977:

1. *West Germany*—156.5.
2. *Switzerland*—162.5.
3. *Austria*—178.0.
4. *United States*—181.5.

5. *Luxembourg*—182.5.
6. *Canada*—185.9.
7. *Belgium*—193.6.
8. *Sweden*—202.0.
9. *Netherlands*—203.0.
10. *Norway*—210.0.
11. *France*—214.0.
12. *Denmark*—224.0.
13. *Australia*—227.0.
14. *Japan*—241.0.
15. *New Zealand*—253.0.
16. *Italy*—257.0.
17. *Finland*—260.0.
18. *England*—292.5.
19. *Spain*—293.0.
20. *Ireland*—304.0.
21. *Portugal*—371.0.
22. *Yugoslavia*—371.0.
23. *Iceland*—397.5.
24. *Turkey*—418.0.

•**IN THE CHIPS.** What would the average American do if he or she suddenly inherited an unexpected $100,000? Here is how respondents in a 1978 Roper poll replied:

1. *Put it in a savings account*—48 percent.
2. *Take a vacation trip*—44 percent.
3. *Buy a new home*—37 percent.
4. *Buy a new car*—26 percent.
5. *Give part to family*—25 percent.
6. *Give part to church*—22 percent.
7. *Invest for old age*—20 percent.
8. *Refurnish house*—19 percent.
9. *Start or buy own business*—15 percent.
10. *Give part to charities*—14 percent.
11. *Invest in stocks*—13 percent.
12. *Quit job*—8 percent.

SOURCES
The Roper Organization.
U.S. Bureau of Labor Statistics.
U.S. Bureau of the Census, *Statistical Abstract of the United States: 1978.*

WHAT WE OWN

No single feature of basic living more widely differentiates Americans from the rest of the world than does the volume and variety of our material possessions. In no other country does the average person own more of the so-called good things in life, and in no other country is as much time and energy devoted to shopping. Here is a brief look at a big subject.

• H O M E B O D I E S . Roughly 70 percent of American adults own their own home, and the proportion of home owners has been rising steadily since 1960, when only about half of the American population owned the place they lived in. Less than 2 percent of American homes are lacking in indoor plumbing, which places the United States just about at the top of the list of countries worldwide in this particular category. The United States also has the lowest proportion of homes (less than 2 percent) with a per-room-living ratio of less than 1.5, although that proportion is considerably higher if you consider only black households. Some other home figures:

1. *Americans who own a second home*—20 percent.
2. *Average price of a previously occupied one-family house*—$15,900 in 1966; $40,000 in 1979.
3. *Americans who own a mobile home*—5 percent.

• I N S I D E   S T O R Y . Here is a look at some of the things— big and small—that Americans have in their homes and apartments, and the proportion who own them.

Big:

1. *Refrigerators*—99.5 percent.
2. *Freezers*—45.0 percent.
3. *Built-in ranges*—20.0 percent.
4. *Washing machines*—75.0 percent.
5. *Clothes dryers*—60.0 percent.
6. *Dishwashers*—42.0 percent.

Small (in alphabetical order):

1. *Air conditioners (room)*—55.0 percent.
2. *Blenders*—51.0 percent.

3. *Electric blankets*—62.0 percent.
4. *Electric can openers*—61.0 percent.
5. *Electric coffee makers*—49.5 percent.
6. *Electric corn poppers*—43.0 percent.
7. *Electric fondue makers*—41.5 percent.
8. *Electric frying pans*—68.0 percent.
9. *Electric hair dryers*—36.0 percent.
10. *Electric slicing knives*—41.5 percent.
11. *Food mixers*—92.0 percent.
12. *Hamburger makers*—15.5 percent.
13. *Hand-held massagers*—5.0 percent.
14. *Microwave ovens*—7.0 percent.
15. *Oral hygiene devices*—15.0 percent.
16. *Radios*—99.9 percent.
17. *Shave-cream dispensers*—8.0 percent.
18. *Stereo or high-fidelity units*—81.0 percent.
19. *Televisions (black and white)*—99.0 percent.
20. *Televisions (color)*—85.0 percent.
21. *Toasters*—99.0 percent.
22. *Toaster ovens*—11.5 percent.
23. *Trash compactors*—2.5 percent.
24. *Waste disposers*—43.0 percent.

• **WHEELS**. A motor vehicle of one kind or another (excluding motorcycles) is present in about 84 percent of American households and is considered a "necessity" by more than 90 percent of Americans. Some additional figures:

1. *Two-car households in the United States*—33 percent.
2. *Suburbanites who own more than one car*—40 percent.
3. *College students who either own their own cars or are the principal car drivers in their family*—53 percent.
4. *Households in 1974 with three or more cars*—20 percent.
6. *Whites who own their own cars*—87 percent.
7. *Blacks who own their own cars*—59 percent.

• **WARDROBE ROOM**. A 1978 *Women's Wear Daily* survey depicted the wardrobe of the average American woman as follows:

1. *Panties*—about 12 pairs, with an average replacement rate of 5 per year.
2. *Slips*—3.

3. *Loungewear robes—3.*
4. *Nightgowns—5.*
5. *Blouses—10.*
6. *Skirts—8.*
7. *Daytime dresses—5.*
8. *Cocktail dresses—3.*
9. *Jacket or blazer—2.*
10. *Coat and heavy jacket—3.*
11. *Raincoat—1.*

And from an R. H. Bruskin survey in 1977, these additions:

1. *Slacks—7.*
2. *Sweaters—5.*
3. *Jeans—2* (more for younger women).

SOURCES
R. H. Bruskin and Associates.
Merchandising, March 1979.
U.S. Bureau of the Census, *Statistical Abstract of the United States:* 1978.
Women's Wear Daily, August 14, 1978.

HOW WE SHOP FOR FOOD

The average American spends more time shopping for food than for any other item in the budget, and probably no feature of our buying patterns has been studied more closely. Two trends are apparent: First, food shopping is becoming more and more a "family" task; and, two, we are spending a larger proportion of our food dollars on meals eaten *outside* the home.

• THE BASIC NUMBERS. Americans now spend three times as much money on food as we spent in 1960, but the actual proportion of our total expenditures that is eaten up by food bills is actually down. The numbers according to Department of Labor surveys:

1. *Proportion of overall average budget spent on food—* 26 percent in 1960; 23 percent in 1979.
2. *Proportion of food dollar spent in restaurants—*19 percent in 1960; 25 percent in 1979.

• **CHEAPER BY THE DOZEN**. Proportional budget expenditures are pretty much the same in all demographic categories, but the *per-capita* expenditure varies considerably. Generally, the richer you are the more you spend on food, but an even bigger factor than income is family size. The larger the family, the smaller the per-capita expenditures. Some representative numbers:

Per-capita food expenditures in an average week in 1978 for:

1. *Americans living alone*—$22.
2. *Family of six*—$11.

Proportion of food budget spent in restaurants:

1. *In families of four*—26 percent.
2. *In families of six*—20 percent.
3. *In $25,000-and-over families*—37 percent.
4. *In $10,000 households*—25 percent.

• **GIVING IN**. A study conducted in 1972 by Scott Ward and Daniel Wackman was designed to find out how often parents give in to children when the kids ask for specific foods and specific brands (usually in response to advertising). The results, based on the percentage of parents who yield on specific foods, are as follows:

1. *Breakfast cereals*—87 percent.
2. *Snack foods*—63 percent.
3. *Bread*—19 percent.
4. *Soft drinks*—46 percent.
5. *Candy*—42 percent.

• **SUPERMARKET TEENS**. Most teenage girls (seven out of ten according to a 1976 *Seventeen* survey) do some food shopping for their family either on their own or as a help to their parents, and the proportion of teen girls who shop for food has gone up about 16 percent since 1972. Here is a sampling of the shopping habits of teenage girls:

1. *Brand consciousness*—60 percent.
2. *Impulse buying*—30 percent.
3. *Nutrition consciousness*—91 percent.
4. *Label reading*—44 percent.
5. *Buying mainly because of flavor*—95 percent.
6. *Buying mainly because of price*—77 percent.

7. *Buying mainly because of past experience with a specific product*—81 percent.

• **TWO ON THE AISLE.** With more American women working, food shopping is becoming increasingly a team affair involving both husband *and* wife. Here is what recent surveys have found out about the trend:

1. *Husbands who help their wives with the shopping*— 55 percent (compared with 25 percent in the early 1960s).
2. *Husbands who actually make food purchases in a supermarket*—23 percent (according to Haley, Overholser and Associates).

• **THE TROJAN DOUGHNUT.** A study by Sandon A. Steinberg and Richard F. Yalch shows that when a free food item—a doughnut, for instance—is offered to shoppers in a supermarket, shoppers tend to spend more money on food than they would if the food item were not offered. The tendency is even more pronounced among obese persons.

SOURCES

Harry L. Davis, "Decision Making Within the Household," 1977.

Sandon A. Steinberg and Richard F. Yalch, "When Eating Begets Buying," 1978.

Seventeen.

U.S. Bureau of the Census, *Statistical Abstract of the United States:* 1978.

Scott Ward and Daniel B. Wackman, "Children's Purchase Influence Attempts and Parental Yielding," 1972.

HOW WE SHOP FOR CARS

A car is the second biggest purchase the average American is likely to make in his or her lifetime (next to a home), and so a good deal of market research has gone into how this process unfolds.

•PICKING IT OUT. A *Newsweek* market survey, done in the late 1970s, showed differences in the shopping patterns of buyers of domestic cars and buyers of imported cars. Friends, for instance, are more likely to influence decision making in the purchase of an imported car, and buyers of imported cars, in general, take a longer time and do more planning on the purchase than do buyers of domestic cars. The reasons cited most often, by both groups of buyers, for selecting a particular car are as follows.

Imported-car buyers:

1. *Better gas mileage.*
2. *In buyer's price range.*
3. *Better-quality workmanship.*
4. *Better overall performance.*
5. *Best value for price.*

And for domestic-car buyers:

1. *Good past experience with car.*
2. *Styling.*
3. *Attractive price.*
4. *Better gas mileage.*
5. *In buyer's price range.*

The verdict: Imported-car buyers are more performance-conscious than domestic-car buyers, but domestic-car buyers put a higher premium on style.

•PAYING FOR IT. More than half the people who buy cars in the United States finance the purchase, but the proportion of installment buyers differs for buyers of domestic cars and buyers of imported cars. The numbers.

Proportion of imported-car buyers who:

1. *Finance the purchase*—72.0 percent.
2. *Use a bank*—45.0 percent of installment buyers.
3. *Finance through the dealer*—27.5 percent of installment buyers.
4. *Take three years to pay*—80.0 percent of installment buyers.

Proportion of domestic-car buyers who:

1. *Finance the purchase*—50 percent.
2. *Use a bank*—45 percent of installment buyers.

3. *Finance through the dealer*—21 percent of installment buyers.
4. *Take three years to pay*—80 percent of installment buyers.

• **WOMEN BUYERS**. About 13 percent of all the cars sold in the United States in 1978 were sold to women, but a survey by J. D. Power and Associates suggests that women are not very happy with the treatment they get in the showroom. Some numbers.

Proportion of women car buyers who:

1. *Feel it is more difficult for a woman, as compared with a man, to buy a car*—62 percent.
2. *Feel that car salesmen take advantage of women*—25 percent.
3. *Take pride in their cars and take good care of them*—70 percent.

• **WALKING OUT**. A 1978 survey by R. H. Bruskin examined the reasons Americans are *not* buying new cars:

1. *Cars are too expensive*—50 percent.
2. *Concern over the U.S. economy on the whole*—33 percent.
3. *Unhappy with performance of cars*—3 percent.

SOURCES
R. H. Bruskin Associates.
Newsweek.
J. D. Power and Associates.

XI ON THE JOB

WHAT WE DO FOR A LIVING:
A CLOSER LOOK

As indicated in Part I, "Americans at a Glance," the trend in American work patterns over the past twenty years has been from blue to white. Here is a closer look.

• THE BASIC NUMBERS. At the end of 1978 there were approximately 90 million men and women in the American work force. Some numbers not mentioned earlier:

1. *Full-time workers*—80.0 percent.
2. *Part-time workers*—20.0 percent.
3. *Unemployed*—10.0 percent of population 16 and older.
4. *Married men in work force*—41.0 percent of all workers.
5. *Married women*—23.0 percent of all workers.
6. *Single men (never married)*—11.5 percent of all workers.
7. *Single women (never married)*—10.0 percent.
8. *Widowed, divorced, or separated men*—4.0 percent.
9. *Widowed, divorced, or separated women*—7.5 percent.
10. *People with two or more jobs*—5.0 percent.

• OCCUPATIONAL DEMOGRAPHICS. There is no arguing the fact that the "best" jobs in the United States are held in the main by white, college-educated males, but the demographic gaps are starting to close up a little bit. Here are some figures to show where we have been and where we are going:

1. *Whites who work in technical fields*—15.0 percent of white male population.
2. *Blacks in technical fields*—12.0 percent (up from 9.0 percent in 1970).
3. *Whites in managerial positions*—11.5 percent.
4. *Blacks in managerial positions*—4.5 percent (up about 25.0 percent since 1960).
5. *Whites in craft fields*—13.0 percent.
6. *Blacks in craft fields*—9.0 percent (and not going anywhere).
7. *Blacks in service industries*—25.0 percent.

• **INDUSTRIAL BREAKDOWN**. Here is a look at how various industries in the United States compare in *numbers* of workers:

1. *Manufacturing*—22.0 percent of work force.
2. *Retail*—16.0 percent.
3. *Construction*—6.0 percent.
4. *Transportation, communications, and public utilities*—6.0 percent.
5. *Elementary- and secondary-school teachers*—5.5 percent.
6. *Public administration*—5.5 percent.
7. *Hospitals*—4.0 percent.
8. *Wholesale trade*—4.0 percent.
9. *Insurance and real estate*—3.0 percent.
10. *Health services (other than hospitals)*—2.0 percent.

• **STUDENT LABORS**. According to a 1972 HEW survey, about 40 percent of American high-school students work at least part-time during the school year. Some other figures:

1. *Twelve-year-old girls who work part-time*—12 percent of all 12-year-olds.
2. *Twelve-year-old boys who work part-time*—38 percent.
3. *Seventeen-year-old girls who work during summer vacation*—56 percent.
4. *Seventeen-year-old boys who work during summer vacation*—84 percent.

• **COMING UP FAST**. A U.S. Department of Labor survey published in 1978 indicates that job opportunities in the future are likely to be the greatest in the following occupations:

1. *Licensed practical nurses.*
2. *Teachers' aides.*
3. *Industrial-machinery mechanics.*
4. *Emergency-medical technicians.*
5. *Air-conditioning, refrigeration, and heating mechanics.*
6. *Dental assistants.*
7. *Sewer-plant operators.*
8. *Iron workers.*
9. *Cement masons and terrazzo workers.*
10. *Home-health aides.*

• **OUT OF IT**. At last glance, about 6 percent of the American people were out of work, but certain groups were clearly worse off than others. Here is a random listing of which groups are obliged to be the most idle:

1. *Teenagers*—19.0 percent are out of work.
2. *Single men*—17.0 percent.
3. *Nonwhites*—14.0 percent.
4. *Laborers*—14.0 percent.
5. *Single women*—12.0 percent.
6. *Married women (those looking for work)*—8.0 percent.
7. *Women over 20*—7.5 percent.
8. *Whites*—7.0 percent.
9. *Men over 20*—6.0 percent.
10. *Married men*—4.0 percent.
11. *Farm workers*—4.0 percent.
12. *Managers, administrators*—3.0 percent.

SOURCE
   U.S. Bureau of the Census, *Statistical Abstract of the United States: 1978.*

HOW MUCH WE GET PAID

Salaries in the United States have gone up in virtually every job category, but some occupations have fared noticeably better than others.

• THE GENERAL PICTURE. Jobs throughout the United States were paying about 75 percent more in 1979 than they were paying in 1970. Some representative figures:

1. *Average hourly pay in American industry in 1978*—$5.50.
2. *Highest paid hourly workers*—construction workers ($8.00 per hour).
3. *Lowest paid hourly workers*—service workers in eating and drinking places ($2.90 per hour, but not counting tips, of course).

• THE COLLEGE EDGE. A college diploma no longer guarantees a good-paying job as it once did, what with plumbers and sanitation workers now pulling in twice as much money per year as do art historians and philosophers, but, statistically, college graduates are still better off financially than high-school graduates and grammar-school graduates. Some examples. Median yearly income for:

1. *College graduates 24 and younger—$9,000.*
2. *High-school graduates 24 and younger—$7,000.*
3. *College graduates 45 and older—$17,600.*
4. *High-school graduates 45 and older—$10,900.*

• FIELD REPORT. Here is what Americans in selected fields were earning as of 1978—on average:

1. *Physicians as a group—$55,000.*
2. *Orthopedic surgeons—$71,000.*
3. *Psychiatrists—$45,000.*
4. *National Basketball Association players—$143,000* (compared with $20,000 in 1967).
5. *Major-league baseball players—$90,000* (twice the average that prevailed in 1975).
6. *National League hockey players—$95,000.*
7. *National Football League players—$55,000* (up 'from $27,000 in 1965).
8. *Policemen—$17,000* in reasonably large cities.
9. *Firemen—$17,000* in big cities; $14,000 in smaller cities.
10. *College teachers—$22,000.*
11. *Teachers—$13,500* (more in New York—$16,000— than in Mississippi—$9,000).
12. *Scientists—$24,000.*
13. *Physicists—$30,000* (they are the highest paid).
14. *Geographers—$20,000* (the lowest paid).
15. *Actors—$8,000.*
16. *Big-city TV anchormen—$200,000.*
17. *Corporation presidents—$250,000* for large corporations.
18. *Postal workers—$17,000.*

• STARTING OUT. While salaries in general have increased around 60 percent since 1970, starting salaries for college graduates have only risen at about half that rate. Here is a random sampling of what the average college graduate can expect to earn in some of the more familiar job fields:

1. *General business—$12,000.*
2. *Engineering—$17,000–$18,000.*
3. *Chemistry—$14,000.*

4. *Mathematics*—$13,000.
5. *Physics*—$12,000.
6. *Humanities*—$10,500.

A graduate with a master's degree can figure an additional 20 percent in earnings, and a doctorate is worth between 25 and 40 percent more, depending on the field. The humanities are the field in which starting salaries have increased the least over the past ten years.

SOURCE
U.S. Bureau of the Census, *Statistical Abstract of the United States: 1978.*

WHAT WE LOOK FOR IN OUR WORK

It does not take an industrial psychologist to figure out that if a job is giving you the things you are looking for in your work, you will be a satisfied worker. So, a good deal of research in the field has tried to sort out some of the rewards that people are looking for. Here is what some of the surveys on the subject have turned up.

Men 18 to 49 who consider each of the following "very important" (from *The Playboy Report on American Men*):

1. *Chance to use the mind and abilities*—79 percent of respondents.
2. *Job security*—70 percent.
3. *Doing meaningful things*—69 percent.
4. *Friendly people to work with*—67 percent.
5. *Chance for personal growth*—66 percent.
6. *Good salary*—63 percent.
7. *Working for a company the employee respects*—63 percent.
8. *Appreciation for a job well done*—63 percent.
9. *New challenges*—62 percent.
10. *Chance for advancement*—62 percent.
11. *Freedom to decide how to do the job*—68 percent.
12. *Good pension plan*—52 percent.
13. *Fringe benefits*—51 percent.

What is important to office workers (from the Steelcase National Study):

1. *Being clear about the scope and responsibilities of the job*—rating score of 95.
2. *Finding their work interesting*—93.
3. *Having necessary resources to get job done*—93.
4. *Feeling that they are making a contribution to the total work done by a work unit*—91.
5. *Feeling like an individual and not a "cog"*—90.
6. *Finding the job challenging*—90.
7. *Having friendly and helpful coworkers*—90.
8. *Having a competent supervisor*—89.
9. *Earning a good salary*—87.
10. *Having the freedom to decide how to do work*—86.
11. *Employee benefits*—86.

Proportion who feel each aspect mentioned is the "one thing" most preferred in a job (from various NORC General Social Surveys):

1. *Important work that gives a feeling of accomplishment* —45.0 percent (down from 51.0 percent in 1973).
2. *High income*—20.0 percent (up from 6.5 percent in 1973).
3. *Chance for advancement*—19.0 percent (up from 18.0 percent in 1973).
4. *No danger of being fired*—7.5 percent (up from 6.5 percent in 1973).
5. *Short working hours, lots of free time*—4.5 percent (no change from 1973).

The factors that most affect job satisfaction (based on Institute for Social Research findings):

1. *Interesting work.*
2. *Opportunity to do what you like.*
3. *Good pay.*
4. *Good security.*
5. *Nice surroundings.*
6. *Time to finish.*

•**ITCHY FEET.** Roughly one out of ten American workers —11.5 percent according to an early-1979 U.S. Department of Labor report—changed jobs in 1978. The turnover rate is slightly up from 1973 when about 9 percent of the work force had made a switch. A little more than one out of three of the workers switching jobs in 1978 were younger than 25.

• **T H E B O T T O M L I N E .** Taken as a group, the various and most recent studies on what the average American worker is looking for in a job provide ammunition for the following observations:

1. *A feeling of personal accomplishment:* clearly the most important single factor in job satisfaction. More important among younger workers and among more educated Americans than anyone else, and more important to men than to women. Showing signs, however, of losing some ground to income.

2. *Income:* probably second for most people, but less important among younger workers than is the chance to advance, and not as important to older workers as job security. Getting more important, though, as inflation gets worse.

3. *Chance for advancement:* difficult to measure, since advancement also carries with it the promise of higher income. Certainly more important for younger than older workers.

4. *Security:* becoming more important for everybody (again, because of inflation). The importance of security as a specific factor in satisfaction rises in periods of relatively high unemployment.

5. *Working conditions, hours, etc.:* important, but secondary among most groups to the aspects already mentioned.

SOURCES
Angus Campbell, *Quality of American Life.*
NORC.
Playboy Report on American Men.
Steelcase National Study of Office Environments.
U.S. Department of Labor.

HOW HAPPY WE ARE IN OUR WORK

Social scientists and opinion pollsters have been measuring the job-satisfaction levels of workers in the United States ever since the early 1930s, and the results throughout most of this period have been strikingly consistent: The majority of Americans (as many as 90 percent according to some surveys) are basically satisfied with what they do for a living. True, there was a precipitous drop in job satisfaction between 1960 and 1970 (fueled in the main by young people), but satisfaction levels have leveled off since then, and although some recent surveys show a large proportion of dissatisfied workers than ever before, there has been an increase in the proportion of "very" satisfied workers.

• THE BASIC NUMBERS. Most job-satisfaction surveys are conducted in the same way. Workers are simply asked to say how they feel about their present job, whether they are "very satisfied," "moderately satisfied," "somewhat dissatisfied," or "very dissatisfied." Here is a sampling of various survey results.

Proportion of American workers in 1972 expressing these levels of job satisfaction (from an NORC General Social Survey):

1. *Very satisfied*—48 percent.
2. *Moderately satisfied*—36 percent.
3. *A little dissatisfied*—11 percent.
4. *Very dissatisfied*—3 percent.

And in 1978 (from an NORC General Social Survey):

1. *Very satisfied*—51.0 percent.
2. *Moderately satisfied*—36.0 percent.
3. *A little dissatisfied*—8.0 percent.
4. *Very dissatisfied*—4.5 percent.

Men 18 to 49 (from the *Playboy Report on American Men*):

1. *Very satisfied*—36 percent.
2. *Somewhat satisfied*—37 percent.
3. *Somewhat dissastisfied*—11 percent.
4. *Very dissatisfied*—10 percent.
5. *Not sure*—6 percent.

Office workers (from the 1978 Steelcase national study):

1. *Very satisfied*—42 percent.
2. *Somewhat satisfied*—40 percent.
3. *Somewhat dissatisfied*—13 percent.
4. *Very dissatisfied*—4 percent.

A final note: Two-thirds of American workers (according to NORC General Social Surveys) say they would continue to work even if they were to get enough money to live comfortably.

• Q U A L I F I E D Y E S S E S. Not every social scientists buys the rosy picture of American work satisfaction that emerges from the various surveys on the subject. The argument is that the question, "Are you satisfied with your job?" does not indicate *true* satisfaction because it does not take into account the way a worker perceives himself or the way he views prospects for other jobs. In one 1971 study, for instance, less than 24 percent of the blue-collar workers queried, and only 43 percent of the white-collar workers, said they would voluntarily choose the same kind of work if given a second chance, and here is what a recent National Education Association poll indicated about the job-satisfaction level of the nation's teachers:

1. *Teachers who say they would choose teaching again if given a second chance*—38 percent.
2. *Teachers who intend to stay in teaching until they retire*—60 percent.

Similar dissatisfaction emerges from a *Psychology Today* poll in which respondents were asked to say how strongly they agreed or disagreed with the statement, "I often feel trapped in my present job":

1. *Strongly disagree*—16.5 percent.
2. *Disagree*—22.0 percent.
3. *Slightly disagree*—7.5 percent.
4. *Neither agree nor disagree*—10.0 percent.
5. *Slightly agree*—18.5 percent.
6. *Agree*—14.1 percent.
7. *Strongly agree*—11.3 percent.
8. *Workers who feel "trapped" (all degrees)*—43 percent.

• S A T I S F A C T I O N D E M O G R A P H I C S. Even granting the possibly deceptive findings of job-satisfaction surveys, some definite patterns show up when you look at how various demographic groupings compare:

1. *Youth:* Younger people are much less likely to be satisfied with their jobs than older people, although the satisfaction level of workers 21 to 30 in the United States has risen noticeably throughout the 1970s (after reaching unprecedented lows in the late 1960s).
2. *Race:* Blacks are not as satisfied with their jobs as whites, but this is probably a reflection of the kinds of jobs many blacks hold and not a reflection of any characteristically racial component at work.

3. *Gender:* Women show more satisfaction with work than men. And the fact that women generally get paid less than men and are in lower-level jobs suggests that there *is* a gender component to job satisfaction, though how long it will last, as women's expectations in the job field rise, is something nobody knows.

4. *Schooling:* Job-satisfaction levels tend to go up with educational levels, but here again the reason has to do more with the kind of work better-educated people do and not with any specific work attitudes fostered by education.

• **WORK HAPPY.** When a sampling of Americans in a 1971 survey were asked if they would select the same career given a chance to do it all over again, the six occupations that fared best were as follows:

1. *University professors*—91 percent.
2. *Physicists*—89 percent.
3. *Biologists*—89 percent.
4. *Chemists*—86 percent.
5. *Lawyers*—85 percent.
6. *Journalists*—82 percent.

SOURCES
National Education Association.
NORC.
Playboy Report on American Men.
Psychology Today.
Steelcase National Study.
Work in America, 1973.

HOW PRODUCTIVE WE ARE

The federal government keeps close tabs on productivity levels in most industries, but these figures are not necessarily a reflection of work performance. Technological advances, strikes, layoffs, the state of the economy—all can have an effect, one way or the other, on what the government's statistical people like to call the "output per hour." So we are obliged to use indirect measures to find out whether Americans are working more productively or less productively than before.

• **THE BASIC NUMBERS.** Without going into the complicated manner by which the federal government sets up its productivity indexes, it is enough to say that the average output per hour has gone *up* anywhere from 25 percent to 50 percent in most major industries since 1965. The industries that have enjoyed the highest increase in output per hour are the hosiery industry, the malt-liquor industry, the pharmaceutical industry, and the man-made-fiber industry. The industries in which the rise in productivity has been the smallest are steel, foundry, and copper.

• **SELF-RATINGS.** *The Steelcase National Study of Office Environments* included a section on office workers' perception of their own personal productivity. The numbers:

1. *Office workers who feel they are now "certainly" doing as much as they can*—42 percent.
2. *Management executives who feel this way*—36 percent.
3. *Supervisory workers*—43 percent.
4. *Office workers who feel they are "probably" doing as much as they can do*—22 percent.
5. *Who feel they could "probably do more"*—34 percent.
6. *Management executives who say they could "probably do more"*—39 percent.

• **SICK LEAVE.** Here is a look at how much we miss work:

1. *Average number of workers off the job on a typical workday because of illness, injury, civic duty, etc.*—6.5 percent.
2. *Average number of days per year missed by American workers*—9 days.
3. *Industries with the lowest absentee rate*—insurance and real estate.
4. *The highest rate*—public administration.

• **GOOFING OFF.** How much does the average American worker goof off on a typical day? Two University of Michigan economists, Frank Stafford and Greg Duncan, did a time study on 1,500 workers. Their findings:

1. *Average amount of "unscheduled idleness" for men workers*—50 minutes a day.
2. *For women workers*—35 minutes a day.

The economists also found that the more money you make, the more likely you will be to waste time on the job.

•OLD GOLD. A study by sociologist Wayne Dennis in the mid-1960s suggests that creative people—philosophers, inventors, playwrights—tend to enjoy their greatest periods of productivity after the age of 40, but the creative field has a lot to do with it.

1. *Creative types who are most productive in their forties* —scholars, artists, and scientists.
2. *In their sixties*—philosophers, botanists, historians, and inventors.
3. *In their twenties and thirties*—chamber musicians.

•ROADBLOCKS. When the office workers who were surveyed for the Steelcase study were asked to name the one thing that "most interfered" with their ability to do their job well, the most frequently given answer was "having too much work to do," but management workers were more likely to cite this reason than supervisory or regular workers. Asked to name the problem considered to be the "most serious" in preventing them from getting their job done, office workers gave these responses:

1. *Not getting good enough instruction and information from supervisor*—15 percent.
2. *Having too much work to do*—14 percent.
3. *Not having enough time to do the job properly*—12 percent.
4. *Being unclear on just what the scope and responsibilities of the job are*—11 percent.
5. *Having to work with tools, equipment, that are now out of date*—5 percent.

•HEAVYWEIGHT WASTES. *Fortune* magazine asked more than fifty corporate chairmen, presidents, and vice-presidents to rank the "ten worst time wasters" of their work time. The list came out as follows:

1. *Telephone.*
2. *Mail.*
3. *Meetings.*
4. *Public relations.*
5. *Paperwork.*

6. *Commuting.*
7. *Business lunches.*
8. *Civic duties.*
9. *Incompetents.*
10. *Family demands.*

SOURCES

Wayne Dennis, "Creative Productivity Between the Ages of 20 and 80 Years," 1966.

U.S. Department of Labor, *Monthly Labor Review*, October 1977.

Frank Stafford and Greg Duncan, "Laziness in the World's Busiest City," *New York*, August 14, 1978.

U.S. Bureau of the Census, *Statistical Abstract of the United States: 1978.*

The Steelcase National Study of Office Environments.

WOMEN AT WORK

Some sociologists contend that the expanding proportion of American women now working has been *the* most significant social development over the past twenty-five years. A big statement, but the figures do support it.

• T H E B A S I C N U M B E R S . As of early 1979, approximately 40 million American women 16 years old and older were officially part of the American civilian labor work force. This is more than twice the number of women who were working in 1960 and represents a jump of nearly 25 percent over the 1970 total. Curiously, though, the makeup of the female work force—that is, the proportion of single, married, and divorced women—has stayed pretty much the same since the mid-1960s. In fact, the most recent figures suggest a slight drop in the proportion of married women who work. Here are some of the numbers that tell part of the story. All reflect the situation as of March 1977.

1. *Proportion of women 16 and older in the work force who are single*—24.0 percent.
2. *Who are married and who work*—61.5 percent.
3. *Widowed or divorced*—15.0 percent.
4. *Married women who work full-time*—32.0 percent.
5. *Married women with no children who work*—33.0 percent.

6. *With children 6 to 17*—36.0 percent.
7. *With children younger than 6*—25.0 percent.
8. *Divorced women who work full-time*—62.0 percent.

Trends? The proportion of married women 20 to 44 years old who work either full- or part-time has climbed nearly 20 percent since 1970, while the proportion of working single and divorced women in this age-group has stayed about the same.

• **THE DEMOGRAPHICS**. The more schooling a married woman has, the more likely she is to be part of the work force, but income is not so predictable a factor. The numbers:

1. *Wives in the American work force who did not graduate from high school*—33.0 percent.
2. *College-degreed wives who work full- or part-time*—69.0 percent.
3. *College-degreed wives, with four years of college and no children younger than 18, who work*—90.0 percent.
4. *Working wives with husbands earning $15,000 or more*—32.0 percent.
5. *With husbands earning between $10,000 and $15,000*—39.0 percent.
6. *Married couples in which the wife is the only wage earner*—4.0 percent.

• **MOVING UP**. Roughly six out of ten working women (married and single) are employed in white-collar jobs. A majority of those remaining are service workers or teachers. Here is how women were represented in some occupations in 1977.
Proportion of female workers in each category:

1. *Accountants*—27.5 percent (up from 22.0 percent in 1972).
2. *Carpenters*—5.0 percent (up from 3.5 percent in 1972).
3. *Computer specialists*—23.0 percent (up from 17.0 percent in 1972).
4. *Dentists*—3.0 percent (up from 2.0 percent in 1972).
5. *Engineers and science technicians*—15.0 percent (up from 9.0 percent in 1972).
6. *Lawyers and judges*—9.5 percent (up from 4.0 percent in 1972).
7. *Physicians*—11.0 percent (up from 10.0 percent in 1972).

8. *Plumbers and pipe fitters*—0.8 percent (or 429,000, up from 389,000 in 1972).
9. *Scientists*—15.5 percent (up from 10 percent in 1972).
10. *Writers, artists, and entertainers*—35.5 percent (compared with 31.0 percent in 1972).

• **IMBALANCE OF PAYMENTS**. It is hard to find a single field in which the median salary for women is equal to the median salary for men in the same job. Overall, the median income for women workers is about $8,000, compared with $13,000 for men. And with the exception of farm workers, as of May 1976 there was not one major occupational field in which women were earning more than 75 percent of men's earnings. The numbers, representing women's earnings as percentages of men's:

1. *Teaching*—66 percent.
2. *Professional and technical*—73 percent.
3. *Sales*—45 percent.
4. *Clerical*—64 percent.
5. *Craft*—61 percent.
6. *Service work*—64 percent.
7. *Farm work*—88 percent.
8. *Self-employed*—25 percent.

• **THE BOTTOM RUNG**. If working women in general are getting a raw deal, black women in particular are getting the worst of it. The numbers:

1. *Black women in female work force*—12 percent.
2. *Black women who work*—50 percent (the proportion is probably higher, since it does not take into consideration domestic workers who do not report incomes).
3. *Female laundry and dry-cleaning workers who are black* —25 percent.
4. *Low-level service workers who are black*—53 percent.
5. *Median annual earnings for black women in 1977*— $7,764 (compared with $8,164 for whites).

• **WORKING MOMS**. In about one-third of the roughly 20 million American households in which both the husband and the wife work, the working mother is between the ages of 25 and 49, has a husband employed full-time, and has at least one child younger than 18 living at home. A survey conducted in 1978 by Kentucky Fried Chicken and *Ladies' Home Journal* elicited the following responses from a sampling in this group.

Proportion of working mothers who say they:

1. *Like their jobs*—97 percent.
2. *Are proud of being a working mother*—88 percent.
3. *Consider themselves more stimulating because of their work*—84 percent.
4. *Get support from their husbands*—92 percent.
5. *Have husbands who are "interested" in their work*—84 percent.
6. *Are working out of necessity*—40 percent.
7. *Are working because the family wants extra luxuries*—20 percent.
8. *Are working for "personal fulfillment" alone*—19 percent.
9. *Find that their children are "more independent" because of their work*—78 percent.
10. *Are more tolerant of both their children and their husband because they are working*—61 percent.

• **MINORITY REPORT**. The relatively rosy picture just painted notwithstanding, most of the sociological studies into working-mother families show that children in these homes have *more* problems growing up than do children in homes where the mother is always there. Here is what some of the studies have turned up:

1. *Delinquency rate:* It is higher in working-mother homes, according to a 1959 study by Harry M. Shulman.
2. *Adjustment:* Children of working mothers are more likely (*a*) to feel uneasy about themselves and (*b*) to have difficulty getting along with their friends than are children of nonworking mothers, according to *The General Mills American Family Report.*
3. *Girls versus Boys:* Comparative studies show that girls have a more difficult time adjusting to a working mother than do boys.

• **WORKING DIFFERENCE**. A report from the Biennial Symposium of the Soap and Detergent Association pointed out some of the life-style changes a woman undergoes when she stops being a full-time homemaker and starts being a full-time worker:

1. *She becomes less interested in trendy, high-fashion clothes.*
2. *She spends about 25 percent less time on household chores than she used to.*
3. *She becomes much less hesitant about buying luxury items for herself.*

SOURCES

The General Mills American Family Report 1976–77.

Harry M. Shulman, *The Family and Juvenile Delinquency*, 1959.

L. Stoltz, "Effects of Maternal Employment on Children," 1960.

Time Out Institute.

U.S. Bureau of Labor Statistics, *U.S. Working Women: A Databook*, 1977.

WHAT IT'S LIKE IN THE OFFICES WHERE WE WORK

More than half the workers in the United States work in offices, but office environments differ and so, obviously, do individual working conditions. Here is what one survey, *The Steelcase National Study of Office Environments*, found out about office living.

• **P L A C E O F B U S I N E S S .** Most American office workers operate out of what is generally referred to as a "conventional" office—a private office in a row of such offices with secretarial reception areas. The next most common environment is the clerical "pool"—a big open room with lots of desks. Finally, there is the "open plan," with cubicles and partitions providing some privacy in an otherwise open environment. The numbers.

Conventional offices:

1. *All office workers*—39 percent.
2. *Executives*—57 percent.
3. *Government workers*—42 percent.
4. *Banking and investment workers*—42 percent.

Pool offices:

1. *All office workers*—14 percent.
2. *Insurance and real-estate workers*—24 percent.
3. *Executives and corporate workers*—7 percent.

Open-plan offices:

1. *All workers*—30 percent.
2. *Business and professional service workers*—45 percent.
3. *Communications and public-service workers*—41 percent.
4. *Executives*—26 percent.

• O F F I C E   B O U N D . Most office workers (about 53 percent) spend between six and eight hours a day lodged within their own "personal work space." Some numbers of office workers who:

1. *Spend four hours a day or less in one place*—14 percent.
2. *Spend over eight hours a day in their office space*—5 percent.
3. *Spend virtually all of their working time at their desks* —7 percent.
4. *Spend 76 to 99 percent*—40 percent.
5. *Spend 51 to 75 percent*—26 percent.
6. *Spend 26 to 50 percent*—15 percent.
7. *Spend 1 to 25 percent*—10 percent.

• R O O M M A T E S . About 54 percent of American office workers share a work space with one or more persons. Here are the figures:

1. *Workers 18 to 29 who share an office*—65 percent.
2. *Workers 40 and older who share an office*—46 percent.
3. *Secretaries who share*—42 percent.
4. *Executives who share*—31 percent.
5. *Clerical workers who share*—68 percent.
6. *Secretaries who work in their own work space*—58 percent.
7. *Median number of workers in shared work spaces*—5.

SOURCE
Steelcase National Study.

XII OUR PROBLEMS

HOW MUCH CRIME WE HAVE TO LIVE WITH

Crime statistics in the United States paint a bleak picture indeed, and the picture gets even grimmer when you take into account the contention of some criminologists that the yearly statistics supplied by the Federal Bureau of Investigation leave out much of the crime that is committed. (The FBI numbers relate to *reported* crimes.) On the other hand, there are indications that the crime rate on the whole—particularly the rate of violent crimes—may finally be leveling off and even dropping, after nearly two decades of relentless growth. Here is a not terribly reassuring look at where we stand today.

• **THE BASIC NUMBERS**. Crime in the United States is usually divided into two categories: violent crimes, that is, those in which people get hurt or are killed, and property crimes, those in which nothing gets hurt except somebody's pocketbook. (Many crimes, of course, involve both property and persons.) The FBI's *Uniform Crime Reports* offer the following general numbers on crime as it happened in 1977:

1. *Crime rate in 1977*—about 11 million crimes committed, translating into a crime rate of 5,055 crimes per 100,000 inhabitants.
2. *Crime rate in 1977 compared with that in 1973*—up about 22.0 percent.
3. *Compared with 1968 rate*—up about 68.0 percent.
4. *Compared with 1976 rate*—down about 4.0 percent.
5. *Violent-crime rate in 1977*—about 466 per 100,000.
6. *Violent-crime rate in 1977 compared with 1973 rate*—up 11.0 percent.
7. *Compared with 1973 rate*—up 12.0 percent.
8. *Compared with 1968 rate*—up 56.5 percent.
9. *Compared with 1976 rate*—up 1.5 percent.
10. *Property-crime rate in 1977*—4,588 per 100,000.
11. *Compared with 1973 rate*—up 22.0 percent.
12. *Compared with 1968 rate*—up 49.5 percent.
13. *Compared with 1976 rate*—down 4.5 percent.
14. *Average frequency for violent crime in 1977*—one committed every 31 seconds.
15. *For property crime*—one committed every 3 seconds.

• Z E R O I N G I N . The scorecard for specific crimes committed in 1977, based on FBI *Uniform Crime Reports*, looks like this.
Murder:

1. *Number committed in 1977—19,120.*
2. *Rate per 100,000 people—9.*
3. *Compared with 1960 rate*—up 60 percent.
4. *Compared with 1970 rate*—down 12 percent.
5. *Compared with 1976 rate*—the same.

Aggravated assault:

1. *Number committed in 1977—522,510.*
2. *Rate per 100,000 people—241.5.*
3. *Compared with 1976 rate*—up 5.5 percent.
4. *Compared with 1967 rate*—up 100 percent.
5. *Compared with 1970 rate*—up 50.0 percent.

Forcible rape (FBI figures on rape are generally considered to be vastly underreported):

1. *Reported offenses in 1977—63,020.*
2. *Rate per 100,000 of population—29.*
3. *Compared with 1967 rate*—up 50 percent.
4. *Compared with 1976 rate*—up 10 percent.

Robbery:

1. *Number committed in 1977—404,850.*
2. *Rate per 100,000 people—187.*
3. *Compared with 1967 rate*—up 80 percent.
4. *Compared with 1971 rate*—about the same.
5. *Compared with 1975 rate*—down 10.0 percent.
6. *Compared with 1976 rate*—down 4.5 percent.
7. *Bank-robbery rate since 1973*—up 90.0 percent.
8. *Mugging rate since 1973*—down 2.0 percent.
9. *Residential-robbery rate since 1975*—down about 12.0 percent.
10. *Gas-station-robbery rate since 1973*—up 36.0 percent.
11. *Since 1977*—about the same.

Burglary:

1. *Number committed in 1977—3,052,200.*
2. *Rate per 100,000—1,411.*
3. *Compared with 1967 rate*—up about 80 percent.
4. *Compared with 1975 rate*—down about 10 percent.
5. *Compared with 1976 rate*—down 2 percent.

Larceny (includes shoplifting, car theft, pickpocketing, bicycle thefts):

1. *Number committed in 1977—5,905,700.*
2. *Rate per 100,000—2,730.*
3. *Compared with 1967 rate—*up 75.0 percent.
4. *Compared with 1976 rate—*down 6.5 percent.

Motor-vehicle theft (technically a part of larceny theft, but reported separately in *Uniform Crime Reports*):

1. *Number reported in 1977—968,400.*
2. *Rate per 100,000—447.6.*
3. *Rate since 1963—*up 4 percent.
4. *Compared with 1976 rate—*less than 1-percent increase.

Crimes committed *most* frequently in the United States (based on rate per 100,000):

1. *Larceny theft—2,729.0.*
2. *Burglary—1,410.0.*
3. *Motor-vehicle theft—447.5.*
4. *Aggravated assault—241.5.*
5. *Robbery—187.0.*
6. *Forcible rape—29.0.*
7. *Murder—9.0.*

Crimes whose rate has *increased* the most since 1968:

1. *Forcible rape—*up 83.0 percent.
2. *Aggravated assault—*68.0 percent.
3. *Larceny theft—*56.0 percent.
4. *Burglary—*51.0 percent.
5. *Robbery—*42.0 percent.
6. *Murder—*27.5 percent.
7. *Motor-vehicle theft—*14.0 percent.

• T o o l s o f D e s t r u c t i o n . Most violent crimes are committed with a weapon. Here is a look at what was used in 1977.
Murder:

1. *Handgun—*48 percent.
2. *Knife or other sharp instrument—*19 percent.
3. *Club, poison, or something other than gun, knife, or fists—*13 percent.
4. *Shotgun—*9 percent.

5. *Rifle*—6 percent.
6. *Personal weapon (fists, feet)*—6 percent.

Aggravated assault:

1. *Gun*—23 percent.
2. *Knife*—23 percent.
3. *Blunt object*—27 percent.
4. *Fists and feet*—27 percent.

• T H E   V I C T I M S . Looked at on a strictly statistical basis, the proportion of Americans who are directly victimized by crimes each year is well under one percent of the population— a statistic that is pretty much borne out in surveys. There is no question, though, that certain segments of the population— chiefly poorer people—are much more likely to be victimized by crime than are other segments. Some representative numbers:

1. *Proportion of murder victims in 1977 in the United States who were men*—75 percent.
2. *Were black*—48 percent.
3. *Homicide-victim rate for white males since 1973*—12 per 100,000.
4. *For black males*—100 per 100,000 black males.
5. *For white females*—3 per 100,000.
6. *For black females*—18 per 100,000.
7. *Victims 29 and younger*—45 percent.
8. *Proportion of murders in which the murderer and the victim knew each other*—80 percent.
9. *In which the victim and the murderer were related*— 25 percent.
10. *In which the murder was the result of a romantic triangle gone askew*—12 percent.
11. *Proportion of rape victims in New York City who were were black or Hispanic*—60 percent.
12. *Proportion of burglarized households in the United States inhabited by blacks or Hispanics*—50 percent.

• C I V I L I A N   V I E W S . Surveys taken among the general public (as opposed to law-enforcement agencies) suggest that a substantial percentage of the crimes that get committed in the United States are never reported. Here is what a Gallup poll turned up in late 1972:

1. *Americans who had been victimized by one or more crimes within the previous twelve months*—21 percent.

2. *Center-city residents who had been victimized by a crime*—33 percent.
3. *Suburban crime victims*—19 percent.
4. *Americans whose home had been broken into*—7 percent.
5. *Who had reported incident to police*—5 percent.
6. *Who had been mugged or assaulted*—21 percent.
7. *Who had reported it to police*—1 percent
8. *Whose home, car, or property had been vandalized*—8 percent.
9. *Who had reported it to police*—4 percent.

• G E O G R A P H Y . Crime is a nationwide problem, but some areas of the country and some cities get hit worse than others.
Murder:

1. *Proportion of reported murders in the South*—41 percent.
2. *In the Midwest (or "North Central" in FBI terminology)*—22 percent.
3. *In the West*—19 percent (up 11 percent since 1976).
4. *In the Northeast*—18 percent.
5. *Murder rate in metropolitan areas*—9.5 per 100,000.
6. *In suburbs*—5.0 per 100,000.
7. *In rural areas*—6.0 per 100,000.
8. *In Cleveland*—39.0 per 100,000 (highest in the nation).
9. *In New York City*—21.0 per 100,000.
10. *In San Diego*—6.3 per 100,000.
11. *In Chicago*—27.0 per 100,000.

Forcible rape:

1. *Proportion committed in the South*—33 percent.
2. *In the Midwest*—23 percent.
3. *Rate in metropolitan areas*—68 per 100,000.
4. *In suburbs*—22 per 100,000.
5. *In Detroit*—97 per 100,000 (highest in the nation).
6. *In New York City*—52 per 100,000.
7. *In Los Angeles*—84 per 100,000.
8. *In San Antonio*—36 per 100,000.
9. *In the Cedar Rapids, Iowa, metropolitan area*—less than 1 per 100,000.
10. *In San Francisco*—89 per 100,000.

Aggravated assault:

1. *Proportion committed in the South*—36 percent.
2. *In the Midwest*—20 percent.
3. *Rate in metropolitan areas*—255.0 per 100,000.
4. *In rural areas*—128.0 per 100,000.
5. *In Eau Claire, Wisconsin*—21.5 per 100,000.
6. *In Cleveland*—1,012.0 per 100,000.
7. *In San Francisco*—815.0 per 100,000.
8. *In Los Angeles*—494.0 per 100,000.
9. *In Philadelphia*—208.0 per 100,000.

Larceny theft:

1. *Proportion committed in the West*—31 percent.
2. *In the Northeast*—21 percent.
3. *Rate in metropolitan areas*—3,093 per 100,000.
4. *In suburbs*—2,546 per 100,000.
5. *In rural areas*—954 per 100,000.
6. *In Dallas*—5,355 per 100,000 (highest in the nation).
7. *In Philadelphia*—1,491 per 100,000.
8. *In New York City*—2,897 per 100,000.
9. *In Johnstown, Pennsylvania*—889 per 100,000 (lowest in the nation).

Motor-vehicle theft:

1. *Proportion committed in the Northeast*—33 percent.
2. *In the South*—19 percent.
3. *Rate in metropolitan areas*—553 per 100,000.
4. *In suburbs*—337 per 100,000.
5. *In rural areas*—118 per 100,000.
6. *In Cleveland*—2,083 per 100,000.
7. *In New York City*—1,262 per 100,000.
8. *In the District of Columbia*—397 per 100,000.
9. *In San Francisco*—1,599 per 100,000.
10. *In Saint Cloud, Minnesota*—107 per 100,000 (lowest in the nation).

Robbery:

1. *Proportion committed in the Northeast*—35 percent.
2. *In the South*—18 percent.
3. *Rate in metropolitan areas*—244 per 100,000.
4. *In suburbs*—198 per 100,000.
5. *In rural areas*—21 per 100,000.

6. *In Detroit*—1,203 per 100,000.
7. *In San Antonio*—191 per 100,000.
8. *In La Crosse, Wisconsin*—7 per 100,000.
9. *In New York City*—994 per 100,000.
10. *In Cleveland*—1,012 per 100,000.

Burglary:

1. *Proportion committed in the West*—32 percent.
2. *In the Midwest*—19 percent.
3. *Rate in metropolitan areas*—1,609 per 100,000.
4. *In suburbs*—1,235 per 100,000.
5. *In rural areas*—767 per 100,000.
6. *In Tucson, Arizona*—3,282 per 100,000 (highest in the nation).
7. *In New York City*—2,391 per 100,000.
8. *In San Francisco*—2,896 per 100,000.
9. *In Eau Claire, Wisconsin*—490 per 100,000.

The five U.S. metropolitan areas with the worst overall crime problem, based on the FBI's "crime index total":

1. *Tucson, Arizona*—9,670 per 100,000.
2. *Las Vegas, Nevada*—9,453.
3. *Stockton, California*—8,373.
4. *Miami, Florida*—8,170.
5. *Fresno, California*—8,118.

The five U.S. areas with the worst violent-crime problem, based on the same index:

1. *New York City, New York*—1,355 per 100,000.
2. *Miami, Florida*—1,084.
3. *Los Angeles, California*—1,004.
4. *Baltimore, Maryland*—971.
5. *Las Vegas, Nevada*—961.

• T R E N D S . Even though the violent-crime rate is three times as high in cities with a population of 250,000 or more as it is in cities with a population of 25,000 or less, the rate since 1970 has been climbing more rapidly in smaller towns and in the suburbs than in the big cities. Here is a little of what has been happening with the violent-crime rate since 1970:

1. *In cities with a population of 250,000 or more*—up 10.0 percent since 1970 but down 8.0 percent since 1975.

2. *With a population of 25,000 to 49,999 (most suburban cities would fit this category)*—up nearly 60.0 percent since 1970 but level since 1975.
3. *In New York City*—up 20.0 percent since 1970 but down 8.5 percent since 1975.
4. *In Chicago*—up 20.0 percent since 1970 but down 4.5 percent between 1976 and 1977.
5. *Detroit*—down 3.0 percent since 1970.
6. *Dallas*—up 10.0 percent since 1970 and up 25.0 percent from 1976 on.
7. *San Diego*—up 87.0 percent since 1970 but very low to begin with.
8. *District of Columbia*—down 40.0 percent since 1970.
9. *Philadelphia*—up 23.0 percent since 1970 but down 28.0 percent since 1975.
10. *Houston*—down 28.0 percent.

• **THE SORE ARM OF JUSTICE.** At first glance, the FBI figures on the number of yearly arrests compared with the number of yearly crimes is highly reassuring—an almost one-to-one ratio. Not quite. The problem is largely one of semantics. A person who is "arrested" is not necessarily "charged" with a crime. Only when a person is *charged* is a particular crime considered "cleared." But there is still the little matter of trial and conviction. All of which helps to explain some of the numbers below.

Violent crimes:

1. *Percentage of violent crimes cleared*—22 percent.
2. *Persons charged*—39.5 per 100 offenses.
3. *Persons found guilty*—11.5 per 100 offenses.
4. *Guilty of lesser offenses*—3.0 per 100 offenses.
5. *Acquitted or dismissed*—8.0 per 100 offenses.
6. *Referred to juvenile court*—6.5 per 100 offenses.

Murder:

1. *Percentage cleared*—82 percent.
2. *Persons charged*—91.0 per 100 offenses.
3. *Found guilty as charged*—33.5 per 100 offenses.
4. *Guilty of lesser offenses*—8.5 per 100 offenses.
5. *Acquitted or dismissed*—18.5 per 100 offenses.
6. *Referred to juvenile court*—6.0 per 100 offenses.

Rape:

1. *Percentage cleared*—52.0 percent.
2. *Persons charged*—43.5 per 100 offenses.
3. *Found guilty as charged*—11.0 per 100 offenses.
4. *Guilty of lesser offenses*—3.0 per 100 offenses.
5. *Acquitted or dismissed*—9.5 per 100 offenses.
6. *Referred to juvenile court*—7.0 per 100,000.

Robbery:

1. *Percentage cleared*—31.5 percent.
2. *Persons charged*—29.5 per 100 offenses.
3. *Found guilty as charged*—9.0 per 100 offenses.
4. *Guilty of lesser offenses*—1.5 per 100 offenses.
5. *Acquitted or dismissed*—5.0 per 100 offenses.
6. *Referred to juvenile court*—7.5 per 100 offenses.

Property crime (total):

1. *Percentage of property crimes cleared*—19.5 percent.
2. *Persons charged*—17.0 per 100 offenses.
3. *Found guilty as charged*—5.5 per 100 offenses.
4. *Guilty of lesser offenses*—0.5 per 100 offenses.
5. *Acquitted or dismissed*—1.5 per 100 offenses.
6. *Referred to juvenile court*—6.0 per 100 offenses.

Burglary:

1. *Percentage cleared*—17.5 percent.
2. *Persons charged*—15.0 percent.
3. *Found guilty as charged*—3.2 per 100 offenses.
4. *Guilty of lesser offenses*—0.7 per 100 offenses.
5. *Acquitted or dismissed*—1.5 per 100 offenses.
6. *Referred to juvenile court*—7.0 per 100 offenses.

•QUALIFICATION. In property crime (and, to some extent, in violent crime as well) a single arrest or conviction may —and usually *does*—involve somebody who commits more than one crime. So the ratio of persons found guilty *to* crimes actually committed may not be as bad as it looks.

•PERPETRATORS. The statistics on persons who commit crimes in the United States are based, in the main, on *arrests* and, as such, do not necessarily reflect the true picture. Here is a sampling.

Arrests by sex, based on 1977 FBI data:

1. *Males arrested for all crimes*—84.0 percent of arrests.
2. *For "serious" crimes (murder, robbery, aggravated assault, larceny)*—79.0 percent.
3. *For violent crimes*—79.0 percent.
4. *Arrest rate for female perpetrators of violent crimes in 1977 compared with 1968 rate*—up 57.5 percent.
5. *For male perpetrators of violent crimes over the same period*—up 13.5 percent.
6. *Crime-arrest rate for women in general*—up 115.5 percent since 1968.
7. *Females arrested for murder*—16.0 percent of arrests.
8. *For robbery*—6.0 percent.
9. *For larceny theft*—33.0 percent.
10. *For prostitution or commercial vice*—66.0 percent.

Black arrests:

1. *Blacks arrested for violent crimes*—47.5 percent of all arrests.
2. *For property crimes*—26.0 percent.
3. *For murder*—51.0 percent.
4. *For forcible rape*—47.5 percent.
5. *For robbery*—57.0 percent.
6. *For aggravated assault*—40.0 percent.
7. *For burglary*—29.0 percent.
8. *For larceny theft*—32.0 percent.
9. *For motor-vehicle theft*—26.0 percent.
10. *For gambling*—78.5 percent.
11. *For forgery*—20.0 percent.
12. *For embezzlement*—13.0 percent.
13. *For driving under the influence of alcohol*—3.5 percent.
14. *For prostitution*—50.0 percent.

Arrests by age:

1. *Kids 15 and younger arrested for violent crimes*—5.5 percent.
2. *Eighteen and younger*—21.0 percent.
3. *Eighteen- to 24-year-olds*—39.0 percent (highest group).
4. *Kids 15 and younger arrested for property crimes*—5.5 percent.
5. *Eighteen and younger*—46.0 percent.
6. *Eighteen to 24-year-olds*—30.0 percent.

7. *Kids 18 and younger arrested for murder—*0.5 percent.
8. *Eighteen- to 24-year-olds—*33.5 percent.
9. *Twenty-five to 44-year-olds—*44.0 percent.
10. *Kids 15 and younger arrested for motor-vehicle thefts—*14.0 percent.

Highest arrest rate, according to age-group for:

1. *Arson—*18 and younger (50.0 percent).
2. *Robbery—*18 to 24 (42.5 percent).
3. *Burglary—*18 and younger (51.5 percent).
4. *Larceny theft—*18 and younger (43.0 percent).
5. *Fraud—*25 to 44 (51.0 percent).
6. *Forcible rape—*18 to 24 (39.0 percent).
7. *Drunken driving—*25 to 44 (46.5 percent).

• **T H E   B O T T O M   L I N E .** According to Frank Schmalleger, only one out of every 100 Americans who commits a serious crime ends up in the slammer, and a substantial number of those who do serve time are given reduced sentences for being first-timers. The imprisonment rate for lesser crimes is now thought to be about one sentence out of 300 crimes.

• **D O I N G   T I M E .** The average American criminal serving time in a *federal* prison is behind bars for about 47 percent of his actual sentence. The average, however, varies according to the crime.

Average sentence for selected crimes in the United States for prisoners for first-time offenders:

1. *Kidnapping—*18.0 years.
2. *Robbery—*12.0 years.
3. *Larceny theft—*28.0 months.
4. *Tax evasion—*13.0 months.
5. *Embezzlement—*20.0 months.
6. *Counterfeiting—*34.0 months.
7. *Fraud—*19.0 months.
8. *Forgery—*29.5 months.

Average time served:

1. *Kidnapping—*38.5 percent.
2. *Robbery—*36.5 percent.
3. *Larceny theft—*38.5 percent.
4. *Tax evasion—*60.5 percent.

5. *Embezzlement*—55.0 percent.
6. *Counterfeiting*—47.0 percent.
7. *Fraud*—56.5 percent.
8. *Forgery*—55.0 percent.

• **REPEAT PERFORMANCES**. Nearly all of the statistical evidence gathered to date points to a population of what might be called "career criminals"—offenders who resume their criminal ways even after imprisonment. One FBI study, for instance, showed that of the 256,000 persons arrested between 1970 and 1975, 64 percent had been arrested two times or more and, as a group, had been accused of more than a million crimes. Another study by the Institute for Law and Social Research in Washington, D.C., found that only 7 percent of the persons arrested for serious crimes between 1971 and 1975 accounted for nearly 25 percent of all such arrests. Then there is the FBI study, published in 1975, that gave these figures for persons rearrested within four years of their release from prison, for each category of crime:

1. *Burglary*—81 percent were repeat offenders.
2. *Robbery*—77 percent.
3. *Car theft*—75 percent.
4. *Rape*—73 percent.
5. *Assault*—70 percent.
6. *Stolen property*—68 percent.
7. *Forgery*—68 percent.
8. *Narcotics*—65 percent.
9. *Larceny theft*—65 percent.
10. *Murder*—64 percent.
11. *Weapons*—64 percent.
12. *Fraud*—63 percent.
13. *Gambling*—50 percent.
14. *Embezzlement*—28 percent.

• **WAITING GAME**. As of early 1979, 464 men and women were awaiting execution in 24 of the 33 states that permit capital punishment. The numbers:

1. *Men*—459.
2. *Women*—5.
3. *In the south*—80.0 percent.
4. *Black*—43.5 percent.
5. *Hispanic*—3.0 percent.

• THE PRICE TAG. From time to time law-enforcement officials are asked to put a price tag on crime in the United States. Their figures, at last look, were as follows:

1. *Overall cost (in terms of stolen property, medical bills, police, etc.)*—$125 billion, which is more than the defense budget.
2. *White-collar crime*—$44 billion.
3. *Financing the criminal-justice system*—$23 billion.
4. *Drug-related crime*—$21.5 billion.
5. *Prostitution*—$10 billion.
6. *Illegal gambling*—$6 billion.
7. *Average per-capita cost*—very roughly $575.
8. *Cost per household*—very roughly $1,600.

SOURCES

Federal Bureau of Investigation, *Uniform Crime Reports*, 1977.

Frank Schmalleger, "World of the Career Criminal," *Human Behavior*, March 1979.

HOW SICK WE GET

The fact that Americans are living longer than ever before has not made much of a dent in the statistics relating to sickness rates in the United States. If anything, the higher proportion of older people in the population has made it appear, on the surface at least, that we are getting sick more often today than we used to.

• THE BASIC NUMBERS. Not many aspects of life in the United States find demographics playing so big a role as it does in the amount of time we spend being sick. Some examples:

1. *Average number of days Americans get sick each year*— 18.0 days.
2. *Average number of days Americans are sick enough to stay in bed each year*—6.0 days.
3. *Sick days per year for women*—20.0.
4. *For men*—15.0.
5. *For whites older than 65*—26.0.

    6. *For blacks older than 65—32.0.*

    7. *For $15,000-a-year earners and above—12.3* days.

    8. *For $10,000- to $15,000-a-year earners—14.4* days.

• OCCUPATIONAL HAZARDS. Americans who work full-time get sick less often than Americans who work part-time (then again, maybe that is why they are able to work full-time). But there are some intriguing differences in the sick-day rates of people in various occupations. Examples:

    1. *Farm workers*—less than 10 sick days a year.

    2. *White-collar workers*—11 days.

    3. *Blue-collar workers*—12 days.

    4. *Service workers*—14 days.

    5. *People who work for the government*—15 days.

• HEALTH COSTS. The average per-capita health expenditure in the United States today is about $600, but only about one-third of this figure comes directly out of the pocket of the average American. The rest comes from health insurance, medicare, charity, or industry. Here is a breakdown of where the money goes:

    1. *Hospital care*—47 percent.

    2. *Physicians' fees*—19 percent.

    3. *Drugs*—10 percent.

    4. *Nursing-home care*—8 percent.

    5. *Dental care*—7 percent.

    6. *Assorted other services*—9 percent.

The largest proportional increase in the categories above has taken place in hospital care, which accounted for only 30 percent of health-service expenditures in the early 1970s. All told, the per-capita cost of health care in the United States has gone up 300 percent, but the actual out-of-pocket expense has gone up by only 60 percent.

• STAYING ALIVE. On any given day in the United States, somewhere between 710,000 and 720,000 men and women are being cared for in a short-term hospital. The rate has gone up some 10 percent since 1970 and nearly 50 percent since 1960. Other averages:

    1. *Average hospital stay in 1976*—7.6 days.

    2. *Average hospital stay in 1965*—7.8 days.

3. *Average hospital stay for women—*7.2 days.
4. *Average hospital stay for men—*7.6 days.
5. *Persons 65 and older only—*11.5 days.

And the reasons we are in hospitals to begin with:

1. *Circulatory diseases—*13.0 percent.
2. *Stomach problems—*12.5 percent.
3. *Childbirth—*12.3 percent.
4. *Accidents—*10.3 percent.
5. *Urinary-tract conditions—*10.3 percent.
6. *Cancer—*6.0 percent.

SOURCE

U.S. Department of Health, Education, and Welfare, *Health United States 1976–77.*

OUR CHRONIC ILLS

About 13 percent of the American population (30 million people) suffer from a chronic condition that imposes some limitation of activity. Limitations vary, of course, according to the severity of the condition and age, but here is a look at the culprits, and the proportion of Americans affected by them.

• **W I T H I N   L I M I T S .** About 24 percent of the 30 million Americans who have chronic illnesses are "limited" by the condition but not to the degree that it interferes with any major activity (work, school, keeping house). Here is what they have, along with the proportion who suffer from each condition:

1. *Arthritis—*11.0 percent.
2. *Leg or hip problem other than paralysis—*9.5 percent.
3. *Asthma—*8.0 percent.
4. *Heart condition—*8.0 percent.
5. *Bad back—*7.5 percent.
6. *Bad eyes—*6.5 percent.
7. *Musculoskeletal disorder other than arthritis (bursitis, or tennis elbow, for instance)—*5.5 percent.
8. *High blood pressure—*5.0 percent.
9. *Hearing problem—*4.5 percent.
10. *Diabetes—*3.5 percent.
11. *Mental or nervous condition—*3.5 percent.

•**LIMITED EDITIONS**. Roughly half the chronically ill people in America are forced to limit their major activity to some degree. Here are the reasons:

1. *Arthritis*—17.0 percent.
2. *Heart disease*—16.5 percent.
3. *Bad back*—8.0 percent.
4. *High blood pressure*—8.0 percent.
5. *Musculoskeletal disorder other than arthritis*—7.0 percent.
6. *Bad leg or hip*—5.5 percent.
7. *Diabetes*—4.5 percent.
8. *Bad eyes*—4.5 percent.
9. *Asthma*—4.5 percent.

•**COMMON ENEMY**. The common cold strikes about 275 million times a year in the United States each time lasting anywhere from three days to two weeks. In 1977 Americans coughed up nearly $850 million for over-the-counter cold and cough remedies, never mind that no remedy to date has proven itself to be a *cure* for the cold.

•**BUGGED**. Influenza—the flu—is the second most common ailment Americans have to put up with. Slightly more than 12 percent of Americans get one variation of it or another every year, but the patterns differ among age-groups. Some examples:

1. *Flu rate from January to March*—24.0 cases per 100 persons.
2. *Flu rate from July to September*—4.4 per 100 persons.
3. *Flu rate in peak season for Americans 6 to 16*—31.5 per 100 persons.
4. *Flu rate in peak season for Americans 17 to 44*—19.0 per 100 persons.

•**BEDDED DOWN**. Roughly one out of four (7 million) "chronically ill" Americans is unable to carry on any major activity without enormous difficulty. Their problems are as follows:

1. *Heart condition*—24.0 percent.
2. *Arthritis*—16.0 percent.
3. *Blindness or near blindness*—8.0 percent.
4. *Mental or nervous condition*—7.5 percent.
5. *Cerebrovascular disease*—7.5 percent.

6. *Paralysis*—7 percent.
7. *High blood pressure*—6.5 percent.
8. *Digestive problems*—4.5 percent.
9. *Musculoskeletal problems other than arthritis*—4.5 percent.
10. *Bad back*—4.0 percent.

• **TOPIC OF CANCER**. Cancer is the second most lethal disease facing Americans (it ranks behind heart disease) but is the most feared disease we have. Here are some of the numbers, which, grim though they are, are beginning to reflect some reasons for optimism:

1. *Americans who currently have cancer*—about 1 million.
2. *Average number of people who get cancer each year in the United States*—661,000.
3. *Proportion of cancer deaths among people 65 and older* —57 percent.
4. *Men cancer patients with lung cancer*—21 percent.
5. *With prostate cancer*—16 percent.
6. *With colonic or rectal cancer*—15 percent.
7. *Women cancer patients with breast cancer*—28 percent.
8. *With colonic or rectal cancer*—15 percent.
9. *With uterine cancer*—14 percent.
10. *Current cancer survival rate*—overall, one out of three cancer patients is being "saved" (that is, surviving for at least five years), but the rate jumps considerably when you exclude lung cancer.

• **HEARTACHES**. Roughly half (51 percent) the deaths that occur in the United States are caused by some form of cardiovascular disease, and diseases of the heart per se account for nearly 38 percent of all deaths. Men between the ages of 25 and 64 are 50 percent more likely to die of heart disease than of cancer, and roughly 30 percent of all the Americans who have chronic conditions suffer from a heart or circulatory problem. Some additional numbers:

1. *Heart-disease death rate for men 25 to 44 years old*— 40.3 per 1,000.
2. *For women in the same age bracket*—12.6.
3. *For men 45 to 64*—554.9.
4. *For women in the same age bracket*—184.4.

• **S H O O T I N G U P**. The big problem with high blood pressure (apart from everything else!) is that a lot of the people who have it do not know that they have it. The numbers:

1. *Americans who have high blood pressure*—18.0 percent of adult population (or 26 million).
2. *White males who have it*—18.5 percent.
3. *Black males who have it*—28.0 percent.
4. *White females who have it*—16.0 percent.
5. *Black females who have it*—28.5 percent.
6. *Black males and females who have a severe case of high blood pressure*—11.0 percent of black American population.
7. *Black males and females who are borderline cases*—13.0 percent of black American population.
8. *Proportion of high-blood-pressure sufferers who do not know they have it*—50.0 percent of high blood pressure sufferers.

• **D E E P - E N D E R S**. Since mental illness is such a difficult condition to define, nobody can say for sure exactly how many Americans suffer from it. The statistics do show, however, that the rate of psychiatric "episodes" (as measured by admissions in mental hospitals) has generally declined throughout the 1970s. Nobody seems to know why, but one guess is that drugs have reduced the need for institutionalization, if not the rate of mental illness. The numbers:

1. *Patient-care episode rate* (*number of persons on the rolls of inpatient or outpatient mental-health facilities*)—847 per 100,000 in 1975; 849 in 1969.
2. *Americans in mental-care facilities*—about 600,000.
3. *Number of admissions and readmissions in 1975*—433,500.
4. *Mentally retarded in institutions*—157,000.
5. *Proportion of mentally ill who are diagnosed schizophrenic*—15.0 percent.
6. *Mentally retarded*—3.0 percent.
7. *Chronic depressive*—12.5 percent.
8. *Organically brain damaged* (*excluding the mentally retarded*)—12.5 percent.

SOURCE

U.S., Department of Health, Education, and Welfare, *Health United States 1976–77.*

PROBLEM DRINKING

There is drinking and there is "problem" drinking. But where one ends and the other begins is a question philosophers are probably better equipped to answer than doctors. "Problem drinkers" are usually defined as people whose drinking habits contribute in some way to a psychological or physical problem. "Alcoholics" are usually defined as problem drinkers whose drinking has become a permanent and destructive aspect of their lives.

• THE BASIC NUMBERS. Depending on whom you listen to, the number of alcoholics in the United States is anywhere between 6 million and 10 million. The lower number comes from surveys based on a complicated formula developed in the early 1940s by E. M. Jellineck, whose system relies mainly on statistics relating to deaths from cirrhosis of the liver. The higher numbers come from surveys conducted by the National Institute on Drug Abuse.

From the Jellineck formula:

1. *Alcoholics in the United States in 1975*—about 5.75 million.
2. *Proportion of men*—84 percent.
3. *Rate per 100,000 (men)*—7,300.
4. *Rate per 100,000 (women)*—1,300.

From the National Institute on Drug Abuse:

1. *Alcoholics in the United States, as of 1978*—10 million.
2. *Proportion of alcoholics who are women*—nearly 50 percent.
3. *Husbands who leave alcoholic wives*—90 percent.
4. *Wives who leave alcoholic husbands*—10 percent.

A number of reasons have been offered to explain the differences in the figures above. One is that women have historically been less reluctant to report their alcohol problems. The second is that the rising divorce rate has turned many "problem drinking" women into full-fledged alcoholics. Some additional numbers based, in part, on Harris surveys:

1. *"Problem drinkers" or "potential problem drinkers"*— about 10 percent of 18-and-older population.

2. *Americans who have alcoholics in their immediate families*—40 million.
3. *Traffic deaths attributable to alcoholism*—23,000.
4. *Members of Alcoholics Anonymous*—1,100,000.

The Harris survey also showed that the proportion of problem drinkers in the population is highest in the 18-to-21 age bracket (27 percent) and second highest in the 35-to-39 age bracket.

• **YOUNG AND FOOLISH.** Probably the most alarming aspect of the latest alcohol statistics in the United States is the numbers involving teenage drinking. A 1978 study by the National Institute on Alcohol Abuse and Alcoholism involving 13,000 youths throughout the country turned up the following percentages:

1. *Teenagers who drink*—74 percent.
2. *Boys*—79 percent.
3. *Girls*—70 percent.
4. *Boys who were drunk at least six times during the previous year*—23 percent.
5. *Girls who were drunk the same amount of times*—15 percent.
6. *Teenagers who drink alone*—35 percent.
7. *Teenagers who are considered problem drinkers*—20 percent.
8. *Teenagers who consider themselves problem drinkers* —3 percent.

• **RISK FACTORS.** A U.S. Department of Health, Education, and Welfare study in the mid-1970s drew profiles of the people most likely to develop an alcohol-related problem and those least likely to do so.
The most likely:

1. *Men.*
2. *Separated, single, and divorced persons.*
3. *Nonreligious persons.*
4. *Beer drinkers (as opposed to liquor or wine drinkers).*
5. *People who see drunkenness as a "sign of having fun."*

The least likely:

1. *Women.*
2. *Persons older than 50.*
3. *Widowed or married persons.*

4. *Jews.*
5. *Rural residents.*
6. *Southerners.*
7. *Persons with postgraduate degrees.*
8. *Wine drinkers.*

•GETTING THERE. Nobody becomes an alcoholic overnight: You have to work at it. From Jellineck, this "typical" progression:

1. *Early teens:* Gets drunk a lot, usually with friends.
2. *Late teens and early twenties:* Continues heavy drinking. Sometimes cannot remember what happened night before.
3. *Early thirties:* Starts averaging a drink a day. Starts to drink when nobody's looking.
4. *Mid- to late-thirties:* Starts going on binges—heavy drinking bouts away from home or work.

SOURCES
Statistics on Consumption of Alcohol and on Alcoholism, 1976.
U.S. Department of Health, Education, and Welfare, Alcohol and Health, 1974.
U.S. National Institute on Drug Abuse.

OUR MINOR HANGUPS

So much for the heavy stuff. Here is a look at some of the less serious mental and physical problems that plague Americans, and the numbers who suffer from them.

•SPOOKED OUT. Nearly 60 percent of American adults (75 percent of women and 38 percent of men) admit to having at least one phobia or persistent fear, with women much more victimized than men. Here is what two surveys, taken in the mid-1970s, uncovered.

Things Americans are "afraid of," based on a 1977 Roper poll:

1. *Snakes*—46 percent (an additional 20 percent say they are "bothered slightly").
2. *Heights*—20 percent.

3. *Mice*—17 percent.
4. *Spiders and insects*—13 percent.
5. *Flying in an airplane*—12 percent.
6. *Thunder and lightning*—9 percent.
7. *Being alone in a house at night*—7 percent.
8. *Dogs*—5 percent.
9. *Being in a crowd of people*—2 percent.

NOTE: Women are nine times as likely to be afraid of mice than are men and twelve times as likely to fear being alone in a house at night.

"Personal fears" of Americans, based on an R. H. Bruskin survey conducted in 1973.

Men:

1. *Speaking before a group*—36 percent.
2. *Heights*—26 percent.
3. *Financial problems*—21 percent.
4. *Death*—18 percent.
5. *Sickness*—15 percent.
6. *Deep water*—13 percent.
7. *Flying*—12 percent.
8. *Loneliness*—11 percent.
9. *Insects and bugs*—11 percent.
10. *Dogs*—9 percent.
11. *Riding in a car*—5 percent.
12. *Darkness*—4 percent.
13. *Elevators*—4 percent.
14. *Escalators*—2 percent.

Women:

1. *Speaking before a group*—46 percent.
2. *Heights*—38 percent.
3. *Insects and bugs*—33 percent.
4. *Deep water*—30 percent.
5. *Flying*—25 percent.
6. *Financial problems*—23 percent.
7. *Sickness*—23 percent.
8. *Death*—20 percent.
9. *Loneliness*—16 percent.
10. *Dogs*—14 percent.
11. *Riding in a car*—12 percent.
12. *Darkness*—12 percent.

13. *Elevators*—11 percent.
14. *Escalators*—8 percent.

• CLOSED IN. An estimated one million Americans now suffer from a condition known as agoraphobia—the fear of going into public places. About 84 percent are women, and nearly 90 percent of agoraphobics are married.

• QUICK HANDS. From Alexander Goldenburg, a dentist at the Mount Sinai Hospital in New York, comes the following data on Americans who bite their nails:

1. *Proportion of population who are nail biters*—about 24 percent.
2. *Proportion of nail biters who are between 21 and 30*— 61 percent.
3. *Older than 30*—14 percent.
4. *Younger than 10*—less than 3 percent.

There appear to be no definitive socioeconomic factors associated with nail biting, but emotional stress is thought to be the chief cause.

• WET BEDS. The proportion of American adults who wet the bed is well under 1 percent and even lower if you do not include people with bladder disorders. Among teenagers, though, the rate is somewhat higher. A 1960 study by the U.S. Department of Health, Education, and Welfare put the number of teenage bed wetters at about 5 percent (5 percent, that is, who wet the bed "on occasion"), but only 20 percent of these children were described by their parents as being in "excellent health."

• STUTTERBUGS. The number of Americans who have a speech defect of one kind or another is about 12 million. And the number of Americans with a serious stuttering problem is 1.5 million. In about half the speech problems that Americans have, the big difficulty is articulation—speaking with a lisp, for instance. There is a strong case to be made for the relationship between speech problems and the attempt early on in a child's life to switch him or her over from left-handedness to right-handedness. There is also some evidence to suggest a connection between premature toilet training and weaning, and the development of an articulation problem.

• PRIVATE AFFAIRS. The number-one—and fastest growing—communicable disease among American adults today is venereal disease, with the 1977 rate showing an increase of more than 80 percent over the 1970 rate. Here are the official HEW numbers, but bear in mind they relate only to *reported* cases. Conservative estimates place the actual number of VD cases at about three times the reported amount.

1. *Gonorrhea cases reported in 1977*—about 1 million.
2. *Reported in 1970*—about 600,000.
3. *Reported in 1955*—about 236,000.
4. *Syphilis cases reported in 1976*—about 72,000. (NOTE: estimates are only 20 percent above this figure.)
5. *Reported in 1970*—91,000.
6. *Reported in 1950*—217,000.
7. *Gonorrhea rate in the United States in 1977*—about 455 per 100,000.
8. *In Canada*—about 225 per 100,000.
9. *In Sweden*—313 per 100,000.
10. *In Japan*—4 per 100,000.

SOURCES
R. H. Bruskin and Associates.
Alexander Goldenburg, D.D.S.
U.S. Department of Health, Education, and Welfare, *Health United States 1976–77.*

HOW PSYCHOLOGICALLY STRESSED WE ARE

Psychological stress has received a great deal of attention throughout the 1970s, with most of the numbers suggesting a definite increase in the number of Americans who suffer from some of the various symptoms of psychological stress and a marked increase, too, in the proportion of Americans who now feel a sense of psychological embattlement.

• THE BASIC NUMBERS. Because it is an almost impossible characteristic to measure with conventional medical methods, much of what we know about stress in the United States is the result of surveys that get people to talk about how stressed they *feel*. One of the few *concrete* measures we have is the level of psychosomatic disease (ulcers, etc.). We shall start with ulcers:

1. *Americans who now have ulcers*—about 8.5 million (5 percent of adult population).
2. *Proportion of ulcer patients who are women*—33 percent.
3. *Proportion of women ulcer patients in 1948*—5 percent.

Americans who report they have felt close to a nervous breakdown (based in U.S. Department of Health, Education, and Welfare surveys conducted between 1971 and 1975):

1. *Men 25 to 74*—8.5 percent.
2. *Sixty-five and older*—5.5 percent.
3. *Women 25 to 74*—17.0 percent.
4. *Thirty-five to 44*—22.0 percent.
5. *Sixty-five and older*—10.0 percent.

Americans who say they have actually had a nervous breakdown:

1. *Men 25 to 74*—2.5 percent.
2. *Fifty-five to 64*—4.5 percent.
3. *Women 25 to 74*—5.5 percent.
4. *Fifty-five to 64*—7.0 percent.

The patterns: Government surveys suggest that a smaller proportion of American men and women were actually *having* nervous breakdowns in the late 1970s than were having them in the early 1960s, but that the number of Americans who feel they are *close to* a nervous breakdown has almost doubled. A possible explanation for this is that while more people than ever feel stressed, drugs or therapy (or both) are cutting down on the number of breakdowns.

•**STRESS DEMOGRAPHICS.** One of the most informative pictures of how psychological stress levels according to life stages and according to life situations came out of the Institute for Social Research study that led to *The Quality of American Life*. Some representative figures.

Proportion of Americans who worry about having a nervous breakdown:

1. *All women*—15 percent.
2. *All men*—10 percent.
3. *Divorced or separated women*—25 percent.

4. *Divorced or separated men*—8 percent.
5. *Single women 18 to 29 (never married)*—18 percent.
6. *Single women 29 and older (never married)*—8 percent.
7. *Single men 18 to 29 (never married)*—13 percent.
8. *Single men 29 and older (never married)*—13 percent.
9. *Married women with a child younger than 6*—19 percent.
10. *Married men in same situation*—12 percent.

• STRESS SCALE. On a scale of one to seven—"one" representing "low" and "seven" representing "high"—here is how the national sampling used in the *The Quality of American Life* study rated the degree of stress they themselves felt they experienced in their lives.

Whites:

1. *Lowest level*—11 percent.
2. *Second lowest*—15 percent.
3. *Third lowest*—14 percent.
4. *Middle level*—16 percent.
5. *Third highest*—17 percent.
6. *Second highest*—16 percent.
7. *Highest*—11 percent.

Blacks:

1. *Lowest level*—9 percent.
2. *Second lowest*—18 percent.
3. *Third lowest*—11 percent.
4. *Middle level*—13 percent.
5. *Third highest*—17 percent.
6. *Second highest*—19 percent.
7. *Highest*—13 percent.

The overall proportion of blacks whose perceived level of stress is moderately high to high is nearly 50 percent, compared with 44 percent for whites.

• FAMILY CONCERNS. Stress as a family problem was one of the areas explored by Yankelovich, Skelly and White in their surveys done for the *General Mills American Family Report 1978–79*. Some representative numbers on how stress is hitting the average American family:

1. *Families who were finding it harder in 1978 to cope with the problems of everyday living compared to a few years ago*—44 percent.
2. *Finding it easier*—19 percent.
3. *Feeling some need to reduce stress in their daily lives* —41 percent.
4. *Feeling a strong need to reduce stress in their daily lives* —41 percent.

SOURCES

Campbell, *The Quality of American Life.*

U.S. Department of Health, Education, and Welfare, *Health and Nutrition Examination Survey, 1960.*

HOW WE GET HURT

The most accurate measures of the accidents that injure Americans each year are reports from hospital emergency rooms, where the yearly case load is now averaging about 12 million. Here are some of the reasons.

• CRACKING UP. More than 5.5 million Americans (based on 1977 National Safety Council figures) get banged up each year in motor-vehicle accidents, and in about one-third of these instances the injury is severe enough to disable the victim beyond the day of the accident. If you like to keep score, it means that a disabling traffic accident occurs in the United States once every two seconds.

• HOME SWEET HOME. Statistically speaking, the best way to get hurt is to stay at home. The reason: more than 90 percent of the nonjob, nonvehicular injuries we suffer each year result from home accidents. (Of course, we spend most of our time at home, too.) Here is a rundown on the most common kinds of home accidents (from 1976 estimates):

1. *Falling down stairs*—538,500 injuries a year.
2. *Stepping on nails or tacks*—309,500.
3. *Getting hurt by a lawnmower or other garden equipment*—195,500.
4. *Bumping into glass doors*—191,000.
5. *Bumping into regular doors*—190,000.

6. *Getting cut by a knife*—184,000.
7. *Colliding with a nonglass table*—165,500.
8. *Falling off a chair or sofa*—138,000.
9 *Falling off a bed (water beds not included)*—133,000.
10. *Getting hurt by metal pieces*—100,500.

• **F U N   A N D   G A M E S** . Nearly three million Americans get hurt each year playing in a game or some sort of participatory sport. The major culprits among sports and sporting equipment, based on injuries caused in 1976, are as follows:

1. *Bicycles*—466,000.
2. *Football*—386,000.
3. *Basketball*—327,500.
4. *Swings, slides, or playground equipment*—158,000.
5. *Skates, skateboards, or scooters*—129,000.
6. *Skiing*—86,000.
7. *Swimming pools*—69,000.
8. *Fishing equipment*—60,500.
9. *Volleyball*—51,500.
10. *Wrestling*—51,500.

• **B I T T E N   U P** . About three million Americans, mostly children, get bitten each year by dogs, with 100,000 dog bites being reported in New York City alone. Meanwhile, about 45,000 Americans get bitten each year by snakes (20 percent poisonous), but hardly any of them in New York City.

SOURCES
National Safety Council.
U.S. Consumer Product Safety Commission, Annual Report.

HEROIN ADDICTION

Coming up with accurate figures on the number of heroin addicts has always been troublesome given the nature of the habit and given the fact, too, that not everybody who uses heroin is necessarily an addict. It does appear, however, that the rate of heroin addiction throughout the United States is dropping somewhat, especially among high-school students.

• **T H E   B A S I C   N U M B E R S .** Researchers and federal agencies have never been able to agree on just how many heroin addicts there are in the U.S. population (federal estimates are invariably higher), but the consensus view today puts the figure at about 300,000. Some related numbers:

1. *Americans who have used heroin at least once*—an estimated 2 million.
2. *Addicts who are black*—60 percent.
3. *Average age of heroin addict*—23.
4. *Estimated "success" rate of methadone maintenance programs*—about 80 percent.

SOURCE
National Institute for Drug Abuse, Washington, D.C.

HOW WE MEDICATE OURSELVES

The average family spends about $230 a year on prescription drugs and packaged medications, such as aspirin, laxatives, nose drops, and antacids. Here are some of the numbers relating to our use of packaged medicines:

1. *Americans who take remedies for acid indigestion*—48 percent.
2. *College students who use antacids more than once a month*—15 percent.
3. *Americans who take aspirin and other pain relievers at least once a month*—50 percent.
4. *Female college students who take headache pain relievers several times a week*—10 percent.
5. *Male college students who use headache remedies at least once a month*—72 percent.
6. *Americans who use laxatives*—25 percent.
7. *Americans who use nasal sprays*—16 percent.

SOURCES
Drug Topics.
Survey of the College Market.

WHAT WE DIE FROM

As living patterns have changed in America over the past twenty years, so have dying patterns, but not all that much. The big change has been a significant drop in the number of deaths caused by infectious diseases, pneumonia, and early childhood diseases, and a gradual rise in the number of deaths caused by cancer.

• THE BASIC NUMBERS. The top-ten killers in the United States as of 1977 were:

1. *Heart disease*—337.2 deaths per 1,000 (38 percent of all deaths).
2. *Cancer*—175.8 (19 percent of all deaths).
3. *Cerebrovascular disease*—87.9.
4. *All accidents*—46.9.
5. *Pneumonia*—25.2.
6. *Motor-vehicle accidents*—21.9.
7. *Cirrhosis of the liver*—14.7.
8. *Arteriosclerosis*—13.7.
9. *Suicide*—12.4.
10. *Bronchitis, emphysema, and related diseases*—11.4.

• THE DEMOGRAPHICS. Here is a comparative look at the causes of death among various demographic segments of the population:

1. *Heart-disease death rate among males 25 to 44*—40.5 per 1,000.
2. *Among females in the same age bracket*—12.5 per 1,000.
3. *Cancer death rate among males 15 to 24*—8 per 1,000.
4. *Suicide death rate among males 15 to 24*—18.5 per 1,000.
5. *Accident death rate among males in general*—67.3 per 1,000.
6. *Accident death rate among females in general*—27.5 per 1,000.
7. *Homocide death rate in the population overall*—9.0 per 1,000.
8. *Homicide death rate among black men*—82.9 percent.

• CRACKING UP. A closer look at the circumstances surrounding the 49,500 traffic fatalities in 1977:

1. *Average traffic deaths in the United States per day—* 136.
2. *Proportion of fatal accidents involving a driver 24 years old or younger—*40 percent.
3. *Proportion of alcohol-related traffic fatalities involving men—*80 percent.
4. *Proportion of fatal accidents in which speed was the chief factor—*75 percent.
5. *Biggest holiday weekend for traffic fatalities—*Fourth of July (700 deaths).
6. *Motor-vehicle-accident death rate for 1977 compared with 1970 rate—*down about 10 percent.

• SELF-RULE. The suicide rate in the United States has been rising steadily since the mid-1950s, although the accuracy of suicide statistics is suspect at best. The chief problem with getting accurate statistics is that many suicides go unreported, the survivors doing their best to make it seem as if the victim died by accident or of natural causes. In any case, here is how some of the numbers look:

1. *Current suicide rate in the United States (total population)—*13.0 per 1,000.
2. *Among white males—*20.0 per 1,000 and holding steady.
3. *Among black males—*11.0 per 1,000 and rising.
4. *Among white females—*9.5 per 1,000.
5. *Among black females—*4.5 per 1,000.
6. *Among white males 65 and older—*39 per 1,000 and dropping.
7. *Among white females 65 and older—*8.5 per 1,000.
8. *Among white females 45 to 54—*14.0 per 1,000.
9. *Among white males 15 to 22—*19.2 per 1,000; holding steady but up 33 percent since 1970.

Trends: Suicide rates are dropping among older males but rising among teenagers for reasons nobody really knows. Another thing: The disparity between the male suicide rate and the female rate may be misleading, since it is estimated that suicide attempts among women outnumber actual suicides by men by nearly ten to one. The difference between men and women when it comes to suicide seems to be that men use more guaranteed lethal means (guns, etc.), whereas women usually rely on pills. Finally, the suicide rate in the United States is about average when compared with rates prevalent in other industrialized countries.

SOURCE

U.S. Bureau of the Census, *Statistical Abstract of the United States: 1978.*

AND WHAT HAPPENS AFTERWARD

Given the changes that have taken place in the way Americans *live*, it is hardly surprising that changes have been taking place, too, in what happens to us after we die.

• THE BASIC NUMBERS. Probably the most detailed look at funeral arrangements in America comes from a Consumers' Union study published in 1977. Some highlights:

1. *Survivors who choose the "conventional" funeral (open coffin, 2–3 days for viewing the body)*—75 percent.
2. *Estimated average cost of a funeral in 1980*—about $2,500.
3. *Cremations nationwide in 1976*—7.0 percent.
4. *In Pacific states*—40.0 percent.
5. *In East South Central states*—0.6 percent.
6. *Among blacks*—less than 1.0 percent of all cremations.

NOTE: The number of cremations in the United States rose by about 12 percent between 1976 and 1977.

SOURCE

Consumers' Union, *Funerals: Consumers' Last Rights,* 1977.

XIII SOME AVERAGE AMERICAN TYPES

LEFT-HANDERS

It is hard to say exactly how many left-handers lurk in America because the very state of left-handedness eludes definition. One estimate puts the number of Americans *born* left-handed at one out of four, but the pressures of a right-handed world cut that percentage down enormously when it comes to *adult* left-handers. One *Newsweek* survey in the mid-1960s put the percentage of adult lefties in the United States at 12 percent. Some of the fields in which left-handers are thought to have an advantage are:

1. *Tennis.*
2. *Blackjack dealing.*
3. *Major-league pitching.*

Some of the things that left-handers have trouble with are:

1. *Egg beaters.*
2. *Scissors.*
3. *Pencil sharpeners.*

SOURCE
Martin Gardner, *The Ambidextrous Universe*, 1964.

FIRSTBORN CHILDREN

Psychologists who have looked into the matter insist that the order in which you are born into your family has a lot to say about what you are like when you grow up. Some of the studies on the subject suggest that firstborn children differ from their later-born brothers and sisters in that they are:

1. *More like their parents in religious and political outlook.*
2. *More achievement oriented (20 out of the first 23 astronauts were either firstborns or only children).*
3. *More likely to attend college.*
4. *Less likely to become delinquents.*
5. *Less likely to be popular with their friends.*
6. *More likely to be neurotic.*

One possible reason for these differences, according to Philip Zimbardo, is that parents tend to set higher ideals for—and place more demands on—firstborns than they do for their other children.

SOURCES
William J. Goode, *Social Systems and Family Patterns*, 1971.
Kenneth Kammeyer, "Birth Order and the Feminine Sex Role," 1966.
Zimbardo, *Shyness*.

JEWS

About 41 percent of the more than 14 million Jews worldwide live in the United States. Indeed, there are almost as many Jews living in metropolitan Philadelphia alone as there are in Israel's largest city, Tel Aviv. From the Gallup Poll, this profile of American Jews.

1. *American Jews who've graduated from college*—58 percent of adult Jews.
2. *Who live in the east*—65 percent.
3. *The midwest*—5 percent.
4. *The south*—13 percent.
5. *The west*—17 percent.
6. *Who earn $20,000 or more (as of 1976)*—43 percent.
7. *Who consider themselves Democrats*—56 percent.
8. *Republicans*—8 percent.
9. *Independents*—36 percent.
10. *Who have a professional or business occupation*—53 percent.

SOURCE
Gallup Poll.

DOG PEOPLE

It goes without saying that most people who own dogs are at least reasonably fond of them, but the Pet Institute of America ran a study not long ago that divided dog owners into five distinct categories. Here they are:

1. *Dog's best friend:* dog owners who see the dog as a companion and member of the family—27 percent.
2. *Platonic dogship:* dog owners who enjoy the dog but are not all that emotionally or psychologically wrapped up in it—17 percent.
3. *Crown jewelers:* dog owners who treat their dog as if it were a piece of fragile china but do not derive any real emotional satisfaction from the animal—19 percent.
4. *Paper chasers:* dog owners who are constantly worried that their dogs are going to do something embarrassing, like mistaking the leg of a guest for a fire hydrant—24 percent.
5. *Dog tired:* dog owners who consider the dog they own a burden and a pain but keep it around for the sake of the kids—19 percent.

SOURCE
Pet Food Institute.

CAT PEOPLE

Cat people also fall into certain categories, according to yet another Pet Food Institute study, but there are only three groups to speak of.

1. *Mirror images:* cat owners who see their pet as a reflection of their own personality and care for the animal accordingly—21 percent.
2. *Strangers in the night:* cat owners who do not get terribly involved with their cats and who like the idea that cats are independent and require little care—59 percent.
3. *Litter lovers:* cat owners who rely on their cats for love and affection—20 percent.

SOURCE
Pet Food Institute.

CORPORATE WOMEN OFFICERS

Corporate women officers are neither as numerous as their male counterparts nor as well paid, but the situation is beginning to turn around. Slowly. A 1977 study by Heidrick and Struggles presented the following portrait of the contemporary woman corporate officer.

Proportion of women corporate officers who:

1. *Are vice-presidents or higher*—25 percent.
2. *Are secretaries (in the corporate sense, not the occupational sense)*—58 percent.
3. *Are married or have been married*—65 percent.
4. *Are widowed*—7 percent.
5. *Are divorced*—30 percent.
6. *Waited until age 30 before they married*—13 percent.
7. *Began career in a clerical position*—66 percent.
8. *Have children*—31 percent.
9. *Quit their jobs for a time in order to take care of their children*—14 percent.
10. *Had fathers who were executives or professional men*—29 percent.
11. *Had fathers who were blue-collar workers*—36 percent.
12. *Hold college degrees*—27 percent.
13. *Hold master's degrees*—18 percent.
14. *Hold doctorates*—3 percent.
15. *Never went past high school*—16 percent.

In addition:

1. *Average salary*—$30,000 (compared with $50,000 for the average male corporate officer).
2. *Average amount of time spent on job during the week*—44.5 hours for women earning less than $20,000; 57.0 hours for women earning $40,000 or more.

SOURCE
Heidrick and Struggles, New York.

CORPORATION PRESIDENTS

A Heidrick and Struggles study of the typical chief executive for a major corporation in the United States today paints the following picture:

1. *Age*—mid-fifties.
2. *Background*—midwestern.
3. *Education*—undergraduate studies in liberal-arts institution; graduate studies in business school.
4. *Length of service*—more than twenty years with company.
5. *Salary*—$260,000 a year or more, not counting perks.
6. *Average time put in each week on the job*—60 hours.
7. *Average number of speeches given a year*—10 to 20.

SOURCE
Heidrick and Struggles, New York.

JOCKS

Do the sports Americans play tell us something about the personalities of the Americans who play them? Quite a few studies have been done in this area, and here is what one of them came up with.

• C O M P A R A T I V E V I E W . A study conducted in the 1960s by Howard Slusher was aimed at finding out how athletes in different sports varied from one another in basic personality characteristics. The groups studied were baseball players, basketball players, football players, swimmers, and wrestlers—all in high school. Here is how they shape up against one another as a group.
Brains:

1. *Football players* (the brainiest).
2. *Swimmers.*
3. *Basketball players.*
4. *Wrestlers.*
5. *Baseball players.*

Nerves:

1. *Wrestlers* (the most neurotic).
2. *Football players.*
3. *Basketball players.*
4. *Baseball players.*
5. *Swimmers.*

The most like nonathletes in basic personality characteristics:

1. *Swimmers.*
2. *Baseball players.*
3. *Football players.*
4. *Wrestlers.*
5. *Basketball players.*

SOURCE
Howard Slusher, "Personality and Characteristics of Athletes vs. Nonathletes," 1964.

TENNIS ADDICTS

Roughly nine million Americans say they play tennis "regularly," and probably a third of that figure are hooked on the game. Here is a profile of the average American tennis addict, as drawn from a *Tennis* magazine subscriber survey.

Proportion of players who:

1. *Have been playing eleven years or more*—25 percent.
2. *Four years or less*—27 percent.
3. *Play both outdoors and indoors*—56 percent.
4. *Play three days a week or more outdoors*—49 percent.
5. *Play in public parks*—76 percent.
6. *At a tennis, beach, or yacht club*—19 percent.
7. *Own two racquets, or more*—82 percent.
8. *Own a metal racquet*—59 percent.
9. *Graphite racquet*—5 percent.
10. *Play with new balls every time they play*—11 percent (men more so than women).
11. *Play with new balls less than every fourth time*—17 percent.

SOURCE
Tennis Magazine.

SKIERS

The number of American adults who have been on skis at some time in their lives is nearly 18 million, but only about three million (well under one percent of the population) does it with any degree of regularity. Here is a look at the American skier, based on a 1978 *Ski* magazine subscriber survey.

Proportion of regular American skiers who:

1. *Rate themselves as either advanced or expert*—57.0 percent.
2. *Ski at least twelve days a year or more*—42.0 percent.
3. *Have ever cross-country skied*—27.5 percent.
4. *Spend more than $200 a year on equipment*—44.0 percent.
5. *Are in college or have graduated from college*—65.0 percent.
6. *Earn $25,000 a year or more*—53.0 percent.
7. *Plan to ski more in the future*—70.0 percent.

Other survey sources show that only 12.0 percent of Americans who ski live in the South, only 2.0 percent are black, 38.0 percent are single, and 7.5 percent are divorced or separated. About 60.0 percent of serious Americans skiers are men.

SOURCE
Ski Magazine.

SUPER-INTELLECTUALS

America is not known for its highbrow intellectualism, but in *The American Intellectual Elite* Charles Kadushin presented an analysis of the 172 men and women who were judged to have the most intellectual clout in the United States (based on a poll he took among contributors to leading intellectual journals).

• THE GENERAL PROFILE. According to Kadushin, the "intellectual elite" in the United States is made up chiefly of men and women who have these characteristics:

1. *They live in New York*—50 percent.
2. *Are Jewish*—60 percent.
3. *Are connected with either Columbia, Harvard, Yale, or New York University*—50 percent.

•INTELLECTUALS' HOME JOURNALS. The reading tastes of the American "intellectual elite" are as follows:

1. *New York Times Sunday Magazine*—81 percent.
2. *New York Review of Books*—74 percent.
3. *New Yorker*—59 percent.
4. *Commentary*—54 percent.
5. *Newsweek*—52 percent.
6. *Time*—46 percent.

•MENTAL GIANTS. The ten most prestigious intellectuals in the United States, according to Kadushin's 1972 poll were (in alphabetical order):

1. *Daniel Bell.*
2. *Noam Chomsky.*
3. *John Kenneth Galbraith.*
4. *Irving Howe.*
5. *Mary McCarthy.*
6. *Dwight Macdonald.*
7. *Norman Mailer.*
8. *Robert Silvers.*
9. *Susan Sontag.*
10. *Lionel Trilling.*

SOURCE
Charles Kadushin, *The American Intellectual Elite*, 1972.

BEAUTY QUEENS

From Frank Deford's *There She Is*, the composite Miss America up to 1971:

1. *Age*—19.
2. *Hair*—brunette.
3. *Eyes*—blue.
4. *Height*—five feet six inches.
5. *Weight*—123 pounds.

6. *Measurements—*35″-23 ¾″-35½″.
7. *Favorite hobby—*dancing.
8. *Favorite sport—*swimming.

SOURCE
Frank Deford, *There She Is,* 1971.

COLLEGE STUDENTS

College-enrollment rates showed signs of slippage in 1978 and 1979, but the number of Americans in degree programs—about 10.5 million—has nonetheless risen by about 20 percent since 1970. About 63 percent of these students were full-time. Here is a closer look.

• **THE DEMOGRAPHICS.** The demographic picture of college students, based on a 1976 study, looks like this.
Proportion of students who were:

1. *Men—*52.5 percent.
2. *Black—*10.5 percent.
3. *Older than 20 when they enrolled—*5.0 percent.
4. *Younger than 16 when they enrolled—*4.0 percent.
5. *From households with incomes of $15,000 or more—* 53.0 percent.
6. *From household with incomes of $10,000 or less—*20.0 *percent.*
7. *From homes where both parents had graduated from high school—*80.0 percent.
8. *From homes where father had graduated from college—* 42.0 percent.
9. *From homes where mother had graduated from college* —20.0 percent.
10. *From homes where father did not finish grammar school—*8.0 percent.
11. *Protestant—*44.5 percent.
12. *Roman Catholic—*35.5 percent.
13. *Jewish—*3.5 percent.
14. *Atheists or agnostics—*10.0 percent.

• **POLITICAL LEANINGS.** Asked to describe their political orientation, college freshmen in 1976 responded as follows:

1. *Far left*—2.0 percent (men slightly more so than women).
2. *Liberal*—25.5 percent.
3. *Middle of the road*—56 percent (women more so than men).
4. *Conservative*—15 percent (men more so than women).
5. *Far right*—1 percent (men more so than women).

• DAY-TRIPPERS. Roughly half the college students in the United States attend a college located 50 miles or less from their home. One out of four goes to a school at least 100 miles from home.

• REPORT CARDS. Here is how the college freshman class of 1976 did in high school.

Men:

1. *A or A+*—6.5 percent.
2. *A*—9.0 percent.
3. *B+*—17.5 percent.
4. *B*—25.5 percent.
5. *B*—15.5 percent.
6. *C+*—14.5 percent.
7. *C*—8.0 percent.
8. *D*—less than 1.0 percent.

Women:

1. *A or A+*—10.5 percent.
2. *A*—14.0 percent.
3. *B+*—24.0 percent.
4. *B*—27.5 percent.
5. *B*—10.5 percent.
6. *C+*—8.5 percent.
7. *C*—5.5 percent.
8. *D*—less than 1.0 percent.

• SELECTION PROCESS. The reasons given by college freshmen in 1976 for choosing their particular college:

1. *Academic reputation*—43 percent.
2. *Special educational programs*—25 percent.
3. *Low tuition*—18 percent.
4. *Location close to home*—11 percent.
5. *Advice from friends*—7 percent.

•**PAYING FOR IT**. College freshmen in 1976 were paying for their education in the following ways:

1. *Parental or family aid*—46.0 percent.
2. *Savings*—14.0 percent.
3. *Some form of scholarship grant*—23.0 percent.
4. *Student loan*—14.0 percent.
5. *Federally guaranteed student loan*—5.5 percent.
6. *Full-time employment*—22.0 percent for men; 13.5 percent for women.
7. *Part-time employment*—15.0 percent for men; 11.0 percent for women.

SOURCE

U.S. Department of Health, Education, and Welfare, *Digest of Education Statistics 1977–78.*

COLLEGE DROPOUTS

Less than half the students who enroll in college drop out before receiving a degree. The factors that seem to affect the dropout rate the most are money, brains, and ambition. Here is what a 1977 HEW report showed.

•**MONEY**. The college dropout rate among students in different socioeconomic groups:

1. *Low socioeconomic groups who do not receive scholarship aid*—52 percent.
2. *Who receive aid*—30 percent.
3. *High socioeconomic groups who do not receive aid*—21 percent.
4. *Who receive aid*—14 percent.

•**BRAINS**. The study divided students (on the basis of grades) into low and high categories:

1. *Proportion of dropouts among "high" academic students*—14 percent.
2. *Low academic students*—37 percent.

•**AMBITION**. Probably the biggest factor of all.

1. *Proportion of dropouts who do not care whether they graduate or not*—71 percent.

2. *Proportion of dropouts among students who express a desire to go to graduate school*—14 percent.

SOURCE

U.S. Department of Health, Education, and Welfare, National Center for Education Statistics, 1977.

THE AVERAGE AMERICAN ROBOT

The average American robot still has a way to go before he matches the smarts or the personality of the various *Star Wars* robots, but here's a progress report all the same:

• STANDARD ISSUE. The typical robot today, made from a $400 to $500 kit, is able to wander around the house and obey simple commands like "go," "stop," "backward," and "fast."

• DELUXE. Slightly more expensive robots can move their arms and shake hands with your guests. They can also bend over and pick up things.

• SUPER ROBOT. The smartest robot around today is Arok, who is 6'8" tall and was invented by a Chicago man named Benjamin Skora. Arok vacuums the carpet, walks the dog and can even serve drinks, although it's reported that he goes heavy on the vermouth when he mixes a martini.

SOURCE

Wall Street Journal, September 7, 1978.

REFERENCES

American Public and the Income Tax System, The. 1978. A survey by the Roper Organization for H. & R. Block, Inc. Kansas City, Mo.

American Soap and Detergent Association. *The National Cleaning and Laundry Census.* New York, 1979.

Andrews, Frank M., and Stephen B. Withey. *Social Indicators of Well Being.* New York and London: Plenum Press, 1976.

Arafat, Ibtihaj, and Wayne Cotton. "Masturbation Practices of Males and Females." *Journal of Sex Research* 10 (1974).

Associated Councils of the Arts, The. *Americans and the Arts.* A survey conducted by Louis Harris and Associates. Associated Councils of the Arts, New York, 1975.

Atwater, Lynn. "Getting Involved." *Alternate Lifestyles.* February 1979.

Bell, Alan F., and Martin S. Weinberg. *Homosexualities.* New York: Simon and Schuster, 1978.

Beller, Anne Scott. *Fat and Thin.* New York: Farrar, Straus and Giroux, 1977.

Berns, Jerry. "21" Club, New York.

Better Homes and Gardens. Consumer Panel. "Building and Remodeling, 1978. A consumer study." Meredith Corporation, Des Moines, Iowa.

"Black Americans in the Seventies." A survey by Yankelovich, Skelly and White, Inc. *Ebony. Black Enterprise Magazine.* New York.

Bradburn, N. M. and Caplovitz, D. *Reports on Happiness.* New York: Aldine Publishing Co., 1965.

Campbell, Angus, Philip E. Converse, and Willard L. Rogers. *The Quality of American Life.* New York: Russell Sage Foundation, 1976.

Canby, Vincent. "The Bottom Line on Hit Films Is Generally Pretty Gross." *New York Times.* April 28, 1979.

Cantril, Albert H., and Susan Davis Cantril. *Unemployment, Government and the American People,* 1978. Public Research, Washington, D.C.

Carns, Donald. "Talking About Sex: Notes on First Coitus and the Double Sexual Standard." *Journal of Marriage and the Family.* November 1973.

Carson, Rubin. *The National Love, Sex and Marriage Test.* New York: Doubleday, 1978.

Carter, Hugh, and Paul C. Glick. *Marriage and Divorce: A Social and Economic Study.* Cambridge, Mass.: Harvard University Press, 1970.

Center, Richard, Bertram H. Roven, and Aroldo Rodrigues. "Conjugal Power Structure: A Re-examination." *American Sociological Review* 36 (April 1971).

Chandler, Robert. *Public Opinion: Changing Attitudes on Contemporary Political and Social Issues.* New York: Bowker, 1972.

Child's Body. New York: Paddington Press, Ltd., 1978.

Chiriboga, David, and Loraine Cutler. "Stress Responses Among Divorced Men and Women." *Journal of Divorce.* February 1979.

Coleman, James S. *The Adolescent Society.* New York: Macmillan, 1961.

"Collective Behavior." *Society Today*. Del Mar, California: CRM Books, 1973.

Consumers Union. *Funerals—Consumers' Last Rights*. New York: W. W. Norton, 1977.

Conway, Flo, and Jim Siegelman. *Snapping*. New York: Lippincott, 1978.

Cooperative Institutional Research Program. *The American Freshman: National Forms for Fall 1976*. Published in the *Digest of Education Statistics 1977–78*. National Center for Education Statistics.

Davis, Harry L. "Decision Making Within the Household." *Selected Aspects of Consumer Behavior*. National Science Foundation.

Deford, Frank. *There She Is*. New York: Viking Press, 1971.

Denfield, Duane. "Dropouts from Swinging." *The Family Coordinator*. January 1974.

Dennis, Wayne. "Creative Productivity Between the Ages of 20 and 80 Years." *Journal of Gerontology*. January 1966.

"Disco Takes Over." *Newsweek*. April 2, 1979.

Drug Topics. Annual Consumer Expenditures. January 20, 1978. Oradell, N.J.

Edminston, Susan. "The Medicine Everybody Loves." *Today's Health*. January 1978.

Elembemp, Alan. "Race and Physical Attractiveness as Criteria for White Subjects Dating Choices." *Social Behavior and Personality* 4 (1976).

Ellis, Albert, and Albert Albarbanel, eds. *The Encyclopedia of Sexual Behavior*. New York: Jason Aronson, Inc., 1973.

Feron, James. "Parents in Suburbs Are Turning Increasingly to Private Schooling." *New York Times*. March 21, 1979.

Fincher, Jack. *Human Intelligence*. New York: G. P. Putnam's Sons, 1976.

Flacks, Richard. "The Roots of Student Protest." *Journal of Social Issues* 23 (July 1967).

Frank, Ellen, and Carol Anderson. "How Important Is Sex to a Happy Marriage?" *Family Circle*. March 13, 1979.

Freedman, Jonathan. *Happy People*. New York: Harcourt Brace Jovanovich, 1979.

Friedman, Meyer, and Ray H. Rosenmann. *Type A Behavior and Your Heart*. New York: Alfred A. Knopf, 1974.

Gardner, Martin. *The Ambidextrous Universe*. New York: Basic Books, 1964.

Gaylin, Jody. "What Do Girls Look for In Boys." *Seventeen*. March 1979.

Gebhard, Paul H. "Postmarital Coitus Among Widows and Divorcees," in Paul Bohannon, ed., *Divorce and After*. New York: Doubleday, 1970.

General Mills American Family Report 1974–75. "A Study of the American Family and Money." Survey conducted by Yankelovich, Skelly and White, Inc. General Mills, Inc., Minneapolis.

General Mills American Family Report 1976–77. "Raising Children in a Changing Society." Survey conducted by Yankelovich, Skelly and White, Inc. General Mills, Inc. Minneapolis.

General Mills American Family Report 1978–79. "Family Health in An Environment of Stress." Survey conducted by Yankelovich, Skelly and White, Inc. General Mills, Inc. Minneapolis.

Goldenberg, Alexander, D.D.S. "Treatment of the Nailbiting Problem in Orthodontic Patients." Monograph. New York.

Goode, William J. *Social Systems and Family Patterns*. Indianapolis: Bobbs-Merrill, 1971.

Graziano, William, Thomas Brothen, and Ellen Berscheid. "Height and Attraction: Do Men and Women See Eye-to-Eye." *Journal of Personality and Social Psychology.* March 1978.

Guilford, J. P. *The Nature of Human Intelligence.* New York: McGraw-Hill, 1967.

Hall, Calvin S., and R. L. Van De Castle. *The Content Analysis of Dreams.* New York: Appleton-Century-Crofts, 1966.

Hartshorne, H. and M. A. *Studies in the Nature of Character.* New York: Macmillan, 1930.

Hite, Shere. *The Hite Report.* New York: Macmillan, 1976.

"How Gay Is Gay," *Time.* April 23, 1979.

Hunt, Morton. *Sexual Behavior in the 1970s.* New York: Playboy Press, 1974.

Institute for Social Research. *Gambling in the United States.* University of Michigan: Ann Arbor, Michigan, 1978.

Institutions/Volume Feeding. 10th annual menu census. April 1, 1978. Chicago.

"Is The U.S. Becoming a Drug Ridden Society?" *U.S. News and World Report.* August 7, 1978.

Jewelers' Circular Keystone. February 1978. New York.

Kadushin, Charles. *The American Intellectual Elite.* Boston: Little, Brown, 1972.

Kammeyer, Kenneth. "Birth Order and the Feminine Sex Role." *American Sociological Review.* August 1966.

Kanin, Eugene J., Karen Davidson, and Sonia R. Scheck. "A Research Note on Male/Female Differentials in Heterosexual Love." *The Journal of Sex Research* 6 (February 1970).

Katch, Frank L., and William D. Mcardle. *Nutrition, Weight Control and Exercise.* Boston: Houghton Mifflin, 1977.

Keeton, William. *Biological Science.* New York: W. W. Norton, 1967.

Kephart, W. M. "Some Correlates of Romantic Love." *Journal of Marriage and the Family* 29 (1967).

King, Karl, Jack O. Blaswich, and Ira E. Robinson. "The Continuing Premarital Sexual Revolution Among College Females." *Journal of Marriage and the Family.* August 1977.

Kinsey, Alfred C., Wardell B. Pomeroy, Clyde E. Martin, and Paul H. Gebhard. *Sexual Behavior in the Human Female.* Philadelphia: W. B. Saunders, 1953.

Klein, Frederick C. "Patterns of Energy Use in the United States Are Changing Five Years After Crises." *Wall Street Journal.* September 7, 1978.

Komarovsky, Mirra. "Cultural Contradictions and Sex Roles: The Masculine Case." *American Journal of Sociology.* January 1978.

Kowett, Don. "TV Sports, America Speaks Out." *TV Guide.* August 19, 1978.

Krech, David, Richard S. Crutchfield, and Norman Livson. *Elements of Psychology.* New York: Alfred A. Knopf, 1969.

Lasch, Christopher. *The Culture of Narcissism.* New York: W. W. Norton, 1979.

Lenski, Gerhard. "The Religious Factor: A Sociological Study of Religion's Impact on Politics," *Economics and Family Life.* New York: Doubleday, 1961.

Lewis, Norman. *How to Read Better and Faster.* New York: Thomas Y. Crowell, 1958.

Livinger, George. "Sources of Marital Dissatisfaction Among Applicants to Divorce." *American Journal of Orthopsychiatry* 36 (1966).

Long, Larry. "Geographical Mobility." *Selected Aspects of Consumer Behavior*. National Science Foundation. Washington, D.C.: U.S. Government Printing Office.

Luckey, Eleanor B. "Number of Years Married as Related to Personality Perception and Marital Satisfaction." *Journal of Marriage and the Family* 47 (1966).

Man's Body. New York and London: Two Continents Publishing, 1976.

"Masturbation Survey." *Forum Magazine*. March 1979.

Mathews, Donald. *Measurement in Physical Education*. Philadelphia: W. B. Saunders Company, 1973.

Merchandising. Statistical issue and marketing report for 1978. March 1979.

Minneapolis *Star*. Metro Poll, 1973.

Mitchell, Curtis. *The Perfect Exercise Book*. New York: Wallaby Books, 1976.

"Most Admired Persons Poll." *Ladies' Home Journal*. July 1978.

"National Diet Survey Conclusions." *Glamour*. July 1978.

National Economic Survey. *New York Times*. January 7, 1979.

National Health Education Committee. *Killers and Cripplers*. New York: David McKay, 1976.

Newspaper Advertising Bureau. *Children, Mothers & Newspapers*. New York, 1978.

———. *How the Public Gets Its News*, 1978.

Newsweek. Market studies on travel and car purchases. New York.

New York Times/CBS Poll of Nuclear Reactor Attitudes. April 10, 1979.

Nguyen, Thanh. *Your Mouth: Oral Care for All Ages*. Radnor, Pa.: Chilton, 1978.

Nicholson, John. *Habits*. London: Methuen, Inc. 1977.

"Nutrition: A Study of Consumer's Attitudes and Behavior Towards Eating at Home and Out of Home." Conducted by Yankelovich, Skelly and White, Inc. *Woman's Day*. 1979.

Oakley, Ann. *The Sociology of Housework*. New York: Pantheon, 1974.

"People Reader's Poll." *People*. March 5, 1979.

Perrier Study of Fitness in America, The. Survey by Louis Harris and Associates, conducted for Great Waters of France, New York, 1979.

Pietropinto, Anthony, and Jacqueline Simenauer. *Beyond the Male Myth*. New York: Times Books, 1977.

Husbands and Wives: A Nationwide Survey of Marriage. New York: Times Books, 1970.

Playboy Advisor. *Playboy*. March 1979.

Playboy Report on American Men. A study of the values, attitudes and goals of U.S. males, 18-to-49-years old. Survey conducted for Playboy Enterprises, Inc., by Louis Harris and Associates. Chicago, 1979.

Ray, Oakley S. *Drugs, Society and Human Behavior*. St. Louis: C. V. Mosby Company, 1972.

Robinson, John P. *Changes in America's Use of Time 1965–1975*. Cleveland State University, Cleveland, 1976.

Rollins, B. C., and H. Feldman. "Marital Satisfaction over the Family Life." *Journal of Marriage and the Family* 32 (1970).

Rubin, Zick. "Measurement of Romantic Love." *Journal of Personality and Social Psychology* 16 (1970).

Schlesinger, Benjamin. "Remarriage as Family Reorganization for Divorced

Persons—A Canadian Study." *Journal of Comparative Family Studies.* Autumn 1970.

Schmalleger, Frank. "World of the Career Criminal." *Human Behavior.* March 1979.

Schulman, Gary I. "Race, Sex and Violence." *American Journal of Sociology* 79 (1974).

Selznick, G., and S. Steinberg. *The Tenacity of Prejudice.* New York: Harper & Row, 1969.

Seventeen. Teen market surveys. Triangle Enterprises, Inc. New York.

Shapiro, Leo J. "Eating Habits Force Changes in Marketing," *Advertising Age.* October 30, 1978.

Shulman, Harry M. *The Family and Juvenile Delinquency.* Boston: Houghton Mifflin, 1959.

Ski. Subscriber survey. New York.

Slusher, Howard. "Personality and Characteristics of Athletes vs. Nonathletes." *Research Quarterly.* December 1964.

Stafford, Frank, and Greg Duncan. "Laziness in the World's Busiest City." *New York Magazine.* August 14, 1978.

"Statistics on Consumption of Alcohol and on Alcoholism." *Journal of Studies on Alcohol, Inc.* 1976. New Brunswick, N.J.

The Steelcase National Study of Office Environments: Do They Work? Survey conducted by Louis Harris and Associates, Inc., for Steelcase, Inc. Grand Rapids, Mich. 1979.

Steinberg, Sandon A., and Richard F. Yalch. "When Eating Begets Buying." *Journal of Consumer Research.* March 1978.

Stoltz, L. "Effects of Maternal Employment on Children." *Child Development* 31 (1960).

Stone, L. Joseph, and Joseph Church. *Childhood and Adolescence.* New York: Random House, 1968.

Stunkard, Albert J. "The Results of Treatment for Obesity." *Archives of Internal Medicine.* 102 (1959).

"Summary of Findings of Book Industry Study." *Publisher's Weekly.* November 6, 1978.

Tavris, Carol, and Susan Sadd. *The Redbook Report on Female Sexuality.* New York: Delacorte, 1974.

Tavris, Carol. "Redbook Report on Male Sexuality." *Redbook,* February 1978.

Tennis Magazine. Subscriber survey. Norwalk, Conn.

United States Government—All publications available through the U.S. Government Printing Office, Washington, D.C.

———. Bureau of the Census. *Statistical Abstract of the United States:* 1978.

———. Bureau of Labor Statistics. *U.S. Working Women—A Data Book.*

———. Consumer Product Safety Commission. *Annual Report.*

———. Department of Commerce. *Survey of Current Business.* July 1978.

———. Department of Health, Education and Welfare.

Age at Menarche. United States Health Examination Survey. Series 11, No. 133.

Alcohol and Health. 1974.

Analysis of Child Abuse and Neglect Research, 1977. January 1978.

Behavior Patterns in School of Youths 12–17 Years. Health Examination Survey. Series 11, No. 139.

Condition of Education, 1976.

Digest of Education Statistics, 1977.

Health, United States, 1976–77.

Height and Weight of Youths 12–17 Years. Health Examination Survey. Series 11, No. 124.

Intellectual Development and Achievement of Youths 12–17. Health Examination Survey. Series 11, No. 128.

Parent Ratings of Behavioral Patterns of Youths 12–17.

———. Department of Labor.

ACTION, *Americans Volunteer.* April 1969 and February 1975.

Monthly Labor Review, April, 1979.

———. Federal Bureau of Investigation. *FBI Uniform Crime Reports.* 1977.

———. Jacoby, John, George J. Szybillo, and Berning. "Time and Consumer Behavior: An Interdisciplinary Overview." Selected Aspects of Consumer Behavior. Washington, D.C.: National Science Foundation.

———. *Mass Media and Violence: A Staff Report to the National Commission on the Causes and Prevention of Violence,* 1969.

———. National Center of Education Statistics. *Digest of Education Statistics,* 1977–78.

———. *Report of the Commission of Obscenity and Pornography,* 1970.

———. *Restoring the Quality of Our Environment.* Report of the Environmental Pollution Panel of the President's Science Advisory Committee. Washington, D.C. November 1965.

———. United States Heritage Conservation and Recreation Service Survey. *Statistical Abstracts.*

———. United States Travel Data Center.

Van Duesen, Edmund. *Baldness.* Briarcliff Manor, N.Y.: Stein and Day, 1978.

Variety. New York.

Walster, Elaine, and G. William Walster. *A New Look at Love.* Reading, Mass.: Addison-Wesley, 1977.

Ward, Scott, and Daniel B. Wackman. "Children's Purchase Influence Attempts and Parent Yielding." *Journal of Marketing Research.* August 1972.

Warner, W. Lloyd, and Paul S. Lunt. *Social Class in America.* Chicago: Science Research, 1949.

Webb, Wilse B. *Sleep the Gentle Tyrant.* Englewood Cliffs, N.J.: Prentice-Hall, 1975.

West, S. G., S. P. Gunn and Paul Chernicky. "Ubiquitous Watergate: An Attributional Analysis." *Journal of Personality and Social Psychology* 32 (1975).

"What You're Getting from Your Job." Results from a reader survey. *Psychology Today.* May 1978.

"Wine and Women, 1977." Market study done for *Ladies' Home Journal.*

Woman's Body. New York and London: Two Continents Publishing, 1977.

"Woman's Wardrobe Survey." *Women's Wear Daily.* August 14, 1978.

Work in America. Cambridge, Mass.: MIT Press, 1973.

Yankelovich, Daniel. "A Second Look at the Sexual Revolution." *Reader's Digest.* June 1978.

———. *The New Morality: A Profile of American Youth in the 1970s.* New York: McGraw-Hill, 1975.

"Your Pursuit of Happiness." Results from a reader survey. *Psychology Today.* August 1976.

Zimbardo, Philip. *Shyness.* Reading, Mass.: Addison-Wesley, 1978.

Additional Sources

American Association of Fund-Raising Counsel, Inc. New York.
American Automobile Manufacturers Association. Falls Church, Va.
American Bar Association. Washington, D.C.
American Cancer Society. Surveys on smoking and health in the United States. Chicago.
American Council of Life Insurance. Washington, D.C.
American Dental Association. Chicago.
American Institute for Public Opinion. Also known as Gallup Poll. Princeton, N.J.
American Kennel Club. New York.
American Music Conference. Wilmette, Ill.
American Telephone and Telegraph Company. New York.
Anheuser-Busch Breweries. St. Louis.
Beatrice Foods Company. New York.
Breck Shampoo Company. East Rutherford, N.J.
Bruskin, R. H., and Associates. New Brunswick, N.J.
Center for Parenting. Palos Verdes, California.
Dunkell, Samuel V., Dr. Conversation. New York.
Gallup Poll. (See American Institute for Public Opinion).
Harris, Louis, and Associates. 630 Fifth Avenue, New York.
Harris Survey (See Louis Harris and Associates).
Hart, Schaffner and Marx. Chicago.
Heidrick and Struggles, Inc. New York.
Magazine Publishers Association, Inc. New York
Metropolitan Life Insurance Company. New York.
Motion Picture Association. New York.
Motor Vehicle Manufacturers Association of the United States. Detroit.
NBC News. Rockefeller Center, New York.
NORC (See National Opinion Research Center).
National Association of Mutual Savings Banks. New York.
National Education Association. Survey on teachers' attitudes.
National Family Opinion Research Center. Toledo.
National Opinion Research Center (NORC). University of Chicago, Chicago.
National Restaurant Association. Chicago.
National Safety Council. Chicago.
Needham, Harper and Speers. Chicago.
Nielsen Company, A. E. New York.
Palace Restaurant, The. New York.
Pepsico. Purchase, New York.
Pet Food Institute. Washington, D.C.
Power, J. D., and Associates. Los Angeles.
Roper Organization, Inc., The. New York.
Simmons, W. R., and Associates. New York.
Slurzberg, Lee. New York.
Television Information Office. New York.
Time Out Institute. Chicago.
Yankelovich, Skelly and White, Inc. New York.

Barry Tarshis, born in Pittsburgh, Pennsylvania, has been a free-lance writer for nearly all of his writing career. His most recent book, What It Costs, *won critical praise for its whimsical treatment of the economics of fantasy building. His previous books include several on tennis, among them* Tennis and the Mind, The Steady Game (*with Manuel Orantes*), *and* Tennis for the Bloody Fun of It, *with Rod Laver and Roy Emerson. A contributing editor to* Tennis *magazine, he has written articles on a variety of subjects for a number of national publications, among them* Playboy, New York, Seventeen, Town & Country, Travel and Leisure, American Home, Apartment Life, *and* Harper's Bazaar. *Mr. Tarshis is married and lives in Westport, Connecticut, with his wife and two children, Lauren and Andrew.*